3702775143

**PARK
LEARNING CENTRE**

The Park, Cheltenham
Gloucestershire GL50 2QF
Telephone: 01242 532721

UNIVERSITY OF
GLOUCESTERSHIRE

NORMAL LOAN

D0784921

British Library Cataloguing in Publication Data
Lewis, David C.
  Healing.
  1. Christianity. Spiritual healing
  I. Title
  615.8'52

  ISBN 0-340-50344-0

Copyright © Dr David C. Lewis 1989. First published in Great Britain 1989. All rights reserved. No part of this publication may be reproduced or transmitted in any form or by any means, electronic or mechanical, including photocopying, recording, or any information storage and retrieval system, without either prior permission in writing from the publisher or a licence permitting restricted copying. In the United Kingdom such licences are issued by the Copyright Licensing Agency, 33–34 Alfred Place, London WC1E 7DP. Published by Hodder and Stoughton Ltd, Mill Road, Dunton Green, Sevenoaks, Kent TN13 2YA. Editorial Office: 47 Bedford Square, London WC1B 3DP. Photoset by Rowland Phototypesetting Ltd, Bury St Edmunds, Suffolk. Printed in Great Britain by Cox and Wyman Ltd, Reading, Berks.

CONTENTS

ACKNOWLEDGEMENTS

A book of this nature requires a specialist knowledge of many different disciplines, including medicine, psychology, sociology, statistics, theology and parapsychology. In some respects the topic is central to the sub-field of medical anthropology, but in other respects it impinges on all the other disciplines mentioned above. I have therefore sought advice from a variety of other specialists, and in particular would like to express my appreciation for the helpful advice of David Wilson, Dean of Postgraduate Medical Education at the University of Leeds, Dr Rex Gardner, former Consultant Obstetrician and Gynaecologist at Sunderland General Hospital, Dr Richard Turner, Consultant Psychiatrist at the University Hospital, Queen's Medical Centre, Nottingham, Michael Flowers, Consultant Surgeon at Leeds General Infirmary, John Sloan, also a Consultant Surgeon at Leeds General Infirmary, Dr John White, a psychiatrist in private practice in Vancouver who was formerly Associate Professor of Psychiatry at the University of Manitoba, Bishop David Pytches of St Andrew's Church, Chorleywood, Rev. Brian Reed of Broadmead Church, Tunbridge Wells, and Rev. Paul Clayton of 'People International'.

For practical help in the administration of my questionnaire, its processing and my subsequent research, I would like to thank New Frontiers in Hove, Vineyard Ministries International in California and the Statistical Advisory Service of the University of Leeds.

I would like to thank the following medical consultants, doctors or other specialists for their co-operation in my enquiries into particular case histories: Dr J. J. Birch, Dr W.

I. Forsythe, Dr Robert Furness, Dr D. W. M. Haw, Dr P. J. Hollins, Dr Illis, Mr G. Jethwa, Mr N. R. M. Kay, Mr D. B. Kilner, Dr I. J. Lewis, Mr R. C. Mulholland, Professor R. W. Smithells, Mr R. C. Todd and Dr G. Watson.

I would also like to thank Miss Jane Restorick of the School of Education at Nottingham University for all her help with the computer analysis of my data and Mrs Sheila Websdale for diligently typing up my manuscript.

My thanks go also to Andrés Tapia for permission to quote a substantial portion of the article on Haiti published in the February 1987 issue of *U* Magazine.

Unless otherwise specified, all biblical quotations are from the New International Version (London: Hodder & Stoughton, 1979).

INTRODUCTION

Fiction, fantasy or fact?

When confronted by reports of supposedly 'miraculous' healing, whether in the Bible or today, people usually respond in
one of three ways. First, there are those who may dismiss the
tales as *fiction*, completely lacking any kind of basis in reality.
A second approach recognises that there might be a kernel of
truth but considers the report to be an exaggerated or embel-
lished account of what 'really' happened. In this book I shall
use the term *fantasy* to refer to such distortions based upon
misunderstandings or misrepresentations of what seems to
be the 'truth'. The third attitude to accounts of healing
accepts them as *facts*, accurate statements of perceived
reality.

Whether or not people's perceptions can themselves be
regarded as accurate depends on the existence or otherwise of
corroborative evidence and on the status of the informant. A
second- or third-hand account is far less reliable than a
first-hand testimony along the lines of 'I once was blind but
now I can see.'[1] Any assessment of the 'truth' of divine
healing has to utilise first-hand accounts wherever possible.

Interlinked with issues concerning the nature of the healings themselves are questions about related phenomena such
as so-called 'words of knowledge'. These utterances which
purport to be messages from God can also be regarded as
fiction, fantasy or fact. Some may consider them to be completely fictitious, others may view them as embellishments of
what might be guessed from clues in people's body language
and a third group may regard them as genuine oracles from
God.

Again, there are differing opinions on some of the physical phenomena often associated with healing, including behaviour such as falling over on the floor or screaming loudly. Some try to explain this away in terms of psychological processes which have nothing to do with God, others consider the behaviour to be partly genuine and partly induced psychologically, while a third group regard all of it as being indicative of the activity of the Holy Spirit.

Each of these different facets of healing as practised among contemporary Christians deserves considerable analysis in itself. Such analyses are contained in the following chapters, which present the results of an in-depth study of a healing conference and its subsequent impact on the lives of participants.

The holy health movement

Throughout the history of the church there have been intermittent highlights characterised by ministries of 'signs and wonders', especially healings. Often these are associated with particular individuals such as St Cuthbert of Lindisfarne, St Francis of Assisi or John Welch of post-Reformation Scotland.[2] In the twentieth century too there are 'famous names' popularly associated with healings and miracles: examples include Kathryn Kuhlman, Oral Roberts or John Wimber in the USA, Archbishop Milingo in Zambia, Paul Yonggi Cho in South Korea and Colin Urquhart in Britain. All of these have written books about healing, but what seems to be more distinctive about John Wimber's ministry is his practical training of large numbers of Christians in healing ministries of their own.

This training has been accomplished largely through conferences held in many cities of North America, Britain, Germany, South Africa and Australasia. Conferences of this nature have generated considerable controversy among Christian doctors, psychiatrists and clergy. It seems difficult to remain neutral on this issue, partly because the so-called 'signs and wonders' themselves provoke decisions about how one should react to them. They also stimulate fresh thought not only about one's view of the nature of God but also about one's personal relationship to such a God.

Reactions can be extreme in both directions. Dr Peter Masters of the Metropolitan Tabernacle in London has described such ministries as belonging to 'the devil's plan for the demise of evangelicalism'.[3] Robert Baldwin, a Consultant Psychiatrist at Manchester Royal Infirmary, describes himself as 'caught in an uncomfortable tension between not wishing to "quench" the Holy Spirit and yet experiencing some nagging doubts about what I have seen and heard'.[4] Bishop David Pytches, by contrast, writes of 'powerful and dramatic' changes in his ministry and in his Anglican church (in the north-west of London) as a result of John Wimber's visit there in 1981.[5]

Others focus on the personality of John Wimber himself. The American magazine *Christianity Today* describes 'the rotund Wimber' as 'a lovable teddy bear' and his style as that of 'an awfully nice neighbor leaning over the back fence, presenting what used to be considered extreme without sounding mean or pushy'.[6] Writing in the *Catholic Gazette*, Leonard Sullivan emphasises Wimber's modesty: 'one clear point about John Wimber is that he diverts attention away from himself . . . His ministry team from the U.S.A. included about 200 ordinary people who had paid their own expenses for the trip, and given their time freely.'[7] Terry Virgo, a leader of what in Britain has come to be known as the 'House Church' or 'Restoration' movement, writes that what he most esteems in John Wimber's life is 'his obvious love for the Lord Jesus and his commitment to Him . . . His burning zeal for the Lord is often camouflaged by his laid back California style of presentation. But how the honesty shines through!'[8]

In all this welter of *opinion* there is a dearth of *facts*. Critics of John Wimber question whether or not the healings are sustained, how far they are due to psychosomatic or other factors, to what extent the associated physical phenomena result from known psychological processes, how plausible it is to attribute to God the supposedly supernatural insights known as 'words of knowledge' – and so on. Various opinions are given, based on what in my view seem to be superficial assessments of merely one or two meetings. There is little, if any, systematic follow-up of cases – merely anecdotal evidence based on those one happens to have encountered. Medical doctors are more likely to come across 'negative' cases in which any apparent healing has not been sustained, simply because those individuals are the ones who feel the need to return to their doctors afterwards. Therefore anecdotal evidence from such doctors is unlikely to be representative. Furthermore, if they are already sceptical about divine healing, then any existing opinions are likely to be both confirmed and reinforced.[9]

Exactly the same process of bias is operative among proponents of John Wimber's ministry, except that their bias works in the opposite direction. Only those who are healed are likely to testify to their healings in public or to write in with accounts of them to Wimber's organisation, Vineyard Ministries International. More spectacular ones might be published in *The Vineyard Newsletter*, which always contains a section for such testimonies. Sometimes an outstanding case of healing may be published in Wimber's *Equipping the Saints* magazine, with eye-catching captions such as 'British Roman Catholic journalist and broadcaster Peter Jennings shares the story of his remarkable healing from sarcoidosis, a rare disease with no known cure.'[10] In this particular case confirmatory medical details were provided because medical tests were administered shortly afterwards which showed that the sarcoidosis had indeed inexplicably disappeared.[11]

A case like this demonstrates that at least some healings following prayer are inexplicable within the frame of reference of conventional medicine. Following Rex Gardner, we may use the adjective 'miraculous' to describe such cases.[12] However, we still do not know how common such events actually are. Neither the faith-reinforcing accounts of dramatic healings reported in Wimber's publications nor the 'negative' cases cited by his critics can be taken as in any way representative. Far more objective facts are required on which to base any realistic assessments of this ministry.

The background to this study

The publication of my report on John Wimber's Sheffield conference as an appendix to his book *Power Healing* generated sufficient interest for me to undertake a much more extensive study of Wimber's next conference in the north of England, held at Harrogate on 3–6 November 1986.[13] In many respects my research on the Sheffield conference was a pilot study which indicated some of the diverse avenues of exploration necessary for a study of this nature. While utilising my professional skills as a social anthropologist, it has also been necessary to consult with medical doctors and psychiatrists about particular specialist areas.

The author's own perspective

While seeking to be as objective as possible, it is nevertheless impossible to dissociate oneself from one's own private views which may produce some bias in one's presentation. This is a problem which is widely recognised within my own discipline, social anthropology, and I have discussed it at some length elsewhere.[14] Essentially I would argue that it is an advantage rather than a disadvantage to have a personal religious commitment when dealing with such topics because: (1) it allows a fuller understanding of the experiences involved, because otherwise one might be like a blind man trying to describe colours; (2) nobody is entirely 'neutral' in this area, but the possession of one's own well-defined belief system enables one to perceive more easily the boundaries of possible bias than if one has a more diffuse or incoherent set of beliefs. Many supposedly 'non-religious' anthropologists are uncertain what they actually believe about the supernormal phenomena they may encounter in the course of their fieldwork.[15]

In this context it may be appropriate to quote a non-Christian anthropologist who has faced up to these issues in his own research:

> We seek to be scientists, but we are also men among men, both in conducting research and in what we make of it . . . What we produce is bounded by our personal limitations; it had better be enriched by our personal assets, which extend far beyond what gifts we may have as scientists in the ordinary sense . . . So long as I tried to exclude my personal feelings and assessments from my intellectual analysis I was divided against myself and unable to proceed . . . An anthropologist is a man – or a woman – and if he strives to be less than a man he defeats his anthropology. This, at least, is surely true when the topic is religion: was it not always absurd to expect to understand religion by excluding value judgements, emotions, and personal experience, which are of its essence? I am indeed a flawed instrument, but so long as I strove to be a narrow social scientist I was maimed as well.[16]

I attended John Wimber's Sheffield conference out of personal interest as a committed Christian with what I would now regard as a relatively limited experience of the gifts of the Holy Spirit. Some of the phenomena I witnessed were new to me, but I attempted to describe them as objectively as possible. Since then my views have been modified or developed considerably through my subsequent research of the Harrogate conference. Most influential in this process have been the facts as I have been able to collect them; it is hard to ignore the evidence obtained from statistical analyses of questionnaires, the administration of certain psychological tests and the documentary evidence of doctors' and patients' reports. Together these build up a picture which I have attempted to present as fairly and objectively as I could, working within my own human limitations.[17] I shall leave the reader to judge how successful my attempt has been.

Methodology

A variety of methods have been employed in this research, as follows:

1 Personal participation in the Harrogate conference and observation of what occurred.
2 The distribution of written questionnaires to all 2470 people registered for the conference. On the Tuesday evening I was given the opportunity to explain publicly about what I was doing and to encourage people to fill in the questionnaires. A reminder was issued on the Thursday morning and the forms were collected in by the stewards just before the final session that evening. The 1890 usable questionnaires represent a response rate of 76.5%, which is very high in comparison with most sociological surveys.[18]
3 The follow-up of a random sample of those who filled in the questionnaires, in order to assess the longer-term impact of the conference on their lives. They were chosen using a random number table in order to obtain as representative a cross-section as possible. An explanatory letter was sent out to each of those selected, after which contact was made by telephone to arrange a date and time to meet, usually in their own homes. The first interviews were conducted towards the end of May 1987, over six months after the Harrogate conference, and the remainder were held throughout that summer until September 1987. My travels took me almost literally throughout the length and breadth of Britain, including places as distant as Cornwall and Orkney. A total of ninety-three people were interviewed in person and an additional seven filled in postal questionnaires. These seven were further followed up by telephone or letter in order to clarify details or obtain extra information.[19]
4 Cases of particular interest which were not included in the random sample were followed up by post, telephone or personal visit, but the postal response rate was less than 50%.[20]

5 Where appropriate, documentary evidence of physical healings was sought by writing to medical doctors connected with the case (not all of whom replied). For psychological healings and deliverance from demonic influences, reports on observable changes were sought, where appropriate, from a minister, spouse, relative or close friend.

Presentation

The information derived from these research methods ranges from the breadth afforded by a statistical analysis of the Harrogate questionnaires to the depth provided by detailed personal interviews with particular individuals. I have attempted to present the more complex statistical information in understandable tables or summaries, while providing more specialist information in the notes.[21] In specific case studies of individuals followed up I have often allowed informants to speak for themselves by quoting relevant excerpts from their accounts.

An overview of participants at the Harrogate conference

Those attending the conference in Harrogate, North Yorkshire, came from all over the British Isles, and even from places as distant as Australia, South Africa, Nigeria, Uganda, Greece, Israel, Iceland, the Faeroe Islands, Finland and many other parts of Europe. Simultaneous translation was provided in languages such as German and Dutch for the sizeable contingents from those countries. Over fifty participants came from Norway, most of them young people in training with Youth With a Mission, while other missionaries came from elsewhere. The 206 people from abroad (including ten from Eire) constituted 8% of those registered for the conference.

Participants were equally divided between men and

women. Many of them had professional interests in healing, as indicated by the high proportions who were either in health-related occupations (such as doctors, dentists or nurses) or else in full-time Christian work.[22]

Over fifty Christian denominations were represented, the largest single one being the Church of England. Anglicans accounted for 35% of my questionnaire sample, Baptists 11%, Roman Catholics 3%, Methodists 4% and Pentecostals 10%. Another 10% wrote 'House Church', 'Restoration church' or equivalent names given to the 'Restoration movement'; to this should probably be added the 3% who wrote 'Community church' and the 3% who styled themselves as belonging to a 'Christian Fellowship' or simply 'Fellowship'.[23] Other denominations represented included Brethren, Lutherans, Mennonites, the United Reformed Church, the Society of Friends, the Salvation Army, the Church of the Nazarene, Presbyterians, the Church of Scotland, Scottish Congregationalists, the Church of Ireland, the Dutch Reformed Church, the Swedish Alliance Mission and Free Independent Evangelical Churches, among others. Some of these denominations have been little affected by the charismatic renewal and may even be antagonistic to it; a few individuals from such churches indicated on their questionnaires that they expected to face difficulties in their own congregations as a result of their participation at this conference.

Differences between the Sheffield and Harrogate conferences

The conference in Sheffield in October 1985 was entitled 'Signs and Wonders and Church Growth (Part I)' and the Harrogate conference the following year was Part II. Many of those who attended the Harrogate conference had also been to the Sheffield one, some having also been to other such conferences elsewhere.[24] Those interviewed who had also been to the one in Sheffield often compared the two, most of them feeling that the Sheffield conference had a greater impact on their lives. Some of them suggested that this may be due to the impact of first encountering this kind of ministry, whereas they were more prepared for Harrogate by knowing what to expect. A general consensus was that the Sheffield conference was noisier and more dramatic.

It is likely that those who wanted to spend time and money in going to a second conference are people who are generally in favour of this kind of ministry. Some of them expressed a certain amount of disappointment, however, when they discovered that 'Part II' actually covered rather similar ground to 'Part I', albeit with somewhat different emphases or topics. This overlap in content may be attributable partly to the presence of some of Wimber's colleagues who spoke instead of him during two of the main sessions, and partly to the fact that there were still a substantial number of people present for whom such a conference was a completely new experience.

The fact that many of those at Harrogate had also been to Sheffield may mean that if they were going to receive any physical healing at all it would have been done at the earlier conference. Fourteen of the hundred people followed up in my random sample mentioned having received physical healing prior to the Harrogate conference for conditions as diverse as migraines, epilepsy, pancreatitis, arthritis or short legs. Half of these healings took place at a conference led by either John Wimber or one of his associates. This kind of prior exposure by many participants to this kind of healing ministry should be borne in mind when assessing the data to be presented in the following chapters.

Theological issues

One of my informants commented that the three American visitors who had most affected the British church in recent years had stressed different but complementary aspects of the Christian gospel: Billy Graham is seen as stressing the *word* of God, Jim Wallis the (social) *works* which accompany that word, and John Wimber the (signs and) *wonders* by which God confirms that word. However, in my study of the impact of John Wimber's ministry in Britain, I have found that these three emphases actually tend to blend into one another. To some extent my sociological perspective makes me consider issues of social class, while my anthropological training brings me to comment on chapter 1 on environmental, political and economic factors which may also impinge on healing.

My research has also led to further reflections on the biblical text, and I comment on such issues in a number of places. Sometimes in the notes I raise questions for which I am unable to provide authoritative answers but which I mention in order to stimulate thought among those who might be better equipped to tackle such issues. In my main text I tend to comment on biblical passages which are more clearly connected with the topics under discussion and which I have found personally more illuminating. It has been fascinating to discover that some of the patterns I have discovered through sociological survey techniques can actually be discerned also in the Bible.

These biblical insights followed on after I had noticed certain sociological trends, but I am aware that there may be unresolved questions about the extent to which contemporary experiences of the supernatural should be allowed to colour our understanding of apparently similar accounts in the Bible. There may be a danger of reading too much into the biblical accounts – and an alternative danger of taking the texts too lightly. What is clear, however, is that the importance we attach to biblical passages is closely conditioned by our own personal experiences. Obviously those with personal experience of angelic visitations or divine communication through dreams will tend to attach more importance to passages referring to such events than will those to whom such experiences are alien. Yet the same principles also apply to biblical references to matters not considered 'supernatural', such as the naming of children, genealogies, inheritance practices, gift giving, marriage arrangements, the status of women and so on. Most people in the Western world skip over biblical genealogies, including those of Jesus in the New Testament, because our backgrounds and personal experiences attach little significance to them. Their import is lost on us, but not on an African or Middle Eastern reader, who is more likely to recognise their significance. Jesus said, in effect, 'If you have eyes to see, then use them': if we are often blinkered in our perceptions of biblical texts dealing with ordinary human phenomena, how much more do we need our eyes to be opened when the texts deal with things of the Spirit?

Prejudice

In this book I attempt to present facts by which an evaluation can be made of John Wimber's ministry, but such information is unlikely to affect those who already have predetermined views one way or the other. I have even encountered what appears to be prejudice in the case of one person whose initial criticism of John Wimber was that he is American, other more rational objections following afterwards. A feeling in some circles seems to be, 'Can anything good come from California?': similar feelings were once held about those who came from Nazareth, and the most sensible reply to such a question is, 'Come and see.'

1

PHYSICAL HEALING

Issues to be considered:

Do the healings last?
What kinds of healings are reported?
How do medical doctors perceive the healings?
Which kinds of people are more likely to be healed?

Among the 1890 questionnaires from the Harrogate conference there are only sixty-eight cases of total healing claimed for physical conditions.

On the surface this seems a poor result from a conference devoted to Christian healing. However, to judge this conference by the numbers healed is actually to miss the whole point of the conference, which was to train 'novice healers' and to equip them to practise in their home situations what they had learned at Harrogate. The fact that a few people happen to have been healed along the way is an 'added bonus'.

In fact the majority of those at the conference were in good health to start with, and whatever physical ailments they had were relatively minor ones. Only a third of all those present received any kind of prayer at all for physical conditions. Because some had more than one condition requiring prayer, the total number of cases of prayer for physical healing is 867, involving 621 people. These figures come from the questionnaires filled in towards the end of the conference and represent subjective assessments of the degree of healing received. On the questionnaire they were given five possible options to indicate the amount of healing: either none at all, a little, a fair amount, a great deal or total healing.

Some, however, felt it was too soon to say whether or not they had received total healing and preferred to bracket together the 'great deal' and 'total healing' boxes. Many of those who ticked only the 'great deal' box probably felt similarly cautious about claiming total healing until their healings had stood the test of time. For this reason those who chose either or both of these two boxes on the questionnaire can be regarded as having received a significant amount of healing, at least by their own accounts. The 279 cases in these categories together account for 32% of all the cases of prayer for physical healing.

At the other end of the spectrum there are those who report little or no healing. I tend to amalgamate these together because I suspect that many of those reporting 'a little' healing are perhaps being optimistic when they really mean there has been little change, as further indicated by some who bracketed the two boxes together. Although there are 132 cases of 'no healing' reported (accounting for 15% of the cases receiving prayer), I combine these with the 166 cases of 'a little' healing and the six cases in which both options are chosen. Moreover, to be on the conservative side, I also include with these the sixty-two cases in which the degree of healing was left blank, even though for some of these the reason may have been simply that the respondent did not see the last page of the questionnaire. The effect of this is to bring my category of little or no healing up to 42% of the cases.

The remaining 222 cases (26%) are almost all those who ticked the 'fair amount' box, but I also include the thirteen cases in which it was bracketed with one or other of the boxes on either side.

These figures can be summarised as follows:

Table 1.1   Degrees of physical healing reported at the end of the
            Harrogate conference

Little or none	Intermediate	High
42%	26%	32%

Examples of healings

The above figures conceal a wide variety of physical conditions for which prayer was received. A detailed list of these is provided in Appendix A, which also shows the maximum, minimum and mean ('average') degrees of healing reported for each condition. Here I shall present merely a few illustrative quotations:

'Endometriosis' (a functional abnormality of the lining of the uterus: 'total healing' was reported).

'Hearing difficulty' (a little healing).

'Abnormal cells detected in cervix' (blank: 'can't tell till biopsies').

'My very sensitive teeth (please don't laugh!)' (total healing).

'Spastic colon' (no healing at all).

'Pain in the right shoulder' (a great deal of healing).

'Spine curvature and stiffness' (a little healing).

'Mouth ulcer' (a little healing).

'Lump in breast' (a great deal of healing).

'Sinuses, Bronchitis, Arthritis, Varicose condition in right leg' (a fair amount of healing: 'Don't know until I get back in home environment and atmosphere conditions. My bronchitis is certainly still with me but a lot better.')

'Heart and blood pressure: to that of twenty-five years of age – before was that of seventy years old' (from a forty-three year old man; total healing).

'Spine just went back into place' (a fair amount of healing).

'Hearing in the higher register due to percussion damage from rifle fire – it is healed' (total healing).

'Hiatus hernia causing heartburn at irregular intervals' (a fair amount of healing).

'Torn tendon of finger' (a fair amount of healing).

'My left ear has a ringing and a distortion. The distortion comes as a result of loud noises. The distortion has gone but the ringing is still there.' (The 'fair amount' box was ticked, probably as an average of the two effects, but I counted this as 'total' for the distortion and 'none at all' for the ringing.)

Follow-up of cases

All these are subjective assessments made towards the end of the conference. The real test comes during the following weeks or months. I allowed almost a year to pass before I began to write letters to a number of people asking about the longer-term effects; some of the replies did not come until well over a year after the conference. Some examples are as follows:

Regarding endometriosis, originally claimed as 'total healing': 'Since that time the condition has been greatly eased but I think that the emotional healing that I received . . . was perhaps more important.'

Regarding pain in the right hip after walking for a fairly short time, claimed as 'a great deal' of healing:

I did have some blood tests to see if I have arthritis or rheumatism but they all came back negative . . . Although mine is a fairly minor problem I felt absolutely sure the Lord would heal me . . . Two men came to pray with me . . . One asked if he could put his hand on my right hip. He did so and we again prayed. I felt what I can only describe as a 'red hot needle' go into my hip and I was very, very conscious of God's love and presence.

During the rest of the conference we had to walk quite a way twice a day . . . Normally that would have brought on a painful hip. At first I felt I could hardly breathe as I waited to see what the Lord had done. He had done a wonderful thing – I had no pain, was I really healed? As a nurse I wondered if it was psychological so decided that time would tell – although I was overjoyed at the freedom it gave me. Now all that time on I have *never* had another pain in my hip . . . but now when I spend a day or half a day shopping in a big town now I only get, in common with most people, aching feet and legs which are cured by a sit down and a cup of tea!

Regarding spastic colon for which no healing was claimed: 'Continued to be troublesome, blood passed 1 week after conference . . . prayed for at Ellel Grange by Wimber team, no further haemorrhage, still spastic. This condition started after . . . my husband died, sat in the car beside me.'

Regarding slipped disc in neck for which 'total healing' was claimed: 'occasional muscle spasm, but not out of place since'.

Regarding 'healing of the eyes', for which 'a fair amount' of healing was claimed: 'I am afraid the healing was not sustained. It is not troublesome and I'm putting it down to "normal wear and tear" of age.'

Regarding varicose eczema, claimed to be 'a great deal' of healing:

. . . a condition that my doctor told me I would have to live with because no blood was getting to the surface. The area was often very inflamed, itchy and the skin broken open. Some years ago I had injections for varicose veins. After the healing prayer I have had no more itching and no more breaking open although the area is still discoloured and after bathing I do use the cream which the doctor prescribed. I do know that I have been divinely healed.

Regarding arthritis of the spine, claimed as a 'great deal' of healing: '. . . during the past year I have had no pain whatsoever due to my spine. I have not had a X-Ray to prove that the arthritis no longer shows up because I know that it is not necessary. I know that I am healed.'

Regarding pain in left hip, claimed as 'total healing': 'My left hip was alright for some months, when I felt the pain coming again . . . So I asked some brothers to pray for me for a second time. Since then I do not feel any more pain in my left hip.'

Regarding 'total healing' claimed for a hernia: 'I have never had any trouble with the hernia whatsoever.'

Regarding 'God has rearranged the bones in my foot and the pain has gone', giving a 'great deal' of healing: there was one recurrence a 'year later after I had sat on my foot in the wrong position. However after prayer and confession it is OK now.'

One man wrote on the questionnaire:

Twisted ankle six months ago not healed and causing aches. A friend and I decided to put what we'd learned to the test. After prayer the pain was gone! I tried to make it come back by twisting to what would have been uncomfortable but it was OK. I didn't feel anything happen during our prayer, some warmth but I put this down to my hand touching the sore point. I didn't totally expect anything to happen. Talk about stunned.

He bracketed together 'a great deal' and 'total' healing, writing 'somewhere here'. Fifteen months later he wrote, 'I've had no problems with my ankle since the healing. I've tested this out with various sports like squash, badminton and some running without any reaction.'

A nurse who reported a 'fair amount' of healing for a spine injury wrote in February 1988:

the physical healing I received for my old prolapsed disc injury was complete for about seven months. I was totally pain free and unrestricted in movement and/or exercise and stress related activities. The pain returned however after a particularly rigorous shift in a geriatric nursing home when I had a twenty-one stone woman shift her weight to me completely as I was assisting her from chair to commode. I prevented her falling to the floor, but my back paid the penalty. I developed severe lower back pain and bilateral sciatica down to the toes in my left leg and to back of knee on right leg. The pain settled after two days but since then I occasionally have lower back pain and sciatica seemingly without much provocation. Whether this pain is due to reinjuring the area God healed I am not sure. I only know that seven months completely free of back pain was a wonderful release.

There are some similar features in the following account:

. . . During the conference, the Lord touched my back. I had had lower back pain, extreme at times, for fourteen or fifteen months before the conference. I believe that I must have injured it through a strenuous programme of exercise. The Lord had touched my back approximately six months before the conference during a healing seminar . . . Once I became pregnant with my son (our third child) my back began to hurt again. By the time I arrived in Harrogate I was limping with the pain. As I was only four months pregnant I was *very* concerned about what would happen to my back as the baby grew.

During the conference, another participant prayed for my back . . . The Lord touched me very simply – no tingles, no rush of spiritual feelings or anything – just a short prayer and I felt something in my lower back slip into place. From that moment I was without pain in that spot. Even during the last weeks of my pregnancy we had *no* pain – and my baby was 8lb 10oz! I'm only 5′3″ – which makes that even more amazing.

Just recently some pain has returned as a result of having to bend over [my son's] hospital bed to feed him. [He was hospitalised with meningitis.] But it has responded to prayer. Just a couple of days ago I was in pain and my children (ages six and eight) prayed for it and the pain went away. As my husband and I are missionaries . . . I do believe that there is an element of spiritual attack involved . . .

Another woman wrote on her questionnaire at Harrogate that she had received prayer for 'general arthritis, not severe but longstanding. My left shoulder has been stiff for nearly a year and my neck for very much longer. As a result of prayer I immediately raised my arm fully and was able to turn my head much more easily.' Over a year later she wrote, 'I can say that my shoulder joint has been moving quite freely ever since that day. Perhaps this doesn't sound a very spectacular healing, but it is a real one.'

Sometimes the person seems surprised at receiving an unexpected healing, as in the next account in which the informant reported 'a great deal' of healing for an 'old whiplash injury':

This was [during] the general prayer from the platform . . . I had what could be described as a very thorough manipulation of my neck. I had *not remembered* I had had this injury ten years previously and had got used to always using the car wing mirrors for reversing. I can now turn my head normally and have nearly full movement of my neck but it does still creak when I do so.

I myself never ever asked God to heal my neck. I just put up with it.

When I returned home that very day I sat up in bed and prayed and thanked God for healing my neck at the conference. As I did so I again had an even more thorough manipulation of my neck – being thrown across my bed. After this I had even fuller movement of my neck . . .

The pain in my neck and stiffness does recur if I carry anything really heavy on my shoulder. I am a nurse and we do have heavy shoulder bags. I carry it in my hand.

A similar report comes from a woman who reported 'a great deal' of healing from 'injuries due to a severe car crash in neck, back, arms and right knee'. When followed up, she said:

The knee is the biggest problem because it got Hoffa's disease in it . . . At the John Wimber conference someone prayed over it. Now it's so much better that the only time I feel it is if I've been for a long walk or bang it against something. [For example], when I knocked it against some steel railings and knocked the knee badly I noticed it for a day or two but not after. I'd say it is 90% to 95% healed.

About my arm – the specialist said it healed four times more quickly than expected. The injuries in my back and arms used to ache a lot. They've not gone altogether but after prayer things are a lot better. For three years after the car accident I had very strong and regular bad migraines. Those have totally gone. I haven't had one since I was first prayed over about them. [She thinks that probably occurred at Harrogate too.]

In many cases followed up there was little point in trying to contact the person's doctor for an opinion because the person either had not been receiving specific treatment for the condition before the conference or else did not feel the need to go back to the doctor after receiving what was believed to be divine healing. Such an attitude is perfectly understandable, even though it frustrates this kind of research! However, in the case quoted above it was possible to obtain the doctor's opinion on the reported healing from Hoffa's disease. I quote from his letter:

> . . . She had a serious road traffic accident . . . on 5.10.83. Amongst her many injuries she sustained injury to her right knee. She had a haemarthrosis of the joint and this was not drained . . . she had physiotherapy three times a week for about nine months. She continued to have physiotherapy on her return [here]. In spite of this treatment she still had pain in that knee.
>
> In 1986 she was seen by [a named consultant] who diagnosed Hoffa's disease of the knee. He described this as post-traumatic intra-patcllar fat pad syndrome. He felt that the condition 'would not deteriorate but unfortunately once it is established it becomes chronic and is virtually incapable of cure other than by surgical excision of the painful piece of fat'.
>
> I gather she is now very much better and she regards herself as cured.
>
> Yours sincerely . . .

This doctor's comments are confirmed by the authoritative text in the UK on Hoffa's disease, Smillie's *Diseases of the Knee Joint*. He recommends physiotherapy and wearing a high heel (*i.e.* high-heeled shoes) to take the strain off the front of the knee. If this does not work then the alternative is an operation to remove the scarred fat pad from the front of the knee joint.[1] Although the condition is not a danger to life, 'it is very irritating and is not one which is expected to clear up overnight!'.[2]

The question of representativeness

The quotations given above are not representative for two reasons: (1) I tended to write more to those who reported significant degrees of improvement and (2) I suspect that those who bothered to write back to me are more likely to be those who have something positive to report. Even among those who did reply the amount of detail given in some cases might be an indication of the degree of actual healing received. For these reasons follow-up of interesting cases gives no clear assessment of how common these actually are.

A much better indication of this comes from my follow-up study of individuals selected at random and therefore providing as representative a cross-section as it is possible to obtain. Most of them were interviewed personally, enabling me to delve into relevant aspects in more depth than is possible from written replies. The twenty-seven people who received prayer for physical healing included five people having two different conditions and one person with four areas of ill-health for which prayer was received. In Table 1.2 I classify any noticeable improvement and I use their own descriptive categories (such as 'backache' or 'knee problem') in those cases where the technical medical terms are not supplied.

Of these thirty-five cases, there are twenty (equivalent to 57%) in which healing has been sustained for at least six to ten months – that is, until the time of my interviews. In most cases the longer-term assessments correspond with the degrees of healing reported at the end of the conference itself. An exception concerns the original questionnaire category of a 'fair amount' of healing, which in the longer-term merges with the categories of a 'great deal' and 'total' healing. Almost all those whose initial self-assessments of healing were in these

Table 1.2 *Maintained change in physical conditions reported by those in the random sample between six and ten months after the conference*

Condition	Noticeable improvement	Little or no improvement
Painful elbows	x	
Arthritis		x
Indigestion (linked with tension)		x
Nausea and vomiting	x	
Back pain	x	
Facial paralysis		x
'Diverticulitis' later diagnosed as hernia		x
Morning sickness		x
Suspected haematoma	x	
Backache	x	
Hip stiffness in mornings		x
Ankylosing spondylitis		x
Cervical spondylosis	xxx	
Diabetes		x
Phlebitis	x	
Short leg	x	
Inability to lift arms/stiff shoulders	x	
Very sensitive teeth	x	
Damaged optic nerve		x
Loss of sense of smell		x
Neck pain after a fall	x	
Lump on side of head	x	
Retroverted uterus	x	
'Problem with leg: can't walk properly'		x
Stiff neck – unable to turn it to the right	x	
'Hearing problem'		x
Deafness in right ear	x	
'Knee problem'		x
Scalp disease	x	
Fungus infection in foot	x	
Swollen lymph glands	x	
Curvature of the spine		x
Club foot (talipes)		x

three categories reported noticeable and sustained improvements when interviewed the following year. However, there is considerable variation in the types of conditions for which healing is reported and a clearer idea of specific circumstances is best obtained through some case studies. In the following examples I include some cases of little or no healing as well as others in which a noticeable improvement was reported.

Case studies of those in the random sample

a) 'Painful elbows' [noticeable improvement]

It began last October, terrible pains in both elbows. Working on land [as a farm labourer] I wondered if it was rheumatics . . . At the conference I was prayed for several times about pains in both elbows but I didn't experience any immediate relief. It didn't seem to get better in any way . . .

By Christmas the pains had gone. I can't locate it more definitely, just that we were in Scotland at the time and I didn't have the pain there. It's never come back since then.

[He had not seen a doctor about the problem prior to the conference and had no other treatment for it. After the conference he felt he had 'prayed enough' about it so did not receive any subsequent prayer ministry for this condition.]

b) Facial paralysis [little or no improvement]

I had a tumour – so round and big (not malignant) but the only thing he could do, to get it out, was to cut the nerve . . . It was a parotid tumour (on the parotid gland) . . . I went to a healing service at York Minster with Morris Maddocks and felt an extraordinary sensation of twitching. At the time I didn't know what it was but people said my face was getting better. It used to be twisted out to the side but my face does seem better.

After they prayed with me at the conference a team member also said he thought it looked better. But it doesn't

matter to me because I felt so different . . . certainly
something did happen because I went home roaring with
laughter – I've never laughed so much in my life. We just
laughed all the way home . . . I always used to be stiff and
starchy, afraid of my emotions. But you can't behave like
that as a church warden – can't go round laughing like a
drunken woman all the time!

. . . The healing of the facial paralysis started at the
healing services here . . . and also the one at the Minster. If
I really think about it I'd say there's some improvement.
My eye has got worse, it waters more but I'm getting older.
But my actual mouth, I don't have so much trouble with
eating or keeping food in. The food at one time got in the
cheek and I had to push it out. Also sometimes when I
drank I used to dribble but it doesn't happen so much now.

c) 'Diverticulitis'/hernia [little or no improvement]

I didn't know what my condition was. I'd been troubled by
it for two years beforehand, but it was intermittent. Then at
the conference there was a word of knowledge for someone
with diverticulitis, so I went out for ministry because I
wondered if it was me. I didn't want to see a doctor before
but I thought all the symptoms were that [of diverticulitis] –
the same symptoms but not the same cause.

A girl prayed with me. She was very nervous, seemed to
be new at it . . . The pain did go away but came back after
Christmas. It started again in early February and I said,
'I have to see a doctor: this is worse than ever.' He said it
was a hernia rather than diverticulitis and a hernia does
come and go. I've got a thin bowel wall . . . I needed an
operation reasonably quickly. That's cured it – mostly, not
100%.

d) Suspected haematoma ('blood lump') [noticeable
    improvement]

I'd had a repair of a prolapse and also a hysterectomy. But I
couldn't stand for more than five minutes without pain and
it shouldn't have been like that after three months. [The

operation was on 1 July 1986.] The week before the conference we'd been staying with friends . . . and she was a
gynae. consultant. She felt that there must have been a
haematoma there to be dispersed. But I didn't need to go
back to the doctor because Wimber came first. There's
been no recurrence of it since the conference . . . I've seen
the doctor and she's discharged me.

e) *Ankylosing spondylitis (a form of arthritis which in this*
   case affected the hips) [little or no improvement]

At Sheffield I felt there was a word of knowledge for me
and I went forward. It was about lameness in the hip –
someone with a stick and trouble with the knees. At first I
thought it was not me but then they mentioned the stick and
I thought maybe it was me. I think my steps were easier –
usually when I've been prayed for my steps are easier . . .
Since then I've lost some movement in my hips. My brother
is encouraging me to see a specialist – I'm happier now
about that than I used to be. There's not so much movement now than last year despite all these encouragements.
It always feels easier afterwards but gradually seems to
stiffen up again . . . After Sheffield I could certainly stride
a lot more and took bigger steps. I could still sleep on my
tummy then but I can't now, or only for a moment or two.
The length of my step did definitely increase after Sheffield
– I don't know if it's the same now . . .

[This elderly lady did indicate on her questionnaire at
Harrogate that she had received further prayer for this condition but was ministered to for her 'whole body'. When
interviewed she spoke of John Wimber's Sheffield conference
as being the more significant time in terms of any physical
improvement.]

f) *Cervical spondylosis ('wear and tear' of neck vertebrae*
   which in many cases may also include arthritis) [noticeable
   improvement]

. . . It's about 95% healed. The hospital were doing

nothing for it and I saw an osteopath regularly but since the conference there's only been three or four times when I've been silly and put my neck out. There's been no trouble . . . I've not had problems with headaches or pain in my back . . . Before it had been reasonably bad: I had to go into hospital for three days for X-Rays and tests but they didn't do anything.

Another informant with the same condition said:

. . . It was diagnosed at the beginning of last year . . . Cervical spondylosis is supposed to be . . . progressive, one of the progressions being that you have a pain and tingling sensation down the arm. I'd had tingling and heat – 'low grade pain', according to the doctor – in my arm for a few months before Harrogate. I was prayed for by two lads who told me to say six times, 'Be healed in Jesus' name' – and I thought, 'Where were you brought up?'! On the Tuesday [one of Wimber's team] prayed for me but I had no particular sensation. The tingling and heat persisted through the conference but sometime in the first two weeks after the conference that stopped and I haven't had it since.

I used to do some normal movement with my neck and then be in agony for a day to a week; that used to be about once a month, and that's not happened since. Also it would ache most days either all day or from lunch-time onwards, but now it doesn't very much. The last time it got quite bad the minister and a friend prayed with me and it's been two months since then. So I've had virtually no symptoms since Harrogate but I wouldn't have said then that God had healed me because I felt virtually nothing and there was no outward sign of anything . . .

[This case is classified as being one of reported 'noticeable improvement' even though the person concerned apparently still has the disease. In a case such as this, the person reports a significant alleviation of symptoms but medically the condition is still present. A similar situation is found in the following case too.]

g) Diabetes [little or no improvement]

I only go once a year to the diabetic clinic. They tested and it was clear. I'm not saying I'm clear – I'm waiting. My blood sugar had gone down to 8.0 or 9.5, the first time in seventeen years that it's been down there. I've had no problems at all. I've felt my diabetes is far better than it's ever been. The two substances that cause the problem – both were totally zero. They told me to slim now. I'm still on medication – I just take the tablets but I have no sickness or dizziness. I'll go in September to the hospital to see what they say.

However, this account does not tie up with a letter received from the hospital consultant:

Mr. —— defaulted from our diabetic clinic during most of 1986. He is a type II non insulin dependent diabetic treated with a nominal reducing diet together with Glibenclamide 5 mg. in the morning plus Metformin 1 g. bd.

A glycosylated haemoglobin in February 1986 was 14.1% (normal range 3–8%) and when he was next seen in April 1987 glycosylated haemoglobin was worse at 15.1%. This was in spite of the treatment having been increased in the interim, the Glibenclamide having been doubled.

We last saw this man in September 1987 when there had been marginal improvement, glycosylated haemoglobin being reported at 12.2%. Nevertheless these results show 1) he remains diabetic, 2) there has been no significant change in his diabetic condition.

This man's feelings of increased physical well-being might be attributed to psychological factors, in which case his perceived alleviation of symptoms may be a real psychosomatic effect, but to claim 'healing' must be put in the realm of fantasy. Or is it actually fiction? Is he 'making it up' or is he sincere in his beliefs, even if possibly overestimating the extent of his healing? He himself told me that he did not regard himself as 'cured' until the doctor told him so, and that he was continuing to take the prescribed medication (although not consistently, because he now doubted the need for it).

A major problem in conducting research on medical matters is that patients can easily misconstrue what has been said to them by a doctor. There are a variety of reasons for this, ranging from misunderstanding technical terms to misinterpreting the doctor's tone of voice or facial expression. This particular informant *might* be liable to such misinterpretations because he also told me that his optician had conducted a number of tests during which he seemed to be surprised to find an improvement in the patient's eyesight. However, I later learnt from his optician that between September 1986 and November 1987 this man had become slightly more shortsighted, a deterioration attributable either to his age or to diabetes. His claims in this area have to be considered either fiction or fantasy. This needs to be borne in mind when assessing the next account, which is from the same informant and for which I have been unable to obtain an independent assessment.

h) Short leg [noticeable improvement]

Claims of legs being lengthened have met with a certain amount of scepticism from doctors because to a limited extent it is possible to create an appearance of lengthening a leg when in fact what takes place is merely an adjustment of the pelvic muscles. This is why claims of leg lengthening of half an inch or so cannot be measured scientifically even if they are genuine healings.[3] Christ's rhetorical question, 'Who of you by worrying can add a single cubit to his height?' still produces the reply, 'No one.'[4] However, is it possible for God to lengthen a leg by one-and-half inches, as in the following account?

> . . . In 1965 I had a bad accident, fell fifty foot out of a crane and was at death's door . . . One of the bones in my leg didn't grow back straight but came out sideways as a spur. They operated on the leg and took away the spur . . . [At Harrogate] a woman with her hand over my heart . . . said

I'd had a problem with my legs – she thought it was my right leg. [In fact it was the left.] We prayed for my leg: I watched the leg come level with my right leg and even heard it grow – like breaking wood. I could not walk right for twenty years but now I can go walking with our vicar. I didn't wear a built-up shoe, just limped. I'd learnt to walk with my hip displaced but . . . my stature had got a wobble on. They prayed for my hip to come back to the position it should be – I feel it has. For the first time in twenty-one years I can walk without discomfort or pain, it seems level to me. People used to ask what was wrong with my leg but now they don't mention it. I know inside myself – I've been twenty-one years with discomfort and an aching left side. If I get aches walking now it's in both sides . . .

The same man also reported healing from phlebitis, saying that on his next visit to the hospital the strapping on his thicker leg was cut off because it had become loose.

i) Very sensitive teeth [noticeable improvement]

All my life my teeth have been sensitive. The dentist said it's because the enamel is worn away and the gums receding. He said it was from incorrect brushing but that can't be right as my teeth never saw a toothbrush till I was twelve or fourteen. (I was not brought up but dragged up!) At one time I'd never been able to bite ice cream or ice lollies but now I chew my way through all sorts. As far back as I can remember if I ever bit ice cream or ice lolly pops I just couldn't do it. The pain would go up me teeth and really hit the nerve if I tried to bite it. If it was winter and I went outside I dared not have a warm drink when I came in even if I'd had my mouth shut – I had to wait half an hour. Sometimes I've drunk through a straw so it wouldn't touch me teeth. In winter I'd dare not go out to peg up the washing without a scarf on – I had to keep my lips together outside or all me teeth would throb. I couldn't hold a conversation outside at the bus stop.

There was a word of knowledge about gums on the top

right side receding. All mine are, but I thought if the Lord is into healing teeth I'll ask about mine . . . He put his hands on my head and prayed. I don't know about feeling anything round me teeth but I did feel slightly drunk. Only two minutes of prayer for healing for me teeth and whatever was causing the pain.

I went out at teatime. It was quite a cold, windy night and I chatted and laughed and did everything I was not supposed to do outside. I expected pain, but no. Then I had a hot drink of tea: normally that would have sent me through the roof but there was no pain at all. But when we went home at night, it was a ten to fifteen minutes' walk to the car park. I were really overjoyed the Lord had healed me teeth so I walked to the car park with me mouth open. But then in the car I got the toothache back. I were quite peeved with the Lord for doing it an' then not doing it. I was quiet and sulking – peeved with the Lord . . . I spoke to the pain and commanded it in Jesus' name to go but it made no difference and the pain was there all the time. I got home and was very discouraged. I told me 'usband and he said, 'Don't worry, maybe the Lord has not finished yet.'

Next day it was very cold. We parked in the usual place . . . It was very cold and I'd got to know one way or the other. I walked down with me mouth open: 'Lord, if you've done it I do need to know.' I had a hot cup of tea when I got there and there was no pain at all, none at all. I couldn't understand it, but that's how it was.

Since then I've only had toothache once. We've gone through a whole winter: I've gone to the shops, bus, pegged washing out and never had to cover my mouth up. It's never come back . . .

When I go into the dentist he asks, 'How's the sensitivity?', and I usually say I keep my mouth shut. I shall go in next month . . . He knows I've got sensitive teeth and once painted some stuff on. But it made no difference. I was due for a check-up three months ago but because we changed address that's probably why I've not had a card about being due for a check-up.

After this informant had been back to her dentist I wrote to him for his opinion. His reply was as follows:

. . . I enclose details from the above patient's record card relevant to your enquiry.

18.1.82	Complaining of sensitivity – Application of Fluocal (Hypersensitive Dentine)
23.11.82	Application of Fluocal on upper right 6 5 4 [teeth]
30.11.82	Application of Fluocal on upper right 3 2 1 and left 1 2 3 4 5 6.
25.4.83	Lower left 8 very sensitive. Prescribed Sensodyne Toothpaste. Suggested must be used all the time in view of patient's hypersensitivity.
6.6.85	Routine examinations. Patient advised to con-
10.3.86	tinue use of Sensodyne Toothpaste to control sensitivity.
18.8.87	Routine dental check-up. Patient no longer complains of sensitive teeth.

j) Lump on side of head [noticeable improvement]

A nurse wrote on her questionnaire about receiving prayer for

intermittent pain behind left ear travelling down to the shoulder and the fear that it might be a growth of some kind. Fear kept me silent and it was never shared with anyone. I asked for prayer after I believed the Lord had healed me, to confirm and make it complete.

When interviewed about it she said:

There was a lump in my head, definitely. It caused pain and could be felt. I got the books out. They were the signs and symptoms of some kind of tumour. I was really very terrified, imagining in what area, and if it was that deep touching a part of the brain and couldn't be operated on. It was really very sore. When we went to Harrogate I said, 'Lord, I would like this removed' – I wanted God to take away the pain and lump so I couldn't feel it. I'd been getting headaches only on the left side and half way round, pain in my left eye and a tingling and buzzing sensation in my ear, so I thought it was a tumour. It was greater or lesser depending on how tired I was.

I mentioned it to two or three nurse friends but not to [my husband] or to church friends who mattered. I tried Panadols *etc*. and could dull it sometimes but not get rid of it. My attitude changed: I shouted at the children, and [my husband] said I was like a bear with a sore head. [At work] I went into the sluice sometimes and kicked the dirty laundry bags – it was driving me crackers.

On the Monday night [at Harrogate] I said, 'Lord, I want this to go.' The pain decreased and became more bearable. Then on the Thursday afternoon session with Blaine,[5] he was talking about faith and said . . . 'Some of you have got things the matter with you and maybe your faith is strong enough to be healed without people praying for you.'

My pain was less but the lump was still there . . . I remember shutting my eyes and clenching my fists and said, 'Lord, I've got faith but I don't know how big it is. You said about moving mountains – I've not got a mountain but a lump in my head. I'm asking now in Jesus' name that it be gone.'

I can't remember feeling different after that but as I went to another person to pray I realised there was no longer any pain, my eye was not sore, my ear didn't buzz and my head didn't hurt. The Lord said, 'Now you've got to ask J. to pray for you.' I thought, 'I'm not hearing this right' but J. was there not far away. 'Why?,' I asked [the Lord], and he said, 'Because you're secretive, stubborn and won't ask someone to pray. You're not to be anonymous in the crowd but it's got to be someone you know.' That was harder than asking for healing. I went to J. and told him the Lord had told me to get him to pray for me. I told him about what I thought was a tumour. 'Silly woman,' he said, when I said why I'd not told anyone and he was laughing as he stretched out his hand and began to pray for me – 'Lord, do it deep, make it permanent and last.' That's when I went down . . .

k) Retroverted uterus [noticeable improvement]

The same nurse also described another healing as follows:

I had a gynae. problem. I was worried that the way it was going it would mean a hysterectomy. I had a D and C (dilatation and curettage) but it didn't do any good. A course of hormones relieved the symptoms but not the root cause, and made me put on a stone in weight. I tried cryosurgery – a freezing technique – with a little success but for a limited time: that helped for a while but then it came back.

I was due for another check-up after Harrogate and they were going to decide what they were going to do. I didn't want a hysterectomy, I had a phobia about it. I prayed this would not be so. I knew I had a retroverted uterus – it was back to front and lying on its side, out of position . . . One night at Harrogate, I was standing there praying and said, 'Lord, you know I don't want a hysterectomy. Please heal it.'

I felt a really strange sensation inside, really weird, like a flutter. I said, 'Thank you, Lord, I'll have that.' I was standing there . . . and manifesting shaking all up the right side while my left side was perfectly still. Some members of the team prayed for me and the shaking got worse. A man at the back of me must have been praying as well because he came up and said, 'It's embarrassing this: I believe you've got something wrong with the insides – the ladies' bit – and the Lord has done a healing.' I flung my arms round him and said, 'Thank you.'

It was not confirmed till March 1987. I had an episiotomy scar with nodules – it gets infected now and again. When they got inside they found a hole, a little tiny tear, and sewed it up with stitches. But they didn't take the womb away as it was completely healthy . . . A hysterectomy was on the cards and I asked the Lord that I wouldn't have it. I had pressure on one side and I was aware of it especially at certain times of the month. But surgically there is no way you can prove that it was because of me and my body. I've seen my own report file and surgically there's no evidence of God's healing . . .

l) Deafness in right ear [noticeable improvement]

A retired missionary was not aware during the conference itself that her hearing had improved but when interviewed the following summer said:

> I'm still slightly deaf – I can't hear acutely but I've not worn a hearing aid since the John Wimber conference. It's not 100% but quite a bit improved.
>
> I can't remember if someone prayed for me about it at the conference. I prayed, 'Lord, give me my hearing' but I didn't mention it to anybody. Before, I couldn't hear my watch tick with my right ear but now I can hear my watch tick with it. Before, I couldn't hear it with either at one time but I particularly prayed for my right ear. I still miss some things at some times but there has certainly been an improvement.
>
> I went to the hospital two years ago because I found I was not hearing very well. They gave me a hearing aid. It was not very satisfactory really because it also exaggerates the other sounds I don't want to hear. At one time I was quite glad to put it on but I've not worn it since and don't think about it now.

[She has not been back to the hospital for further tests since the conference because the hospital does not recall such patients for check-ups and they only need return if they have problems.]

Assessment

In many cases when a patient visits a doctor, the doctor relies largely on the patient's own report. A few additional tests for temperature, pulse and so on might provide further information but these are evaluated in the light of the patient's own account. For some kinds of ailments it may be necessary to refer the patient on to a hospital for more specialised examination through blood tests, X-Rays or other procedures. These more specialised examinations are undertaken for what is in fact a minority of ailments, whereas the majority of cases receive treatment from the local GP – if they are even brought to the doctor at all.

For this reason there is often very little documentary medical evidence for claims of healing. In many cases all the doctor would be able to say is that the patient has ceased requesting repeat prescriptions for a drug or that the patient no longer reports having various symptoms. It is the patient's own account which is the primary evidence of the person's state of health.

In this connection it is appropriate to quote some comments by David Wilson, Dean of Postgraduate Medical Education at the University of Leeds. Commenting on the initial draft of this chapter, he wrote to me:

As a doctor I am troubled by the way in which you give 100% credence to the 'doctor's diagnosis'. Perhaps you have to do so to have a reference point for your case discussion, but I am so conscious that (a) doctors are not always right, (b) they are very reluctant to admit that anything other than the treatment they prescribed can have benefited the patient. I'm not suggesting you can do anything about this! You are just reflecting the lay public's blind faith in the medical profession.

At several points there is a conflict between 'diagnosis' and 'complaint'. This perhaps occurs most clearly over cases of cervical spondylosis. The X-Ray shows the typical ageing process or degeneration in the joints between adjacent cervical vertebrae. If there is pain in the neck spreading to the arm, the patient (complaint) and the doctor (diagnosis) are in agreement. If the patient is healed and the complaint disappears then patient and doctor may be in disagreement because the X-Ray appearance hasn't changed. But surely what matters, what is important, is what the patient feels (or doesn't feel), not the doctor's intellectual concept of cervical spondylosis. What I am trying to express is a belief that patients matter more than doctors; the doctor is the servant of the patient, not vice versa!

Anthropologists have often drawn a distinction between the worldview of the people they are studying and the supposedly more 'scientific' categories of analysis used by the Western anthropologist.[6] However, the validity of this distinction is being increasingly questioned because of the substantial areas of overlap between the two worldviews. This is particularly the case in my anthropological study of part of our own society and culture. Those who report these healings are aware of medical categories and in some cases are themselves employed in medical or health-related professions. They accept the validity of doctors' opinions on their conditions even if they also happen to have divergent views on the possible spiritual causes of certain ailments. Their worldviews do overlap considerably with those of their doctors.

For the doctors, however, professional integrity may be at stake if they are willing to acknowledge that a cure is 'supernatural'. This is outside their professional areas of competence and all they are able to report are the facts as these are presented to them, of which a significant part consists of the patients' own accounts of their conditions. Therefore the doctors are able merely to state that particular patients no longer report various symptoms: it would be overstepping their professional boundaries if the doctors then drew conclusions that certain cures were actually 'miracles', even if they are unable to explain the cures on medical grounds.

This is the approach of the doctor who wrote about the patient with Hoffa's disease and of the dentist reporting on the patient with hypersensitive teeth. In other cases medical reports are able to give even less information, even if they are available. For example, if the retired missionary in case (l) above were to have her ears tested again it may be possible to quantify the extent of her gain in hearing but it would not add very much to the basic facts of her own account which has been quoted.[7]

Some Christian medical doctors are also prepared to accept patients' accounts as evidence of divine healing even in the absence of corroborative evidence. In Rex Gardner's excellent book *Healing Miracles* (1986) there are a number of medically documented cases of healing, but in case record 8.2 he mentions a woman in India who was healed of backache and of urinary stress-incontinence. Gardner as a professional gynaecologist was convinced by the testimony she gave him even in the absence of corroborative hospital records.[8]

For these reasons I have generally allowed the testimonies to speak for themselves but I have included quotations from doctors' reports where appropriate. In cases such as the ones involving Hoffa's disease or hypersensitive teeth the nature of the ailments seems such that the cures cannot be attributable to psychosomatic or other factors as conventionally understood. These would appear to be among the better documented cases of divine healing among those which I have followed up. However, there are many other testimonies, not all of which are included in this book, which from the informants' own accounts would also appear to indicate the possibility of divine healing.[9] The *fact* of divine healing is to my mind adequately documented by Rex Gardner's research.[10] What I want to do now is to go beyond this to explore some of the other issues raised by my data.

Recurrence or Achilles' heel?

If in October I have a sore throat, often find myself sneezing and have other symptoms of a cold, but the symptoms disappear shortly afterwards only to come back again the following February, we say that I have caught 'another cold', not that my cold has had a remission and recurrence. This is because we attribute the cold to an external agency such as an influenza virus. We also assume I have come into contact with a slightly different form of the virus to which my body has no existing antibodies.

However, the sore throat is often produced by bacteria called streptococci which are found in the throats of many people who do not have colds, even if they multiply more when someone does have a cold. This suggests a different model of how one catches a cold, namely that there is an equilibrium between the attacking forces and the body's resistance in most healthy people, but if our resistance falters the opposition gains an advantage. Linked with this model are other models, perhaps equally valid, which point to some of the factors affecting our resistance to infection. These can include environmental agents like the weather, nutritional factors like the amount of Vitamin C in the diet and psychological influences to do with our attitudes and general feelings of well-being.[11]

If this is the case with the common cold, what about other illnesses? During my interviews I came across people who reported healings from arthritis at some point in the past who had a recurrence as much as five years later. For a long while they genuinely thought they were healed, but then the symptoms came back so they decided they were not healed. My question is whether it is indeed a 'recurrence' or if it is parallel to 'catching another cold' at a later date. Is it the 'same' disease or not?

As an example, consider the following account from a middle-aged nurse:

From 1972 when I suffered my first attack of cervical spondylosis, a particularly painful form of one of the arthritic diseases, affecting my neck bones, leading in time to osteo-arthritis of the third and fourth cervical joints and as an indirect (but not proven) cause of frozen shoulders, left twice and right once, due to calcium deposits in the shoulder joints. I have been on traction . . . three times and a cervical collar four times . . . and I can't remember how many injections *into* the shoulder joints. I am a state registered nurse of twenty-three years experience . . . This severely handicapped me. Sometimes it would be agony to work and to lift and I used to consume painkillers – you name it, I've taken it!

. . . [At John Wimber's conference in Brighton in 1985] . . . suddenly Mr Wimber stepped to 'my' side of the stage and said, 'The woman in the cream shirt (me), I command in the name of Jesus that the arthritis in the third and fourth joints of the neck to be gone and the joints to become perfect.' I felt as though I was being grabbed by an unseen hand. I had been *so* bent forwards shaking, my shoulders had been *so* curved forwards and my backbone bent, I was almost double. Suddenly I was straightening up and my shoulders were uncurving, and my back was being straightened up and my head was being taken right back and my neck was being forced back and I found myself looking up at the ceiling, as I couldn't see anything else! I said, 'Oh Lord, I'm in such pain,' for it was. It was agony, and I couldn't move, every muscle was being pulled and straightened. I felt the Lord say, 'This is what I suffered for you,' and I just saw him on his cross, bent double for me. Suddenly it stopped, it seemed like I'd been there for ever, and I started to laugh, and John said, 'Another satisfied customer.'

. . . The noise in my neck had gone! I'd had a slight crunching noise in my neck for years. I felt as though a donkey had kicked me the next day and I ached for weeks after. But since, we've had the coldest February on record, and I've had no trouble. I have *never* had such pain since. I've been tired and aching when I've come home from work, but after twelve hours night duty, wouldn't you? I have had the odd slightly stiff neck, but I notice only when I'm tired . . . I have had my healing for over a year now, and as a cynical hardened nurse who is accustomed to dealing with people for twenty-three years I would not have accepted this in the past, but now I know the Lord loves and heals.

This testimony was written in November 1986, but a letter to me dated 6 January 1988 had a different story to tell:

> . . . It is with the very deepest regret that I have to tell you that I am unable to be of any assistance. Believe me I am so very sorry to tell you that as of Monday 4 January I have had an 'attack' of cervical spondylosis, confirmed by my GP.
>
> It started at the beginning of December . . . and I thought I had 'pulled' a muscle. However, it did not clear up and it remained a nagging ache, slowly increasing . . . I was, by now, almost certain what it was and staggered and disappointed, and very confused spiritually. For I am absolutely convinced that I received a healing from God . . . Slowly I have come to terms with this reoccurrence. Incidentally my GP thinks it arises from C 7 (the seventh cervical vertebra) whereas before it was C 4 and 5 or C 3 and 4, I cannot remember.

This account has been quoted at length because it shows how a dramatic healing appears to have been sustained for over two years but what was interpreted as a recurrence led to the person being 'very confused spiritually'. My question, however, is whether the arthritis in the seventh cervical joint is actually a recurrence of that which had been in the third and fourth joints – or is it a 'different' illness? The third and fourth joints appear still to be healthy – and these were the ones specified in the apparently supernatural information about her condition given to John Wimber.

The same is true of accounts in which a back condition has come back after a while because of heavy lifting, as in the case of the nurse who had to support a very overweight patient who fell on her. Is it that an 'Achilles' heel' or an area of weakness in our bodies is particularly prone to certain ailments? If there is no recurrence of arthritis in the third and fourth joints, are there predisposing conditions which make it easier for arthritis to occur in the nearby seventh joint? I speculate that some of these areas of weakness may be linked with factors such as diet or general lifestyle which may mean that a similar kind of problem might occur in a similar part of the body because external factors such as one's type of work remain unchanged.

'Divine physiotherapy'

From the available evidence it seems as if God can heal in a variety of ways. There are cases in which natural healing processes seem to be miraculously speeded up, other cases in which physical healing follows on after ministry for deliverance or inner healing, and still other cases in which there appears to be a supernatural work of power resulting in healings inexplicable by 'natural' processes. All these are aspects of divine healing but it is the third type which tends to be the most spectacular.

A fourth, less commonly recognised form of divine healing involves 'divine physiotherapy'. One instance was quoted earlier in the account of 'a very thorough manipulation' of the neck which had received a whiplash injury. One of those I interviewed said that she witnessed a rippling of the skin on a girl's leg which looked like the effects of massage by invisible hands after the body of this girl had received a certain amount of battering during the manifestation of a demon prior to its expulsion. Another informant said that while praying at Harrogate for a man with badly damaged feet a team member said, 'Everybody, hands off.' Then

> the man could feel hands on his leg but no one was touching him: he was told it was the Lord . . . He felt there was someone's hands on him and it was warm. I felt that the team leader had a word of knowledge about taking hands off, so that the touch the man felt was a confirmation that God was healing him.[12]

Ginny, the woman whose healing I mentioned on pp. 272–273 of *Power Healing* (in my report on the Sheffield conference) described a similar experience:

I was tired and sceptical because I had the attitude that I hadn't seen any signs and wonders yet. I very nearly didn't go to the meeting . . . but as I entered the building and sat in the disabled section I got a sense of being lifted inside: the tiredness and scepticism lifted. I got a sense that tonight I'd see signs and wonders – but I didn't think it would be me!

The meeting began with praise and worship and we all stood to sing. As we were singing I started feeling various physical sensations very slightly in my back, as though someone were going up and down each vertebra pinching each one with a finger and thumb. By the time we'd finished worshipping, I sat down and it dawned on me I'd stood for forty minutes continually. Also I noticed I had no pain in my lower back when I moved from standing to sitting. It never dawned on me that God was doing something. John [Wimber] began to speak and all the time the sensations were getting stronger and stronger. My right leg . . . then tingled and it felt like it was being moved about. My back felt hot, especially in the area where I'd had the operation. Also heat in my neck. The feeling of somebody pressing on each side of my vertebrae lasted till the coffee break. I still didn't think God was doing anything but it was so pleasant I didn't want it to stop . . .[13]

Another informant described her healing from cervical spondylosis and back pain through a process of 'divine physiotherapy' which began one night during a visit to her church by one of Wimber's teams after the Harrogate conference:

. . . the Spirit came very powerfully, my hands shaking and my head started nodding. I was very frightened and asked God to stop it if it was not from God; it started again . . . That night I had lots of dreams and the team was still ministering to me in my dreams . . . In the middle of the night I woke up and my hip was going round and round but I was not frightened by it. Another time I woke up and I was pushing my face upwards. God said I had to put my hands on my back . . . [and] to invite the Spirit to come on my back. I got an anointing in my hands for my back, then my head started to go from side to side . . .

[Two nights later.] Still I hadn't had prayer for the odd head shaking thing . . . They prayed for me and I felt very terrified as they prayed . . . They ended up praying against a spirit of torment. So much had been coming up in the week that was very painful. It was like as if something was on my back – my back arched and I screamed and screamed and was hoarse afterwards . . . I do think I was delivered of something. I still felt very low but that night I slept well for the first time in four nights.

The next day I felt very bereft . . . Then I let the Lord hug me and his Spirit came on in and a real sense of release. I was full of joy and it was fantastic. That night . . . at 11.45-ish I was standing in the kitchen praising the Lord. Then all of a sudden . . . I felt God saying, 'Just relax, put your hands down by your side' and my head started to go up and down. Normally that would be incredibly painful because of my spondylosis. There was no way I could do that. The Lord proceeded to give me physiotherapy in the Spirit over the next two hours. I started to put my shoulders or arm this way and that and got into a rhythm. I had my eyes shut and felt the Lord even warning me not to hit the fridge or put my hand in the fire. I'd say, 'That was a funny one, Lord' as he made me do something: . . . at one stage I was with my tummy on the floor and my legs on the fridge above me. There was no way I could do that. This physio went on for an hour in the kitchen – I took off my clothes as they were restricting . . . A lot of [the exercises] are actually exercises where the motor action was from the muscles in one part of my body moving muscles elsewhere, such as legs to hips or arms to shoulders . . .

Relationships with 'words of knowledge'

In chapter 3 I shall discuss further the relationship between healing and messages believed to be from God, called 'words of knowledge'. In particular I shall discuss how high degrees of healing are associated with more specific 'words of knowledge'. However, less specific 'words of knowledge' have associated with them some cases of high degrees of healing and other cases of little or no healing. For example, the woman who was healed of hypersensitive teeth was not the only one to respond to the word of knowledge about receding gums. Two men who also responded to it reported no healing as a result. I wrote to them both in February 1988. One of them replied that his condition was caused by following, over the years, an incorrect tooth-brushing procedure but when he changed the way he brushed his teeth the recession of the gums halted. He had no pain or sensitivity to begin with and had none afterwards. The other man had a cold-sensitive area in his upper right jaw so that he could not, for instance, rinse his mouth out using water straight from the tap without intense pain. His condition had lasted 'some time' and his dentist had been unable to treat it successfully. The sensitivity remained but had diminished during the year following the conference, so that it was 'now far less than it was'. He remarks that he has no way of knowing whether this is a natural progression or was aided by the prayer, but he considers there still to be a problem there somewhere.

During one of the afternoon workshops at Harrogate there was a word of knowledge about 'swollen lymph glands under the left arm which have been painful in the last few days'. As approximately a quarter of those attending the conference were at any one workshop, this was a somewhat more specific word of knowledge than the one about receding gums. Only one man (to my knowledge) felt this applied to him. His account is as follows:

The minute this was spoken it was as if the volume to me suddenly increased . . . a subliminal thing, I knew it was for me, like a scripture standing out. The pain went as I was prayed for – I could touch things without pain. The amazing thing was that the day before it had been very painful but I was not so aware of the pain that day. That was in an afternoon session – by the evening the swelling had gone.

At the end of the conference he claimed the healing was total. When interviewed about it the following September, he said:

> Before Harrogate I got it regularly, probably monthly, and if it lasted for a chunk of one week at a time it meant I was under the weather and in pain. It's only a thing I've suffered from since I went into full-time Christian work – I don't remember it when I was in senior management in industry for fifteen years and worked quite hard . . .
> It has come back but is totally different from what it used to be: it used to last one or two weeks, but in Thailand at the most it lasted two days, and also this August . . . at the beginning of my holiday, and I'd moved house the week before and helped someone else to move . . . So to me it was total healing and the fact that there's only three days recurrence in the last ten months to me ranks as very close to total healing because there are clear reasons for it . . . In Thailand in February I had a monumental work load, I'd never worked so hard in my life. In one month I led worship thirty-five times and spoke seventeen times . . .

This attribution of recurrence to times of unusual stress or tiredness is also a feature of some accounts of the recurrence of arthritis. Nevertheless, informants perceive a marked difference in their ailments before and after prayer and the extent of this difference does seem to be relatively greater for most of those who responded to more specific words of knowledge.

Can healing be conditional?

The occasional recurrence of certain conditions raises the question of whether these are due merely to stress or are also linked to moral or spiritual factors. Sometimes conditions which recur at times of Christian ministry are attributed to demonic agencies. However, in a few cases the recurrence of certain ailments is attributed to a relapse in the person's own spiritual life.[14] The next account is one such example but refers to a healing which took place two years prior to the informant's first contact with John Wimber, while she was at a meeting led by someone else:

> I was playing the piano that night and didn't really want to be there . . . I wanted to go home. That evening he spoke about God wanting to heal people and spoke about David dancing and Michal laughing at him, which led to her barrenness. He said, 'All you cynical people, be careful' . . . I was sitting by the piano thinking it was about time I was home.
>
> I had alopecia; my hair used to drop out in bald patches. It was concealed: I used to wear wigs and never admitted to it or told anyone. Before this I used to get a lot of bald patches. I thought it was from stress but now I don't believe that: God said, 'This is a sign of rebellion and disobedience if you're not walking close to me.' It's taken me seventeen years to find that out.
>
> This man prayed for everyone because there were many people there . . . I said to myself, there's nothing wrong with me except my scalp. As I did so, I had a tingling on my scalp – I thought it was auto-suggestion. About a week later I found that in every single area where I'd had a bald patch there was a week's growth. I suddenly realised I'd been healed by this man I didn't even like!
>
> . . . Later I mentioned it to a Christian consultant friend and he was fascinated: it was never heard of because alopecia doesn't recover like that, there was no logical reason why it should all grow back. He told me to write to a dermatology journal but I never bothered.
>
> I don't have alopecia now. It has come back but the closer I am to God then it doesn't recur. When I don't back-pedal then it stays; it's a sign of my closeness to God.

It is interesting that another person interviewed should also view the condition of his scalp as a barometer of his walk with God:

I've got bald patches on my scalp from a skin disease – *lichen planus* – but there's no cure for it. It's like a scab that grows and kills the hair follicles: once dead, they're dead. Two years ago I had a course of steroids but it didn't work. I get very itchy patches on my scalp – there are remains of it now. It's not restored my hair but the development has stopped; it's not ravaged my scalp in the same way as before.

Blaine [Cook, who was leading one of the workshops] described clearly a skin disease going up the back of the head . . . At the same time I was healed of a fungal infection in my foot. There was no word of knowledge about my feet, just about the creeping thing on my scalp. But both have totally gone.

His wife, a nurse, was also present during the interview and commented:

Occasionally when [my husband] gets uptight about something I will see it pinking at the edges so I suspect it's a tension thing . . . I feel his scalp condition and the return of the growth of his hair is like Samson: there's an association in the growth of his hair being somehow tied up with the growth of the parish – I feel a conviction that it's all tied up.[15]

What counts as an 'illness'?

One of those interviewed reported a temporary alleviation of morning sickness symptoms which returned after the conference. Rex Gardner asks, 'When does the nausea of pregnancy cease to be normal? When are aching joints merely due to age?' He goes on to write, 'I do not believe that we can always draw a clean line between health and disease,' mentioning also menopausal problems as a further example of the similarities between changes due to natural ageing processes and those due to disease.[16] In the previous section certain scalp problems were reported to have been healed by God, but is it right to pray for relief from having grey hairs or baldness as one becomes older? God says, 'Even to your old age and grey hairs I am he, I am he who will sustain you' (Isaiah 46:4). He does not promise to heal the grey hairs. The prophet Elisha, who had one of the greatest 'signs and wonders' ministries of the Old Testament period, became bald (2 Kings 2:23).[17] Rex Gardener quotes Walter Stockdale (a doctor in York) as saying that when God heals us he heals us into dying bodies.[18]

Nevertheless there are pop stars and others in our own culture who pay for plastic surgery to remove wrinkles caused by the ageing process. Their wrinkles are what anthropologists would call a 'culture-bound illness' – one which is perceived as a medical 'problem' by certain people but is not perceived in the same way by outsiders. In the same way there is a certain degree of subjectivity in the way each one of us regards our own health. Moreover, that state of 'health' can be measured on different axes – physical, mental and spiritual – and it is sometimes assumed that spiritual health may be at the expense of physical health. To some extent this idea lies behind the practice of fasting – even if the discipline involved in fasting also happens to bring about some side-benefits in our relatively over-fed society!

Fasting produces a discomfort to ourselves brought about voluntarily for the sake of a desired benefit. The same is true of having a surgical operation. Those who question the necessity of surgery should consider the fact that some mutilation of the physical body was divinely ordained in the Old Testament (Genesis 17:9–14; Exodus 21:6). Christ himself voluntarily suffered piercing with nails on our behalf.[19] While his crucifixion is different from surgery for one's own sake, it raises questions about the extent to which God allows us to suffer physically for the sake of greater goals.

The same may be true of persecution. Persecution is often mentioned in the book of Acts and it forms the background to the first letter of Peter. Several of Paul's letters as well as the book of Revelation were written from prison or exile, and we are warned that 'everyone who wants to live a godly life in Christ Jesus will be persecuted' (2 Timothy 3:12). However, the attitude to these physical trials is that they produce spiritual benefits (1 Peter 1:7).[20] A very similar idea is found in Matthew 5:11–12, which is immediately followed by comments about salt losing its saltiness: is there an implication that persecution maintains a Christian's saltiness?[21]

A theology of suffering

The nurse quoted earlier who believed she had been healed of arthritis at Brighton in 1985 wrote of being 'very confused spiritually' after her doctor diagnosed cervical spondylosis in a different joint in 1988. Over the centuries, religious people have tried to come to terms with the fact of suffering, illness and death in the world. They have come up with a variety of rationalisations or part-rationalisations, but often these ideas provide little comfort for those actually suffering. These 'explanations' for suffering can be modern equivalents to the theological positions of Job's so-called 'comforters'. A rather different approach is that associated with the name of John Wimber, which expects God to intervene actively in healing people, instead of trying to rationalise why one should put up with suffering.

However, what is not so widely appreciated in Britain is that Wimber also has a theology of suffering. To some extent this is discussed in chapter 8 of *Power Healing*, but it is expounded in more detail in the Winter 1988 issue of *Equipping the Saints* magazine, which is published by Wimber himself.[22] In essence he writes that 'God uses our suffering to fulfil his purposes and bring maturity to our lives.' In many respects this is similar to the approach of Paul Billheimer's book *Don't Waste Your Sorrows* (1977), which puts our suffering now in an eternal context through what in many ways is an exposition of the text 'For our light and momentary troubles are achieving for us an eternal glory that far outweighs them all' (2 Corinthians 4:17). Billheimer's view is that God is working to produce in us *agape* love, and he may use suffering in order to mould our characters (Romans 5:3–5).[23]

Repentance and emotional healing

Some of those I had followed up reported that during prayer for physical healing it was discerned that what God really wanted for the person's life was repentance of some kind. However, certain individuals who have repented of homosexuality or a past adulterous affair did not afterwards receive physical healing – although as far as I am aware they did not have subsequent prayer for physical healing following their repentance. Even if God uses suffering to produce purer characters, the repentance in itself apparently does not necessarily lead to physical healing.

Similarly, prayer for a physical problem may be interpreted as a sign of God's care and lead to emotional healing even if the physical condition afterwards remains unaltered, as illustrated by the next case:

In the autumn of 1986 . . . I was told that I needed to be cut off from 'something wild', possibly in my family line. I was mortified by this. My confidence that what I had been doing was OK was greatly undermined. I then allowed myself to be subjected to a thorough purging of anything and everything, even from years back, things which I thought had been dealt with during the normal course of Christian forgiveness. This left me feeling exceedingly battered and vulnerable and humiliated and open to all sorts of attack from thoughts wondering . . . if it was complete, *etc*. [There was actually a word of reassurance and comfort at Harrogate to people who had been through this sort of thing.] I did not feel reaffirmed in the love of God or the church. I had repented of everything imaginable, whether I had done it or not . . .

At Harrogate . . . when the Holy Spirit came . . . I had pins and needles in my arm *and I couldn't move* . . . So I asked the man in the next seat to pray for my neck. He did, then I said that what I really wanted to know was that God loved me with all my peculiarities. So the man said I must ask *for a sign* – nothing too wild – and he went.

Then a woman came up to me and said the Lord had told her to pray for my hands. I thought she was probably a bit daft as there was nothing wrong with my hands. She . . . picked up my hands and began to look at them and saw my peculiar bent fingers (which I had entirely forgotten about as they have always been like that and never really bother me). She started to pray for my hands. I suddenly knew that this was God's sign to me telling me that he really did love me with all my peculiarities . . .

Prevention is better than cure

Physical sickness may be caused by emotional conflicts which in turn might have demonic roots (as I shall explain further on pp. 116–128). Sometimes it is necessary to 'dig deep' in order to discover and minister to the causes of a problem rather than trying to alleviate its symptoms. I would go further than this, however, and suggest that a wider context for therapy may be appropriate too.

1   *Diet* Kenneth Vickery has pointed out the problems which may arise from poor nutrition even in Britain, let alone in the Third World. He attributes many common illnesses to what he calls Deplete Food Disease – often caused by the commercial preparation and treatment of food before it is sold in supermarkets.[24] One of those I interviewed described how at Harrogate she was involved with a group praying for a twenty year old man who was 6′6″ tall. She told him he needed cod liver oil, vitamins and calcium, because he needs vitamins A and D (found in cod liver oil) to enable the calcium to deposit. She called this 'sanctified common sense', not a supernatural insight; the man confirmed this was his doctor's diagnosis.

2   *Medicine* Wimber recognises the need for conventional medicine and does not suggest that divine healing should replace it. Some medical techniques like vaccinations are preventative instead of therapeutic but both kinds of medicines can at times produce undesirable side-effects. Some-

times the side-effects can be so damaging as to cause major ill-health: thalidomide babies are the best-known example of what are technically called iatrogenic illnesses.[25] What was originally intended as an instrument for producing health has instead produced ill-health and grief – perhaps rather like boiling a kid in its mother's milk.[26] Partly as a reaction to such side-effects, there has in recent years been an increasing interest in 'natural' or herbal remedies. This movement is partly a return to the roots of conventional medicine, which originally derived drugs like quinine from isolating the active ingredients in the plants. However, according to some recent experiments, these active ingredients might actually be less effective as medicines than the original crude extract. This is because the trace elements and other molecules hitherto considered unimportant in fact play a vital role in ingestion by limiting the reaction of the drug in the body, so that it does not go too far and cause unwanted side-effects.[27] For the Christian, these properties of the original plants could be perceived as divinely ordained. Just as dock leaves can be found in the same environments as stinging nettles, to provide a readily available antidote, so some medicinal plants can contain in themselves the antidotes to their own side-effects. These unwanted side-effects can result when man tries to separate what God has joined together.

3 *Ecology* If God has provided food for healthy bodies and plants containing medication, man's responsibility is to look after God's creation as his representative and as stewards of his resources (Genesis 1:28). A plundering attitude to nature can have long-term deleterious results on the health of mankind, through the degradation of the very environment which is essential for life. Short-term profit can lead to long-term loss, like selling one's birthright for a bowl of stew (Genesis 25:29–34).

4 *Politics* Often collective effort is required to effect long-term benefit or damage to man's environment, and it is the responsibility of human governments to organise collective resources wisely. Political forces have powerful influences upon the availability of resources, including food-

stuffs and medicines. They also permit or hinder exploitation, both of the natural environment and of the human beings under their jurisdiction. 'Healing' in a broader context includes the provision of water supplies and sanitation, legislation on safety at work or the use of toxic materials, measures to enable people to have decent housing, defending the rights of the weak and underprivileged, showing compassion for refugees and protecting citizens from injustice.

5 *Economics* Political and economic forces are closely interlinked, but if we are to address issues of health and healing we need to recognise that in most societies those suffering the greater degrees of ill-health are the poor. Poverty is closely linked with malnutrition, inadequate housing and, in some countries, the lack of amenities such as domestic water supplies or sanitation. In many countries the poor are trapped by a cycle of debt which perpetuates their poverty. The Bible forbids the exacting of interest on loans to one's fellow countryman and provides legislation for the return of land which has been alienated as a result of poverty (Exodus 22:25–27; Leviticus 25:25–28, 35–38; Deuteronomy 15:1–11; 23:19–20).[28] In today's credit card society, few people stop to consider the crippling effects of debt in perpetuating cycles of poverty both within our own countries and internationally.

6 *Prevention is better than cure* The biblical injunctions against exacting interest and the regulations favouring compassion for the poor and needy (*e.g.* Exodus 23:11; Deuteronomy 24:14–15, 17–21) are preventative rather than therapeutic. In the same way, Vickery points out that rules on covering up excrement prevented the spread of disease (Deuteronomy 23:12–14).[29] It may be said in general terms that the thrust of the Old Testament legislation bearing on health is 'preventative medicine'.[30] Promises of health following obedience to God's laws need to be considered in this light.

Does God have a bias?

All these approaches to health and healing nevertheless fail to answer the fundamental question faced at the pragmatic level by some of those who have sought divine healing but are still not healed: Why does God seem to heal some and not others?

My studies have shed some new light on this question, indicating that God does seem to have a bias, and that in particular directions, because God seems to heal younger people more than older ones. Ironically, however, the proportions of those who seek prayer for physical healing increase among the older age groups. Whereas only 15% of teenagers at Harrogate sought such prayer, the percentage steadily increases for older age groups to reach 48% of those aged sixty and over.[31] By contrast, there is a statistically significant difference among age groups in the degree of physical healing actually reported.[32] In particular, those aged sixty and over are much less likely to report high degrees of healing than are younger age groups. Instead, they are more likely to report a 'fair amount' of healing, suggesting perhaps a more cautious approach in their self-assessments of their degrees of healing. This might be influenced by the amount of chronic or degenerative illnesses among older people, whereas younger people may be more aware of what seem to be instantaneous cures. We could rationalise these findings by the observation that younger bodies generally seem to have more 'vitality' and heal quicker than older ones.[33] Whatever the cause of this finding, its effect is that a high proportion of those seeking physical healing are older people who do not seem to receive it so often as the minority of younger ones who do.

In part this result is influenced by 'words of knowledge' because the more specific public ones pick out those individuals whom it is believed God wants to heal. In chapter 3 I shall discuss how the reported degrees of healing in response to the more detailed public 'words of knowledge' is greater than that in response to less detailed ones. All those responding to the highly specific public messages are aged in their twenties, thirties or forties, and 85% of them are under forty. By contrast, the proportion who are aged less than forty responding to 'words of knowledge' of medium specificity is 60% and for those of low specificity the percentage falls to 46%. This clearly indicates that the 'words of knowledge' are not randomised but are focused upon younger rather than older people.[34]

Does God have a bias for the young? I believe there is some biblical evidence to support this. We do not know the ages of most people whom Jesus healed but we do have some evidence of the ages of the few people who are reported to have been raised from death. Of these, one was a girl about twelve years old (Jairus' daughter: Luke 8:42), one was a teenager or young man (the widow of Nain's son: Luke 7:14) and one was of unknown age (Lazarus: John 11). So in the known ministry of Jesus, two-thirds of the accounts of raising the dead refer to younger people – and it might be that Lazarus was not too old either if he had two unmarried sisters.

A similar pattern can be found in accounts of raising the dead elsewhere in the Bible. Two were young children (the sons of the widow at Zarephath and of the Shunammite: 1 Kings 17:17–24; 2 Kings 4:8–37), one was a young man (Eutychus: Acts 20:7–12) and one was of unknown age (Dorcas: Acts 9:36–42). Therefore in the Bible as a whole the predominance of younger people being raised to life is the general pattern.[35] These cases all involve specific prayer for the raising of the dead, but God can also raise people to life in the absence of such prayer (2 Kings 13:21; Matthew 27:52–53).

Among the three cases of raising the dead described by Rex Gardner for more recent times, one involves a girl aged about thirteen or fourteen, one a 'young man' and the third a woman aged about fifty.[36] Of these, the first two were raised to life following specific believing prayer. The exception is the woman of about fifty, who was the first person to become a Christian in a tribal area of North Thailand; she was apparently raised to life as a divine sign for her people without the missionaries themselves having the faith to pray specifically for her to be restored to life. David Pytches also cites a number of modern-day examples of raising the dead, one of which is the thirteen or fourteen year old girl mentioned by Rex Gardner. Among the other cases quoted by Pytches in which a dead person was successfully raised to life, six are children, two are stated to be young adults and four are apparently older adults, of which only one is described as 'elderly'.[37] No mention is made of the ages of those involved in other cases referred to, including a dozen occasions during the ministry of Smith Wigglesworth and two other occasions in Indonesia. Pytches also cites Trevor Martin's attempt to raise to life a fourteen year old girl, but 'his attempts were frustrated and he saw no resuscitation' despite his sensing 'amazing power pulsating through him'. Taking together the twelve cases in which Pytches indicates the ages of those raised to life, plus the three cases mentioned by Rex Gardner and the seven biblical accounts in which the dead were raised following specific prayer, we find that ten are children, five are young adults and seven are more mature adults. One of these seven was raised to life without intercessory prayer – the tribal woman of North Thailand – and only one of the others is described as 'elderly': both of these occurred in public settings as 'signs' to unbelievers.[38] Other cases which I have heard of anecdotally also involve younger people.[39]

This does not mean that God neglects the old, as shown by the retired missionary whose hearing was restored. Perhaps what it does indicate is that when God does choose to heal, it is often because he still has purposes to fulfil on this earth in the lives of those whose bodies are restored in some way.[40] Those particular purposes involve the need for these areas of health. For other people it may be that God has purposes which involve, like Jesus, learning obedience through suffering (Hebrews 5:8). After that comes the fuller healing when they are with Christ.

Good news to the poor

Jesus praised God because he had 'hidden these things from the wise and learned, and revealed them to little children' (Luke 10:21). Though we may interpret this metaphorically to mean those who receive the kingdom of God like a little child (Luke 18:17), it seems that God also has a special concern for children in terms of healings. In the same way, Jesus came to preach 'good news to the poor' (Luke 4:18), but the revelation of the gospel to 'little children' and to 'the poor' was accomplished in works of power as well as in words. This seems to be a deliberate choice: 'God chose the weak things of the world . . . He chose the lowly things of this world and the despised things . . .' (1 Corinthians 1:27–28).

Most of the healings of Jesus were accomplished among the poor. Partly this was because those who were blind or lame often had no other available occupation except begging, while lepers were social outcasts. However, it seems significant that the only recorded healings of people belonging to the upper echelons of society involved children – Jairus' daughter (Luke 8:41–42) and the nobleman's son (John 4:46).

At Harrogate the majority of those present belonged to the higher social classes. Using the official categories of the Registrar General, I classified people into social classes according to their occupations. As this is an occupational ranking it does not include housewives, students or retired people. Among the 1444 people who could be classified according to social class, there were 545 (38%) belonging to Social Class I – such as doctors, university academic staff and clergy. A further 550, again about 38% of the group, belonged to Social Class II, which includes business managers, teachers and nurses. Social Class III, which includes bus drivers, sales representatives, plumbers and secretaries, accounted for 18% of the sample (265 people). Only 1.5% (twenty-two people) were in Social Classes IV and V, who are mainly manual labourers; to these I add the sixty-two who are unemployed to make a grouping which accounts for 6% of the sample. It should be noted also that West Indian churches appeared to be considerably under-represented at this conference.

It can be seen that the sample is 'top heavy', with a preponderance of professional people and relatively few in manual occupations. When analysing the degree of physical healing reported according to social class, however, it is found that those in Social Class I report significantly lower degrees of healing as compared with other social classes.[41] Are those in this class somewhat more sceptical and therefore lose out, or is it that those in the lower social classes have more 'faith'? However, the greatest deviations from expected patterns do not occur so much in the lower social classes – and in fact the lowest group reports more in the middle than the high range of healing. Rather, Social Class I reports considerably lower degrees of healing than expected whereas Social Class II actually reports rather higher than expected frequencies. This would seem to indicate that those whose academic backgrounds incline them not to expect healings are precisely those whose expectations are confirmed in their own experiences.

This is borne out by analysing the reported degrees of physical healing according to education. The result is statistically highly significant and shows that the amount of healing is considerably less among those with university education.[42] By contrast, those who attended a technical college or equivalent show considerably higher than expected results.[43] Whatever effect 'faith' may have in producing healing, it is clear that an education in disciplines which may tend to undermine that faith by producing more scepticism does seem to reduce the level of reported healing.

The doctors, clergy and university academic staff who form the majority of those in Social Class I at this conference are the educated elite who correspond to the teachers of the law at the time of Jesus. When such people asked Jesus for a miraculous sign, perhaps to satisfy their intellectual curiosity, the reply was, 'A wicked and adulterous generation asks for a miraculous sign!' (Matthew 12:39). A similar refusal to perform miracles on demand was given to Herod (Luke 23:8–9).

Only in the case of the ritually polluting disease of leprosy did Jesus instruct those healed to present themselves to priests for verification of their healing (Mark 1:44; Luke 17:14). In other cases Jesus explicitly forbade those healed from exhibiting their healings in public (Mark 7:36; 8:26). Was this to prevent the equivalent of 'scientific' investigation by the authorities? Such investigations were conducted in the case of another blind man, as recorded in John 9, and the fact of the healing could not be doubted. Gardner comments that the command in Mark 8:26 'sounds a futile instruction as even if he said nothing his newly acquired sight would be obvious within hours. Presumably it was those hours Jesus needed to get away on his preaching mission to the next village, before the mob prevented him.'[44]

That God is not averse to scientific verification is indicated by the timing of the healing of a nine year old girl who had been nerve deaf in both ears and whose condition was regarded by the consultant as incurable. She had attended the audiologist on 8 March 1983, the following night experienced complete healing and on 10 March had further tests showing her audiograms and tympanograms to be normal. The girl's mother remarked that 'God's timing was remarkable, the fact that Rebecca's aid was damaged the day before her hearing returned emphasised that her return of hearing was instantaneous. The audiologist knew she was deaf the day before.'[45]

Such documented cases are relatively rare simply because most cases of healing do not involve sophisticated measuring instruments. For example, some of the remarkable accounts from those living in poverty in Mexico have little or no medical documentation because such proofs are not available when the people are unable to pay for medical help.[46] In cases like this, it seems that God is far more concerned with *faith* than with scientific verification. In the words of Jesus, 'Blessed are those who have not seen and yet have believed' (John 20:29).

2

INNER HEALING AND DELIVERANCE

Issues to be considered:

What biblical basis is there for the practice of 'inner healing'?
Is 'inner healing' merely · a Christianised form of psychotherapy?
For what kinds of problems do people receive inner healing or deliverance?
Can the effects of the healing be perceived by others?

In *Power Healing* John Wimber includes a chapter on 'Overcoming the Effects of Past Hurts', conventionally referred to as 'inner healing'. The book cites cases of people whose physical ailments were healed only after some 'inner' hurt had been dealt with (pp. 92–94, 210–211). At Harrogate too a number of those who requested prayer for physical complaints in fact received prayer for 'inner healing', discerned to be their more pressing need. Is this a 'cop out'?

From a medical point of view, it is by no means a lame excuse. In the medical professions it is widely recognised that very many of our common ailments are to at least some degree psychosomatic. This means that disturbances in the mind have effects on the health of the body. Very often it is due to the (mis)management of stress situations. The problem is that the range of conditions which can involve possible psychosomatic aspects has grown to encompass the majority of routine cases dealt with by General Practitioners. Not only are there the 'classic' stress illnesses such as peptic ulcers or asthma but there are also some psychosomatic aspects to ailments such as rheumatoid arthritis or certain cancers: the timing of the onset of such conditions and their rate of spread can depend on a variety of mental attitudes towards the disease and towards life in general. Rex Gardner writes that we even know something about the bodily mechanisms involved:

> . . . both the hormonal and immunological defence mechanisms are eventually controlled by the fore-brain which is the seat of the emotions. Just as emotions are benefited by the loving care of Christians, acceptance into a warm-hearted fellowship, experience of sins forgiven, the realisation of welcome by a loving heavenly Father, and by the peace with God which allows acceptance of oneself; so there will inevitably be beneficial physical effects mediated through the psychoendocrine pathways. The patient who is healed by these or by biochemical alterations, is healed by mechanisms devised by our creator God . . .[1]

From a medical point of view, therefore, the practice of inner healing is both justified and necessary in preventing further recurrence of illnesses with psychosomatic components. The problem for many Christians, however, is finding a theological justification for the practice.

Biblical precedents?

On the face of it there seem to be few examples of 'inner healing' in the ministry of Jesus or his disciples. Rita Bennett claims 'the Originator of inner healing . . . was Jesus Christ himself. He began healing broken souls and mending broken hearts nearly two thousand years ago . . .'[2] As justification for this statement she quotes a paraphrase of Luke 4:18, emphasising the words 'He [my Father] has sent me to heal the broken-hearted . . . to set at liberty those who are bruised.' The problem with this, however, is that Luke actually *omits* the line 'He has sent me to bind up the broken-hearted' in his quotation from Isaiah 61:1. We can only speculate on the reasons for this omission, whether it be accidental or deliberate.[3] A more useful question may be to ask whether or not there are more specific examples of inner healing in the ministry of Jesus.

A possible text occurs in the next chapter of Luke's gospel. When a paralytic is brought to him, Jesus first announces, 'Friend, your sins are forgiven' (Luke 5:20). The man's physical condition is not healed immediately, but only when Jesus demonstrates his authority to those who considered his words to be blasphemy. This might be interpreted as showing that in some cases Jesus assigned greater priority to one's relationship with God (involving 'inner healing') than he did to physical healing.

To another man who had a very similar condition – who could not walk because he was either lame or paralysed – Jesus first administered physical healing and then said to him, 'Stop sinning or something worse may happen to you' (John 5:14). These words might imply that the inability to walk was somehow linked with some sin in the man's life. They might also imply that the degree to which healing was sustained was perhaps conditional upon the man's repentance from sin.[4] It is noticeable also that in both these similar cases Christ's words were almost identical: 'Get up! Pick up/take your mat and walk/go home' (John 5:8; Luke 5:24). There was no rebuking of the illness itself or deliverance from a demon; rather, the man himself was commanded to undertake a specific act of faith. (The same is true of the crippled beggar in Acts 3:6.)

Words similar to John 5:14 are found again in John 8:11, where Jesus tells the woman caught in adultery, 'Go now and leave your life of sin.' No physical healing or deliverance from an unclean spirit is recorded: if anything, it was what in today's jargon we might call a case of 'inner healing'.

More specifically in terms of 'healing of the memories', there is the reinstatement of Peter in John 21:15–19. Exegesis of this passage quite rightly compares it with Peter's earlier denials that he was a disciple of Jesus, but it should be noted that Jesus did not refer directly to the earlier incidents. Instead, he called forth a positive reaffirmation of Peter's love and then commissioned him to a fresh pastoral role.

Although these passages might be interpreted as precedents for a ministry of 'inner healing', most biblical passages relevant to inner healing are not concerned at all with *therapy*: instead, they are concerned with *preventative medicine*. It is better to prevent the problem in the first place, and this may account for the repeated emphasis on forgiveness in the New Testament (*e.g.* Matthew 6:12–15; 18:21–35; Luke 6:27–42; Romans 12:9–21; 1 Thessalonians 5:12–24, *etc.*). The Old Testament also had the same emphasis in setting out laws prohibiting adultery, envy/covetousness and so on. Prevention is better than cure.

Methods

Rita Bennett writes that the 'two main ways to pray' are 'Reliving the Scene with Jesus' and 'Creative Prayer'.[5] Both involve what at first sight appear to be imaginary visualisations of hurtful scenes, but then rewriting the script in a positive way through the agency of Jesus. John Wimber's chapter on 'Overcoming the Effects of Past Hurts' makes very little reference to such methods, and I believe I have heard him remark during the Harrogate conference that he does not encourage such visualisation unless the Holy Spirit himself does it. The example of a healing procedure given on pp. 235–236 of *Power Healing* makes no reference to such visualisations, although he then describes (pp. 236–237) how deep memories and hurts may arise in people when the Holy Spirit is invited to minister to them.

Some Christians are wary of 'inner healing' because it seems to be a form of secular psychotherapy dressed up in Christianised clothing.[6] Wimber recognises this possibility when he writes:

I am using the term 'inner healing' sparingly and judiciously in this chapter, because different authors use it to mean so many different things, many of which I do not agree with. In many instances inner healing is based on secular psychological views of how our personalities are formed and influenced. But where these views contradict the biblical teaching, they must be firmly rejected.[7]

It is easier to assess 'views' or theories according to biblical criteria than it is to assess methods. For physical healing we are prepared to concede that Jesus used a variety of methods. For conditions which are described as 'blindness' (though we do not know what caused it in each case) Jesus on one occasion spat in a man's eyes, producing partial healing, after which he put his hands on the man's eyes (Mark 8:23–25); on another occasion he spat on the ground, made some mud with the saliva, applied it to the man's eyes and told him to wash it off in the pool of Siloam (John 9:6–7); for blind Bartimaeus he simply said, 'Go, your faith has healed you' (Mark 10:52), but another man who was both blind and dumb appears to have received his sight through a deliverance ministry (Matthew 12:22). If there is this variety for physical healing, might it be the case for emotional/psychological healing too?

Another problem arises if we consider the well-attested cases of physical healing through the miraculous filling of dental cavities. These are reported both in Catholic contexts in North America and in Protestant contexts in South America.[8] Gardner suggests three reasons why God should have filled teeth miraculously rather than making new ones grow: (1) out of compassion for suffering, (2) as a witness to his power, (3) to show his approval of human medical or dental technology. Expanding on the third point, he writes, 'I tentatively suggest that now, by filling teeth, God signals his approval, sets his seal of blessing on the use of technology. Man's healing skills and techniques are acceptable. In this specific case it is dental surgery . . . but obviously the implications are far wider . . .'[9]

One of these wider implications concerns the use of what

may appear to be 'secular' techniques in a Christian counselling context. There are no biblical precedents for the miraculous filling of teeth, just as there is scant precedent for some of the techniques advocated by some of those practising so-called 'inner healing'. But if God can work through a technique commonly used by dentists of all religious persuasions or none, then can he do the same with psychotherapeutic techniques? In the Bible we see divine healing making use of a poultice of figs (Isaiah 38:21) and spit (Mark 7:33; 8:23): does God also make use of modern psychotherapeutic techniques in the same way? Many Christians allow that God can work through conventional medical or dental therapies but may draw a line at psychiatry. Douglas McBain tells about a girl suffering from deep depression for whom there was a predictive prophecy that 'a man will come from Hamilton and she must do whatever he tells her'. Later that same day a visitor from Hamilton arrived to see her: he was a

> consultant psychiatrist to whom the family G.P. had spoken earlier in the day. He assured Rosemary that a little drug treatment was all that she needed in order to get better, and much to everyone's surprise . . . she accepted his advice and . . . was soon totally well again . . . Yet she would never have felt able to receive advice from a psychiatrist without the word because of the suspicion with which they were regarded in the church by some of its members . . .[10]

For any therapeutic technique, whether medical, dental or psychiatric, one can take one of at least three different views: (1) it is consistent with what God wants for mankind and appears to have his blessing; (2) it is morally neutral but is a second best to what God really designed human beings to be; (3) it is contrary to God's will for mankind.

One of the most remarkable accounts of inner healing related to me during my interviews concerns a seventeen year old girl whom I shall call 'Jill'. She had come to live with her pastor's family and it was the pastor's wife who told me the following story:

. . . Her parents divorced when Jill was four years old. Her mother was anti-Christian and would have nothing in the house which was Christian. Jill became a Christian when she was ten and had to carry her Bible with her and sleep with it under her mattress or else it would be destroyed . . . Her mother's boyfriend subjected her to all forms of abuse – everything. Jill's sister who is two years younger had everything lavished upon her but Jill was totally deprived . . .

[After coming to live with the pastor's family] she woke every night screaming with nightmares from what her mother's boyfriend had done to her. No man could go near, only I could . . .

[One night we] heard her rattling the door in her night-dress. We took her back to bed and as we were doing so we were aware she was talking – in a very childish voice . . . She talked as a four year old . . . It was the time of the divorce and she relived it: horror and horror. ([Her mother's boyfriend] sexually handled her, burned her, choked her – she was literally going red in the face and not breathing: we couldn't believe what we were experiencing.) She would even say what she had for dinner – but at the end of the day said, 'My Jesus is coming. He's so *big*.' It was so delightful. She gave a full description of how he was dressed: 'Long, white and shiny, and a shiny thing round his waist. Gold varnish on feet and hands, a pretty sticky-up thing on his head – and his eyes, his eyes . . .' – four year old language. The first one was 'Mummy's friend' but '*My* friend is big – my friend is bigger than your friend. Mind your head, Jesus, don't bump your head on the door.' Then he'd come and minister to her. He had pockets on his robe: 'I wonder what he's got for me?' Cream to soothe bruises or beating, plasters to put on. Something to eat – she was starved as well. She would go through the motions – a big strawberry milkshake . . .

There is much more to Jill's story which deserves a book in itself, and all I can do here is provide a small glimpse of it. On one occasion, when Jill was reliving a time she had been denied a knickerbocker glory ice cream which her younger sister had been allowed, Jesus brought her a knickerbocker glory with a large strawberry in the bottom. I was later shown a photograph of when the family on holiday all bought knickerbocker glories – Jill's first taste of a 'material' one – and Jill's one alone had a large strawberry at the base!

An account such as this convinces me that God does meet with people in this kind of way and does allow hurtful memories to be relived – but then the pain of them is taken away as Jesus ministers appropriately to the situation. Jill's description of Jesus is strikingly reminiscent of Revelation 1:12–16, with the additional detail of a crown on Christ's head, and there is no indication at all that she visualised Jesus as a result of suggestion. Her reliving of past events became a regular nightly event for a few months, with the pastor and his wife taking turns to be in attendance while Jill relived a whole day from her childhood before Jesus came to minister to her. Later, to avoid the trauma of reliving the atrocities committed against her, they did suggest to Jill that she wait until Jesus arrived and then tell him directly about the day's events, but there is no way by which I can attribute Jill's initial experiences to any human psychological technique. Rather, the 'visualisation' appears to have been a genuine spiritual visionary experience in a context which ministered healing and wholeness through reliving painful memories in the presence of Jesus.

Jill's story also confirms to my mind the accuracy of some of Dr Wilder Penfield's conclusions which Wimber quotes on pages 102–103 of *Power Healing*, to the effect that our memories not only store all of our experiences but also our perception of the feelings associated with these experiences. The present is also affected by these memories of the past. Penfield came to these conclusions as a result of neurological studies involving the electrical stimulation of the cerebral cortex of the brain.[11] However, Dr Rupert Sheldrake has pointed out the fact that it is virtually impossible to find a particular locus in the brain where 'memory' is stored: it appears to be 'everywhere and nowhere'.[12] He then suggests a controversial theory that perhaps the brain should be viewed not so much as a kind of computer but rather like a television set. 'Memory' might actually be stored outside the physical body but transmitted through it. Loss of memory following brain damage is analogous to not being able to pick up Channel 4 because of a faulty TV set – it does not mean that Channel 4 is 'no longer there'.

I am not necessarily endorsing Sheldrake's theory, because I do not see how Penfield could then have stimulated artificially the recall of dream-like memories. However, I do find Sheldrake's theory worth consideration because some people who have come close to physical death and have found themselves outside of their physical bodies sometimes describe how they were able to see their whole past lives portrayed before them with a clarity surpassing the 'dream-like memories' artificially stimulated by Penfield. (The best example of this actually comes from a Christian psychiatrist named George Ritchie.[13]) Those who find themselves outside their physical bodies are also able to recall in detail what happened to them during that disembodied state – suggesting that memory may actually be stored in a non-material aspect of our beings. If so, then it seems highly appropriate that 'healing of the memories' should occur through *spiritual* means: what Rita Bennett describes as 'soul healing' may actually require non-material or spiritual sources of healing.

Overview of areas of healing

Many of those receiving inner healing at Harrogate gave rather vague descriptions of it on their questionnaires. Often they would simply write 'hurts in the past' or a general area such as 'resentment', '[sense of] worthlessness', 'anxiety' or 'knowing God as Father'. Sometimes a cause of the hurt is mentioned in general terms, as when a thirty-seven year old woman simply wrote 'the wounds I got in my divorce'. The following quotations are taken from among the more specific examples and provide an overview of some of the areas for which healing was sought.

'[Received prayer] to be freed from resentment and anger towards my husband who seems to be misdirecting my life. To exercise love during times of abuse and rejection and to give the situation to Jesus in faith' (from a fifty-four year old woman);

'Repentance of old sins, especially of an abortion an ex-girlfriend had had' (from a twenty-four year old man);

'Divorce, adultery, pornography, hurts from childhood, to forgive mum and dad, nuns in orphanage' (from a fifty-two year old woman);

'Healing for unforgiveness of incestuous child abuse by three members of my family and not believing that God was there at the time of my hurt and that he was hurt deeply as I was' (from a twenty-nine year old woman);

'Felt spiritually drained after a hard year when my husband was ill for six months so I needed to feel the Lord's love, presence and reassurance and a new infilling of the Holy Spirit' (from a thirty-seven year old woman);

'Repented of involvement in abortions in assisting to nurse and in giving drugs that terminated pregnancies' (from a twenty-six year old woman, a State Registered Nurse);

'I would not let go of my father, who died eighteen months ago. Subconsciously I was blaming God. I have now given him over to Jesus' (from a forty year old woman);

'Forgiveness of *past sin* – immorality and alcohol abuse. Forgiveness for *present sin* – the ambition to be a great preacher' (from a twenty-nine year old man, an Anglican curate);

'Needing to know the love of God more fully as a reality rather than a theory' (from a thirty year old man, a theological student);

'Rejection, self-hate, self-condemnation, anger, lack of acceptance with God. After all this was dealt with God bathed me in his love and filled me with his Spirit and gave mc a prayer language' (from a twenty-eight year old man).

Sociological patterns

An analysis of the kinds of people who report receiving prayer for inner healing shows the following patterns: (1) those receiving prayer for inner healing are more likely to be women than men and are more likely to be younger than older people;[14] (2) the degree of healing reported as a result of this kind of prayer is higher among women than men. It is also higher among those from lower social classes or who have received less education than it is for higher social classes or better educated groups.[15]

Some of the examples given above of areas in one's life for which inner healing is received largely explain why more women than men should receive this kind of prayer. The inner emotional pains associated with being the victim of sexual abuse, going through a divorce or having an abortion are all likely to affect women far more deeply than men. If this is the case then any relief from the hurts associated with the memories of these is likely to be more keenly felt among women than men. They are therefore likely to report higher degrees of emotional healing.

To what extent might the same reasoning apply to people from lower social classes or having less education? It is well known that the urban priority areas of many British cities contain a high proportion of unemployed people, manual workers and single parents.[16] They also have relatively high crime rates. In other words, social problems of one kind are often linked with those of other kinds: single parents, for example, may also be unemployed and live in inadequate housing. For these people, who in official statistics are classified as belonging to the lower social classes, there may be considerable inner healing necessary in order to restore their self-esteem or to heal their feelings of rejection or inadequacy.

Many churches assume a relatively high literacy rate among their congregations (requiring a reasonable standard of education) as well as an aptitude for reading books. The social environments of these churches themselves may produce feelings of inadequacy among less literate people who are more used to the television than to books. It is not surprising that many churches, with few exceptions, tend to remain predominantly middle class.[17]

An example of how these social attitudes can affect those with lesser education comes from the inner healing reported by a young man whose occupation is a manual one. He wrote about receiving a release from feelings of inadequacy because of his lack of academic qualifications: 'The Lord said, "I was master carpenter of Nazareth and didn't have CSE wood-work".'

Follow-up of healings

At the conference in Harrogate 748 people (40%) received prayer for inner healing of some kind. Because some of these received prayer for more than one area of their lives, a total of 1275 cases of inner healing are reported. By the end of the conference the amount of healing felt to have been received showed the following proportions:

Table 2.1   *Self-assessments of the degree of inner healing received at Harrogate*

High	: 50.5%
Medium	: 28%
Low	: 21.5% (including 7% who left blank their degree of healing)

As these are self-evaluations after a time of relatively intense spiritual activity, it might be that people are being over-optimistic: the real test comes after they return to their normal environments and have to face situations of stress. For this reason my follow-up study beginning six months later gives a more realistic picture of the longer-term effects.

Categorisation in this area is not always easy, and I am aware that the categories I am using are sometimes over-simplifications of the real situations involved, as will become clear from some of the case studies to be presented later. Nevertheless it is helpful first to provide a general overview, as follows:

Table 2.2 *Overview of degree of improvement reported among those followed up in random sample*

Area of need	Number of cases	Noticeable improvement	Little or no improvement
Resentments	3	2	1
Tension	2		2
Sense of rejection	3	3	
Feeling of being unloved by mother	2	2	
Developing a substitute mother-daughter relationship	1	1	
Relating to God as Father	1	1	
Release of emotions/ not being 'stiff and starchy'	2	2	
Knowing the love of God more personally/ reassurance of God's love	2	2	
Sense of forgiveness from God	2	2	
Being able to forgive another person	1	1	
Self-forgiveness	1	1	
Habit of picking skin spots	1	1	
Sense of guilt	3	3	
Guilt of past adultery	1	1	
Lifting of sense of oppression	1	1	
Gain in confidence	2	2	
Blushing and embarrassment	1		1

Table 2.2 continued

Area of need	Number of cases	Noticeable improvement	Little or no improvement
Sense of inadequacy because of inability to speak in tongues	1		1
Increase in maturity	2	2	
Attitudes to mother-in-law	1		1
Post-natal depression	1	1	
Sense of peace	4	4	
Reassurance	4	4	
Insecurity/loneliness	1	1	
Sleeping patterns/laziness	1	1	
Giving up smoking	1		1
Attitudes to women	1	1	
Healing of the effects of sexual abuse as a child	2	2	
Masturbation	4	4	
Memory of attempted incest	1		?
Thoughts of murdering husband	1	?	
Marriage relationship	1		1
Attitudes to others in church	2	2	
Fears	2	2	
Anger	1	1	
'Pendulum swings' in life	1	1	

Noticeable improvement of some kind is reported for 85% of the cases followed up (*i.e.* fifty-two out of sixty-one cases).[18] Among the remaining 15% (*i.e.* nine cases), there were sometimes temporary improvements sustained for a short while. Similarly, among the cases of noticeable improvement, the informants sometimes mention infrequent recurrence of the problems but feel the problem is very much less than it used to be. Where appropriate I later telephoned a pastor or other person who could give an outsider's assessment of the degree of observable change in the person. In all but two cases these corresponded with the person's own assessment.

My allocation of individual cases into one of two categories according to their degrees of improvement actually conceals a gradation between the two categories. A better picture comes from presenting a selection of case studies illustrating some of the problem areas involved.

Resentment/inadequacy

. . . My father died in 1981 and my mother in 1985, just two months after we married. She had to come to the wedding in a stretcher from hospital. She'd lost the use of her legs, was paralysed from the waist down, in a terrific amount of pain from cancer. I had resentment about the way my mother died: I'd never known her ill, she'd always been so strong. She also became very dependent on me and unable to cope – a reversal of roles.

It was also very traumatic because my husband's first wife had died, leaving two children, and I felt inadequacy because of not knowing how to cope with the children . . .

On the Thursday night [at Harrogate] . . . one of the team came by and said God wanted to minister peace to me. He prayed with me and said something along the lines of God wanting to give me joy and release me in that way . . . I began to scream – the memories came back. (It was as if joy was the end product desired – I felt it was not something I could put on or be because there was something there stopping it.) As I screamed I was completely unaware of the presence of other people except I was aware of voices speaking to me – as if I was screaming into a box, or a chamber protecting me from what was outside, though I realised it was not a physical container. I was surprised afterwards how loud it was – I now wish they hadn't told me.

Two other team members, a married couple, then came and the woman counselled me and told me how to cope with my feelings when they came up, reassuring me that God accepted me and I was not inadequate. When the feelings came again what helped me most was recognising that it's alright to feel this way but then to give the feelings over to God and let him deal with it. There was probably guilt there also that I felt I couldn't cope . . .

Immediately there was a physical release and I did feel better, but that could have gone overnight – it's only over a process of time that I've seen things build on that . . . It was like taking a cork off a bottle so I could deal with the situation with my mother. I don't feel any resentment or hurt about the way she died. Ten months after she died a friend's mother died of cancer but it was a relatively quick end process – only a week. (My mother had been in and out of hospital for ten months and it was a progressive illness, and previously she'd had major surgery – it took three years altogether.) This provoked a reaction in me of bitterness or anger: why should my mother go through all this and hers not? Why can she accept it like this and I can't?

I needed to deal with my feelings rather than wallow in them – also recognising that it was something God understood and he accepted me in it. Three or four weeks ago J., another woman in church – her mother died. She'd been ill for years but was taken into hospital and died in a week. I hadn't had any reaction to it except for empathy for J. It was quite parallel to the earlier case but it didn't provoke a reaction. I went to the funeral of J.'s mother and that experience was quite upsetting but it wasn't a bitter experience. I was able to empathise with J. and feel for her . . . because it brought back memories of my own mother but there wasn't any of the bitterness there.

This account has been quoted at length because it illustrates how there are often multiple factors involved in the circumstances leading to a person requiring ministry. Moreover, there are two specific instances, one prior to the conference and the other afterwards, in which the informant's reactions to similar circumstances were clearly different, apparently as a rcsult of the ministry she had received.

The accounts of outsiders also corroborate her own account. Another person in my random sample was probably the one who initially prayed for her – not a team member in fact, though in her later account she assumed he was:

> . . . I saw a woman there: looking at her I felt she needed prayer and volunteered to pray for her . . . I sensed she felt out of things during the week. I began to pray for her along those lines and within twenty seconds she was in tears. That encouraged me. I continued praying and tried to apply some of the things we'd learned . . . I prayed the first thing that came to mind, can't remember what it was. Then her husband came along and I remember feeling her husband was the type of man that would get involved in church affairs but would leave his wife behind to some extent. I prayed about that and continued to pray for a while. Then she let out an almighty scream – it echoed around the hallway. Then some of the American team came and took over.
>
> I felt a bit uncomfortable but her husband came along afterwards and explained that it was to do with a remarriage (her first, his second) and the children's reactions to it. There were problems with the children and he was really grateful . . .

Her pastor's viewpoint also corroborates her account:

> Three to four years ago she was very, very timid and withdrawn, painfully timid. Then she came out of that, a great big jump for a while. She seemed to go back into it again two years back. There was a lot of trauma in the family. Her father was tragically killed, and there was her mother's serious illness and . . . she married and her husband was very involved in the leadership of the church. All these together . . .
>
> There was not an immediate overnight transformation

and there might be other factors . . . but there has been a consistent improvement in her whole personality and demeanour. In all honesty it started before Wimber but has continued since then . . . she had ongoing pastoral counselling from my wife . . . There were deep levels of adjustment in areas where she had difficulties before. John Wimber was a significant piece in the jigsaw. The other day she was speaking to me about a possible involvement in a counselling ministry, being a counsellor herself.

Tension

Two people received prayer about tension but neither of them showed any significant change when interviewed the following summer. In both cases the opinions of others shed light on other possible factors involved.

One of these is a businessman shouldering heavy responsibilities for his firm. During the interview I thought these business pressures were the cause of his ongoing problems of tension, but in a confidential telephone call with his pastor I learned that another major contributing factor to the tension was his sexual relationship at home, with 'a great deal of frustration there'. His wife is not so fully committed to the church and despite pastoral counselling the circumstances 'haven't changed – over the last couple of years have got slightly worse'.

The other person reporting no healing at all for tension is a sixty-two year old woman who asked to be interviewed in the presence of her vicar and his wife. She spoke of inner healing at Harrogate concerning resentment: 'I poured out everything to him and felt clean inside. I wanted him as my Counsellor, not anyone else.' These resentments were linked to a sense of inferiority which went back to her childhood, living 'in a village with an aristocratic society and feeling very under the thumb of the lord of the manor. We had to address the gentry as "Sir" or "Mr So and so" and I always felt very inferior as we belonged to the lower class of society.' She spoke of other tensions later in life, partly in her former work and partly now through being made to feel guilty by others who say she ought to go to live with her brother who lives by himself, instead of her living her own life. These continuing frictions or pressures have not changed.

One of my standard interview questions asked about other spiritual experiences, including an item on feeling oneself to be in the presence of someone who has died. This woman mentioned such experiences after the deaths of three of her relatives, so that by the third time she was expecting it and 'felt quite happy that they visited'. I later contacted her minister about this, who said he had not taken it further because, 'it's the sort of thing I wouldn't like to go further with'. He said his parishioner 'used to talk about experiences of the supernatural that we couldn't understand and all we could do was pray for her and assure her of the Lord's desire to set her free'. When I suggested that such experiences might be indicative of demonic influences, his wife acknowledged that for a long time she had thought there was 'something there that was not right, feelings that some things aren't of the Lord and she needs releasing from; just a feeling I had'.

In both these two cases there are ongoing external factors contributing to the continuing tension. The second case also raises questions about other possible factors which may need dealing with first, but I shall defer discussion of such experiences of the dead, dealing with them instead in the section on demonisation towards the end of this chapter (pp. 121–124).

Sense of rejection

Often those mentioning 'rejection' as a problem had felt rejected by parents or other close relatives, as in the following example from a Scandinavian pastor:

> I felt rejected since my father left us when I was two weeks old. This made it impossible for my mother to take care of me and I went to an orphanage. After that I went to a foster-home and my foster-mother, who didn't love me, treated me badly – which I remember though I was only two

years old. When she fell pregnant she didn't want me to stay with them any longer and I was sent to another foster-home. These foster-parents later adopted me and they were really loving and caring, and they gave me a very happy childhood.

I think the fact that my mother and father didn't take care of me made me feel rejected. This rejection problem made me insecure. When people said that they loved me I didn't trust them. I wasn't sure of my wife's love or God's love . . .

I contacted my mother in 1983 . . . my first foster-parents I haven't seen since I left them when I was a child. As a teenager I resented my mother, and when she tried to contact me I didn't want to see her and I never saw her until 1983. These feelings that I felt as a teenager changed when I got married and became a father. My mother was very happy when I contacted her in 1983 and our relationship has been very good since then. I thought that I was free from all bad feelings until this team-leader spoke straight into my situation through a word of knowledge. He made me aware of these hurts in the past and that it was the reason why I couldn't trust my wife when she assured me of her love for me. The team-leader prayed for me and broke every bloodline that caused the hurt. The rejection I felt has left me. When he prayed for me I had a *strong* experi-ence of God as my father. For the first time I really trusted him. He kind of embraced me with his love.

This experience has changed my relationship with God. I can now both give and take love from my mother and it's a wonderful feeling to know that I'm accepted and loved just as I am.

. . . My wife told me over and over again how much she loved me, and for her to know that I didn't trust her was very painful to her. Our relationship is different now. The hurt we both felt is now gone.

A few people mentioned feelings of rejection by individuals or groups who are critical of either the charismatic movement or the particular form of ministry associated with John Wimber. The following example, however, illustrates how a woman with a long-term physical problem felt a sense of rejection by those who attributed her lack of healing to some presumed sin in her. My quotation describes how she felt when encountering these attitudes at the conference, but she also encountered them later from certain individuals in her own congregation:

I felt terribly rejected on the Monday when those around me [praying for physical healing] said there must be something blocking it. The next day I was separated from my church group and was sitting among people I didn't know, and felt even more rejected. After the break I found some of our church people who prayed for me – it took away the feelings of rejection but I still felt more tired than I would have expected. On the Wednesday I was next to A., who felt a spirit of fear and cast it out. There was no big manifestation but I felt lighter and the feelings of rejection and fear had gone.

If my self-esteem had been higher at the time I wouldn't have taken it so personally because God had told me many times that there was nothing in me blocking my healing. If my self-esteem was higher I'd have known I was right and they were wrong. The people from church praying for me on the Tuesday also helped.

Her minister's opinion is worth quoting:

. . . she bounced back. I have a great respect for her tenacity and stickability. I was well aware of her feelings about self-worth and feel she's come a long way. Her house group at the time contained one or two people who are rather triumphalistic and gave her regular double messages which were very undermining if you have self-worth problems: 'Why was she not healed?' *etc*. But I've seen her come through with flying colours and she's stood up under pressure – and I'm not sure it would have happened pre-Harrogate.

Relationships with one's mother

. . . I was made aware that all was not right with what I thought of myself and of my mother. I was not conscious of it and it came as a shock to me, but through words of knowledge and images by mostly members of our group and one of the team – I feel I had a deep-rooted thing that anything I did was rubbish and no good to anyone and no one loved me. It took the full week of the conference and a bucket of tears . . .

The root of it was an incident when I was about four years old . . . I was across in a neighbour's house in the corner of a courtyard and a ram that had been spoiled since it was a lamb charged at me. I couldn't escape as I was a child and if I'd have run it would have chased me. So I believe God lifted me out: there was no way I could have escaped but now I have a conviction that the Lord lifted me out.

Next I was . . . I can't remember where I was, but I was out of that corner and away. I went to my mother crying and she said it was nonsense and couldn't believe what I said. My 'can't do anything right' syndrome stems from that, especially from my mother's point of view (not from my father). But since then I've appreciated that my mother was brought up in the same kind of way, with no affection from her mother, so she couldn't give it to me.

I closed my heart to everyone, even the Lord. Before then I'd always believed in him and talked with him but didn't then afterwards, and after becoming a Christian still tended to do so. I became a Christian when I was eighteen, but can't say I was not aware of God all through that – . . . but since becoming a Christian I've been up and down, not falling away, but no certainty and nothing to show for it. But during Harrogate and afterwards I could freely worship the Lord because all this had been broken away, this unforgiveness. I could honestly say I loved him, not just a thing to say . . .

I had to receive love and forgive my mother. Yes – there has been a difference in my relationship with her since the conference: a general appreciation from my side that she didn't mean things she said in the way I'd understood them. It had begun to get better before Harrogate and has continued to improve. I think we're a lot more open. Things were packed away in my own memory that were dealt with – it was more my little self that needed dealing with. On the surface my relationship with my mother was fine and no problem, but she has noticed a change in me since going to Harrogate. She says I'm happier and says, 'Are you going on another course so you can get another top-up?'

This informant's minister confirmed that there had been noticeable changes in her since the conference, notably:

1 'She is more relaxed and not so intense about things since the conference. For example, she's more "laid back" about changes in the staff and organisation at [the place where she works] – is willing to let God be in charge of it and take care of it.'
2 'She is more confident about getting involved in ministry, including going up to people to pray with them, and also in giving words of knowledge to people . . .'
3 'She's more relaxed and free in worship, even at times during the morning service allowing herself to express her worship by a big smile on her face, *etc.*, instead of being as formal as most of the congregation are.'

Developing a substitute mother-daughter relationship

When I was in the overflow hall . . . John Wimber was talking about reconciliation in families . . . Then a face came on to the big screen . . . She wasn't actually there, but her face came over the speaker's face – a superimposition just for a moment, then faded. But it made a strong impression on me. I jotted it down for her reassurance . . . It was [the vicar's] wife, R. At times a vicar's wife gets a lot of criticism and talking about. She's a shy person . . . At a church retreat we were talking about bereavement and I told her that the worst thing was knowing that I'd never be cuddled again. At a Communion service she did something lovely and gave me a cuddle. John Wimber said we need to be more demonstrative, even if we're misunderstood . . . Now R. will pop in when things are getting her down. That relationship is developing with her now – like a mother-daughter relationship with a younger woman, something I didn't look for. Her face came up on the big screen so I had to tell her what I think about her. She's often in the shadow of her husband. At that time I told her of things about bereavement which I'd never have told others.

Habit of picking skin spots

After the person was speaking on inner healing about things that had been said in childhood, something stirred in me that I had a dislike of myself that I felt stemmed from things in childhood. I don't know quite what they were. A kind of rejection? It's difficult to analyse it. It was to do with hating myself. I can't exactly say how that came about – something clicked through the address.

I felt when I was knocked over that it was a confirmation that I was released from that. Sinful habit patterns are symptomatic . . . Something's clicked with me. Simply, the habit has been picking spots. It might seem trivial, but my husband says it's symptomatic of disliking one's looks. To me it was quite major, stemmed from a dislike of myself.

I can honestly say it's decreased – I'm more in control. I think personally, in my opinion, it could be far less if I was more self-controlled. It's lack of self-control now rather than a deep-rooted thing, something that could be and will be easier to give up . . . I did it under stress, but there have also been stressful times in the last month when I haven't.

Guilt of past adultery

. . . He asked anyone who wants prayer for healing to stand up and move into the aisle . . . I said, 'Lord, if I'm to be healed, I want someone to come and speak to me.' D.

came. I explained about [a physical problem] . . . He began to pray for me but nothing happened. He asked if the Lord was saying anything needed to be put right. There was – about immorality a long time ago. I needed to put it right . . .

I was in a quandary because I didn't really want to put it right and I didn't want to be 'slain in the Spirit'. He began to pray with me, . . . I remember I was there and nothing was happening to me. I remember saying to myself, 'If nothing happens I'll get up and walk out, I'm being conned.' I can only explain it as my ankle and then leg, then arms, then my whole body began to twitch. He prayed harder, 'Lord, let him see your love.' I shook quite uncontrollably against the seats around me and there was nothing I could do to stop it.

In the middle of all this what was happening was like a ray of light came into my presence – like I am there in this seat shaking and I know where I am, I've got my eyes shut, but it seemed as if in the darkness of my eyes shut a beam of light came in and a burden lifted off me.[19]

The peace and the overwhelming security that came with that was quite remarkable. I didn't want to let it go, but I came back into reality when he ended his prayer. It seemed as if I was free and hadn't been free for a long time. After that I was able to join in worship – I hadn't been fully able to for three days. I also realised I'd been hardened in my attitude and now wasn't so.

When I got home I had to put it right with my wife and confess to her. On the Monday at work I was looking out the window at the landscape garden: it was as if the beauty of the Lord came into that garden and I began to cry – it's not like me, I'm not a person who cries – and so I knew that what had happened was a real experience.

Sense of inadequacy because of inability to speak in tongues

A woman who on her questionnaire wrote 'I think so' in the box about receiving the gift of tongues for the first time at Harrogate, later when interviewed said:

I came to the conclusion I didn't. I was making these noises and they were saying, 'Come on, that's right,' but I don't think it was at all – I think it was their enthusiasm and not [real].

I've got a real hang-up about it. I also had it before I ever went there, nothing to do with the conference; I'd had it for eighteen months – since my husband did [speak in tongues]. Certainly there was some . . . jealousy in it, and all sorts of other things as well.

I was sitting with a friend one day, talking about this and that, and suddenly God told me I was jealous. In the past I thought I had a good imagination, but this was so clear and there was no doubt about it. I said, 'I know, yes.' I know what God's forgiveness feels like – as if someone lifted a ten-ton weight off me. That day and the next day I felt on top of the world.

I can't remember what happened after that – this person said something to me and it was just as if they'd pulled the plug out and everything went flat. I've always felt I've played second fiddle to my husband and it was as if God thought so too . . .

A minister's opinion described this informant as a

well-together person – no recurring needs, very competent in her family and as a wife, very supportive. No particular jobs in the life of the church but a lot of support for her husband . . . It's difficult to say about any change because there have been other things like Spring Harvest. Over the last year I'd say there's been progress, rather than retrogression or staying the same, but I didn't know her very well before . . .

Attitudes to mother-in-law

My father-in-law died of cancer in August 1986. I had a lot of pressure from my mother-in-law, a feeling of responsibility towards her; she lives locally. She's a Christian, and my father-in-law became a Christian shortly before he died. God really helped us even though it's awful to see someone suffering in pain. In the end we asked God to take him if he's not going to be healed. It made me embarrassed for my mother-in-law because we'd prayed for healing and he wasn't healed. My mother-in-law accepts he's in heaven but it's still a long process to accept the loss . . .

At Harrogate I had inner healing for facing up to this and not being angry. At one of the meetings [John Wimber] asked the Holy Spirit to come. I was thinking about morning sickness and suddenly this came to mind, that I should have been dealing with my mother-in-law and not morning sickness. I started blubbering all over the place. I was feeling a bit knocked about with my father-in-law dying and feeling I had to go to visit my mother-in-law almost every other day or ring her up – three or four times a week. I used to pop in for a couple of hours after work. Also I was pregnant and had morning sickness. So a bit of resentment got in there. And she was saying things I didn't really agree with, in the presence of my parents [non-Christians], but I didn't want to hurt her, so that got bottled in – as anger and so on.

I started crying and a friend prayed with me about it – about the bitterness and the feeling I could have done more when M.'s Dad was there – but I don't think I could have done. He really found God then and always wanted you to pray with him before you went home.

I was crying. For a couple of minutes I was quite hysterical but I felt it was all bubbling out really. I suppose I felt it was all unfair – why should I be expected to do all these things and other people don't realise it? It's good that God shows you these things and I wouldn't want it any other way really – it's just at the time . . .

Also I'd been worried about my mother-in-law with time on her hands interfering with the baby when the child would be born . . .

After someone prayed with me I felt a lot better – confessing it to God and realising I shouldn't have been thinking these things . . . I felt really able to praise God then, as if this had been blocking . . .

At the time of the interview this woman's problems had apparently been resolved, but I have counted this as a case of 'little or no improvement' because of the contents of a letter which she wrote to me two and a half months later. After giving details about their baby's birth she went on to describe what she initially called 'post-natal depression', but at the end of the letter she supplied the technical term for her condition as puerperal psychosis. A few extracts are sufficient to convey some of the main points:

> I've felt as though I was a baby curled up in bed, also I've seen [my husband] M. wrapped up in a white sheet looking like a baby. I've seen other hallucinations and had night-mares. Also looked in mirrors and I've looked so evil and felt as though my teeth were too big for my mouth. At one stage I had lots of voices calling to me inside my head. Also the television and radio were also sending me messages. As you can imagine, it was very frightening. I had to take one day at a time. On the other hand sometimes I would be extremely happy, too happy.
>
> I must admit I feel foolish when I think about, and so very hurt, when I think of who I thought M. was – John Wimber if you would believe it. It may have been triggered off by my interview with you. You might smile at that, but everything was so clear in my mind that he was . . .
>
> Sometimes I feel upset, especially as I've to ask M.'s mum not to come near me, for the time being that is. I feel as though she's trying to organise my life, and I may say something I'll regret if I do see her . . .
>
> I managed to sort things out in about five weeks. Then soon after, my Grandma died. I believe this has slowed down my recovery. My Grandma had milk fever when she had my mum. (Another name for it is post-natal depression.) We were very close as she nearly adopted me when I was born . . . Someone did mention that it is hereditary, post-natal depression that is.

This informant's minister says she is a very 'giving' sort of person who tries to do a lot for other people. He is aware of her situation and it appears that she has benefited considerably from subsequent ministry in her local church.

Healing of the effects of sexual abuse as a child

I've never been mothered – my mother didn't love me . . . I'd had prayer and counselling before I went there but the Lord continued through prayer and counselling at the conference. I met two women who mothered me. One lady put her arms round me and said she felt the Lord saying she had to put a garment of some sort round my shoulders like a cloak. She was a motherly figure but couldn't have known what she was doing.

When I was young I was sexually abused by a neighbour. My mother knew about it but it didn't seem to me that she was doing anything about it. She let it happen . . . Sometimes when I'm praying Satan presents to me that the Lord is a man, so I'm unable to speak to the Lord candidly about that part of my life.

I stood up to pray at the conference . . . I was conscious that a lot of people were there. When you have an awful secret like that you feel as if everyone knows about it. I stood up to pray and felt exposed with a lot of people there. It was of significance that the woman put her arms round me and said she was covering me with a robe of – something – and mothering me all the time.

I've known mothering as an emotion for my own children but I've rarely felt it as an emotion with my own mother and me. I went to hug J. and was bonded in mother-love; I held her and wept in buckets. W. also mothered me . . . Next day another woman standing at the side of me was saying the same things. Since then I've been aware that the mother-love of J. and W. and another two women is what mother-love is like and what the Lord wants to restore in my mother and me . . .

As far back as I can remember – I could only have been five or six or four, one of my earliest memories [is of sexual abuse]. I'm not sure how long it went on for, I only remember three specific occasions, but I guessed more because when I found out my mother knew about it – when I was fifteen or sixteen, when I got round to telling her about it – I tried to suss it out. She said she did know about it but didn't try to do anything in case it became a major thing in me. But she's the kind of woman who doesn't.

She still let me go out and play with him – an eighteen or nineteen year old boy . . . When she comes I ask the Lord to give me love for her. There's a part of me that can only be healed when I know why my mother felt unable to do anything about it. How do you know when you've completely forgiven someone? I'm just waiting the Lord's time. Every time she comes the Lord gives me love for her – I don't know if he gives her a love for me but I'm sure there's a gradual awakening that something has happened between us. She told my sister that she thought she was not a good mother to us when we were young. I don't know if she was unable to cope or unwilling: probably a bit of both . . .

When I first met my husband I was seventeen and he had a terrible time convincing me he did really love me. He knew I had a problem somewhere. Over the years we tried to sort out why I didn't like him to touch me. When you grow up with an idea you think it's normal. I thought sex and love were incompatible. Your sex life should also progress more in marriage . . . but over the last year it's progressed more than in the whole of the previous twelve years . . . Since the problem was brought to the surface it has an influence on all parts of my life, not least the sex side.

Sometimes I fall back on habit – I was about to sit next to a man on the bus but instead I went one back and sat next to a woman: small things become part of life, a habit . . . But I've only just got over the bitterness and rot of thinking of my mother not doing anything about it. I thought it would be the first thing to be sorted out but in fact it was the last . . . There were also the nightmares: they started when the abuse started and continued. Ministry for that started before the conference and working through the conference. I've had no more prayer and counselling sessions –

the Lord is still working on the bits he's shown me. Its *years* that the Lord is sorting out . . .

Problems of this nature tend to colour the rest of life. You come to regard your body as a sort of threat. Your view on life is distorted: men become monsters with one interest in a woman. These ideas were formulatcd before I could explain what had happened. I grew up mistrusting the whole of life. I didn't know the Lord could do anything about that . . . The Lord only surfaced the problem in the last year or two. I was amazed when I first received the Spirit that I quite naturally began to embrace people, even men. But I only do it when it comes naturally because otherwise – well, I just think people know when you're not sincere, they sense the insincerity. I do it when it occurs naturally. Its something I've never done before. I think that's when the healing started but I didn't recognise it as that.

Masturbation

Three men and one woman, all of them unmarried, reported receiving prayer at Harrogate concerning lustful fantasies leading to masturbation. All reported a noticeable lessening in frequency during the weeks following the conference: one man, for example, said, 'Before it was about twicc a week but now it's about once every six weeks to two months.' The woman similarly said, 'I thought I'd been healed totally for about three months. Since then, whereas previously I'd been troubled two out of four weeks now it's once or twice a month, but I might miss a month: it's hardly anything . . .'

The clearest testimony in this area comes from a young man whose account is worth quoting at some length:

I went forward about lust, masturbation and impure thoughts (*not* pornography). A Scottish woman had two words, 'Love yourself.' It took me by surprise, but since then I realised it was spot on – you're part of God's creation and he loves you. Therefore you should love yourself . . .

To love your neighbour as yourself, you've got to love yourself. (I checked where it says about 'lovers of self' and the word is *philia*, which is selfish love, but I interpret her word to mean *agape* love.) It's true I tended to feel guilty about all the things God had given me. To be told to love yourself was a tremendous release for me, not to feel guilty about all that God has done for me. That verse about Jabez – 'Oh, that you would bless me'[20] – I can accept and know God wants to give. I used to despise myself for my weaknesses . . .

Then someone else, a man, said that he thought my problem was not with lust but with feelings – that was spot on.[21] Some years ago I had a trough-like experience where God took away my feelings so I could trust him. I had been feelings-orientated and God broke that during a dry period when I had only the promises to go on – during a whole term at university. Then I was baptised – a watershed. But I felt my feelings were not really restored. Someone said feelings are a part of you: 'Do you have faith God will restore feelings?' They prayed for me – I did feel something deep within, an inner warmth. On the way back this warmth was still there: no overpowering sense of feeling but now emotions do rise up as praise. A healthy attitude to feelings – they may come or not; if not, then go by faith.

Another thing – a girl had a vision that God wanted me to get up early in the morning, throw open the windows and let in the wind of the Spirit. I hadn't done it, a lifetime problem of not getting up in the morning. It was a standing joke, my reputation for being late at work – a bad witness. I prayed, 'Lord, wake me up when you want me to get up.' As a one-off I woke up tremendously early and had a tremendous time with the Lord . . .

As a kind of New Year resolution I felt it was right to try to tithe my time: two and a half hours a day. To begin with I had two days holiday and a weekend. Then I thought, 'What will I do when I get back to work?' (A few years earlier I had tried to get up early, at 7.00 a.m., but failed after a month.)

The first day I set the alarm for 7.00 a.m. but woke at 6.00 a.m. The second day the same. The third day 2.55 a.m.; I prayed for an hour in bed and got up at 3.45. Next it was 1.50 a.m. – I went back to sleep but did get up about 6.00 a.m. Next morning it was reasonably early. On Saturday I caught up a lot of sleep. Sunday 4.30 a.m. Monday 3.30 a.m. I was not going to bed any earlier. That week I was going to a customer in W. – how will I cope? What I need is the gift of deep sleep. I prayed about waking when he wants – but also to give me deep sleep . . . After that I was thinking about deep sleep and saw a Gideon Bible in the hotel. Where the binder was opened the first verse was, 'For the Lord has poured out upon you a spirit of deep sleep' – it was out of context from Isaiah but I trusted that and believéd it. At lunchtime I began to feel tired but said, 'I can't be tired. These feelings are of the devil. Feelings of tiredness, I command you to go.' Two minutes later they went.

Since then my life has been completely revolutionised. Now I seem only to need about five hours sleep. There's an amazing difference at work. People have seen the difference. This year I've only once been late – at 9.04, because I was late leaving an early morning prayer meeting . . . It's made an amazing difference in praise: sometimes there's been a struggle when I've not prayed so much and old things begin to creep back. At one time I seemed to be losing it but said, 'No, the gifts and the call are irrevocable.'

After that victory in the first few weeks of the year I realised God had broken a lifetime habit. Then I thought about lust and masturbation. Before it had gone for a little while but I went back to it. Now this year I'm focusing on the fact of being a new creation and am beginning to stand on the scriptures of being a new creation and old things are dead and buried.

On January 18th I fell again – despaired. Then I realised nothing has changed – I am still a new creation . . . 'I believe God's word – the old lustful nature is nailed to the cross and I know it's true. I know I've been set free – Go away.' From that day to this [31 July] I've had no problems. I have occasional lustful thoughts but I tell them to go. When the thought comes – I'm not sexless but now I can have the victory and [do] not think about it as I did previously.[22]

It has also led to victory in other areas – about what the Bible is saying about me versus feelings of rejection *etc*. . . . As a result of spending time in prayer, I feel the day works out better and when I pray I'm very quickly aware of the presence of the Lord and have more victory over temptation because of the power of prayer and praise. There's been a significant increase in my spiritual life – one thing leads to another . . .

Memory of attempted incest

While I was going forward for prayer for those involved in leading groups at church, Ed Piorek [one of Wimber's team] had a word of knowledge about incest. I then said I'd come forward initially for leadership prayer but now I think I ought to receive prayer also about incest in the past with my sister.

When I was three and my sister five, an older man looking after us encouraged us to try to have sex together. Also when I was twelve and not yet potent my sister and her friend encouraged me to try to have sex with them too. I don't know what effect this prayer has had on my life since Harrogate but perhaps it may have affected the way I feel about that area of my life and my relationship with my sister.

Thoughts of murdering husband

There were three specific things in words of knowledge including people who have been thinking in their thoughts about murdering people. I'd felt like killing my husband and thought and dreamed of it for a long time. I received prayer – nothing great or terrific happened, but I just felt peaceful afterwards.

[By the time she was interviewed, she and her husband had divorced.]

Attitudes to others in church

There were two people in particular. One was a woman who had lost her husband . . . She is the manageress of a shop, and it's very much as if she knows best. After prayer and meditation with the minister we both feel there is something within her, possibly since childhood, causing her to be as she is. She's a very serious person and if you don't do things her way she automatically alienates you. She won't take teaching from anyone else but the minister because she feels no one else can match her. The Lord has used her in youth work and Crusaders, but a lot of people have been hurt by her attitude. Each of the three pastoral assistants before me had been involved with Crusaders, but the previous one had felt it was taking up too much time so I didn't go into Crusaders. This automatically alienated me from her. When her husband died I got no welcome from her – I was kept on her doorstep and she more or less told me to go away. I'd been here only a month; that began a resentment in me.

At the conference I received prayer for that and had a great peace about it. Sometimes I get hot under the collar but it does not express itself in anger or resentment, but instead in sorrowfulness: I feel like crying not with her but for her.

The other person was brought up in a very strict Christian church . . . He is very dour and serious in all he does. I've never seen him smile for months, he's so serious, but he does have a real love for the Lord. He's always the first person out of the door and takes you up on a couple of points about what you should have said. He's very precise – I always had to be careful to do everything right. Because of my extrovert nature he had to be sure of my commitment – I found that hard to accept; he interrogated me.

Now I've been given a great love for the guy and he's even begun to smile and laugh – a miracle for him. He's really coming on . . . and I no longer feel as if I'm being criticised or summed up; the Lord has been working in both our lives.

'Pendulum swings' in life

Since my late teens I've always had a profound lack of confidence. As a child I had terrible nightmares: the whole prospect of school was terrifying . . . Aware of a pendulum swing – either I was very calm and relaxed and able to function or else very tensed up and confused, unable to function properly. I told a friend about this pendulum swing in my life and he said it'd be much less by the end of the conference. I found that living under the principles of John Wimber – the way we're supposed to operate – and the denuding of personality is part of the process: living in risk . . . Living in the Word had a healing effect . . .

Two people came and began to pray for me. They prayed for half an hour or so. One person got several words of knowledge. The first two were ridiculous: 'Do you have any greyhounds in your family?', 'I can see the pavement you walked on as a child – did you talk to God?' – No. Then he told me I would feel God's power now. I had a problem area in my life . . . I was told to cultivate a Father relationship with God as I would be on my own a lot in a way other Christians aren't. He said some very encouraging things to me that were very important to me . . .

Now the pendulum swings have virtually gone from my life. Harrogate was pivotal in this. When I would get befuddled one minute and not the next it would produce strain in my life – I'd be fluent, then awkward. That led to tension. A lot of that's gone. I don't know how that's happened.

A friend who is a minister reports:

There's definitely been a big growth in maturity in him, and Harrogate had a lot to do with that. His relationship with his parents and a lot of other relationships, and his ability to handle relationships have changed. Also his relationship with the people he works with . . . has changed – going from strength to strength. From someone who was seen as 'suspect' and not generally accepted he's been promoted to being a union rep. . . . and is well accepted without any compromise in his witness.

Also he had a number of difficult problems to deal with . . . not his personal problems but people very closely related to him . . . Both of these he'd handled extremely well and I feel Harrogate was a turning-point for him in dealing with these things. He still speaks about Harrogate and quotes John Wimber quite a lot – so obviously the impression it made has been great.

Comments on particular problem areas

The selection of case studies presented above illustrates a diversity of problems, some of which appear to have been successfully resolved and others not. Several pastoral applications as well as questions arise out of this kind of material, many of which are discussed elsewhere by Mary Pytches or Rita Bennett.[23] Often there are no clear-cut answers, and it is necessary to treat each person as an individual in the context of his or her own circumstances. (Those circumstances include past memories as well as present social situations and future anticipations.) Here I shall restrict my comments to a few of the areas in which there do appear to be at least some continuing problems for certain people.

Disappointments over not receiving charismatic gifts

The woman quoted earlier who was jealous of her husband's having received the gift of speaking in tongues nevertheless could describe other times in her life when she believed she had received messages from God. For example:

A family vaguely connected with the church – their son had meningitis . . . was very, very ill and they thought he was going to die. Ten of us from the church got together after the evening service and prayed for this lad. One person had a picture of knights on chargers but no one knew what it meant. A minute later this whole picture he'd had came into my mind and someone shouted forcefully into my head the word 'Victory!' At that moment we knew he was going to live and get better. I was thrilled to bits when he did. They said by rights he should be dead, it was as bad as that.

On another occasion she felt strongly that she had to go to pray with a minister whose mother had died, even though she felt very foolish at doing so – 'I'm not in the habit of praying with ministers' – but later she heard via another minister that her prayer had been described by the pastor as 'one of the most helpful things that had happened to him since his mother's death'.

Perhaps one pastoral application might be to encourage individuals to recognise what gifts they have already received and to be thankful for those, because 'There are different kinds of gifts, but the same Spirit' (1 Corinthians 12:4).[24] Another approach may be to recognise that God equips with his gifts as and when we need them, as illustrated by the testimony of a forty-three year old man who previously had not spoken in tongues:

[At Harrogate a team member] . . . was looking for someone to support her. I climbed over a couple of rows of seats. She said, 'This man is' – in a trance or whatever. 'We can't question him on what his feelings are . . . he's just incommunicado. We have to pray in the Spirit and ask the Spirit to intercede.' I couldn't speak in tongues. I prayed, 'Oh, God, Oh, God!' – and out it came! It was not by the laying on of hands or anything, just meeting a need . . .

A not dissimilar attitude is expressed by another person interviewed, who seemed content to wait:

I was sitting next to a lady and somehow got talking about baptism in the Spirit. She said, 'I'll pray for you' . . . She and a friend prayed . . . It was not a dramatic experience but I was aware of a lightness and joy coming through me. More a sense of warmth coming right through me . . . I didn't speak in tongues but they felt that one day when I'm by myself I would speak in tongues. I was really not quite kind of drunk but was very bubbly and lightheaded. Not stumbling and all over the place but strange that it was a bit like as if I'd had wine. B.'s comment was that I was shining, looked radiant . . .

I've had no charismatic gifts since the conference. I've not spoken in tongues – I personally feel something's there still as a blockage but I don't know what. I'm hoping that when I join the house church in W. I'll learn how to minister in the gifts of the Spirit in that environment.[25]

[Her church at the time was not very open to charismatic gifts: probably this social context is also an important factor in facilitating or hindering the development of such gifts.]

One man interviewed who had not to date spoken in tongues described how at Harrogate he had received his first word of knowledge. When I contacted his minister some time later, the minister told me that in the interim there had been a word of knowledge in the church which specified the man's name.[26] As a result this man began to speak in tongues, the minister describing it as 'not under great pressure'. (He then described other noticeable changes since the Harrogate conference, including the comment, 'I do put Harrogate down as a formative time for him in listening to God.')

'Listening to God' is a key element in the development of several charismatic gifts; the ways of listening do vary, however, in different denominational traditions. In my question on gifts received in the past a Roman Catholic man wrote 'prayer of absolute silence' and 'prayer of gift of tears'. When asked to elaborate on these during my interview with him, he said:

Both are listed by some people as charismatic gifts, though they're not scriptural. Absolute silence – when you're very definitely in the company of God. Tears – more extensive than people realise. They can be of joy as well as sorrow.

Again this is linked to being in the company of God. You never know when it's going to come. The prayer of silence is more likely in my experience in a church, with the fewer people the better because of the noise, but it can occur anywhere. The prayer of tears – again you don't know when, more often when alone. I have had it in company. You are praying and your eyes water like mad for a few minutes. You feel what I can only describe as 'the peace of God'. Tears of joy are more common for me – joy of being in a relationship with God. Sorrow – may be sorrow associated with when things are going wrong . . .

Over the last twelve years I've had a whole change in the nature of prayer. My traditional idea was that prayer equals words thrown at God. Now I'm far more relaxed in prayer. One of the greatest of gifts that has come my way is a sense of relaxation in prayer – like the prayer of absolute silence.

Tongues I've only had noticeably on one occasion. At a conference I had my tape recorder with me. I volunteered for something and was separated from my tape recorder. Suddenly I broke out into tongues but it was a distraction in the service so I stopped. It was the Lord's purpose that I shouldn't tape it – because of my inquisitive mind . . .[27]

In his book *Walking on Water* Barry Kissell describes how he (a Protestant) had been inspired by reading a book on the Russian mystics, as a result of which he began 'to see the link between seeking God and silence'. He also writes of how the gift of tongues 'after a relatively short period . . . always leads me into an awareness of the presence of God'.[28] This combination of verbal and non-verbal modes of prayer blends together strands of different traditions. For the Roman Catholic man quoted above the 'prayer of absolute silence' seems to be almost functionally equivalent to Barry Kissell's use of the gift of tongues in personal devotional prayer. Those who have difficulty in receiving the gift of tongues might be encouraged to seek the presence of God through other forms of prayer – while also trusting God to give this gift for intercessory prayer as and when the need should arise.

Compulsive habits

A man who received prayer about giving up smoking said it had no effect at all except to make him feel more guilty when he did smoke. Another man wrote on his questionnaire that healings in two other areas were 'successful', but for giving up smoking was 'unsuccessful'. It is clear that this is an area which is not easily amenable to prayer.[29]

The woman with a compulsive habit of picking spots claims it has decreased, but it has by no means disappeared. Another woman, aged seventy-two, wrote on her questionnaire about 'contamination of the house due to the death of a relative', which produced compulsive hand-washing. Over a year after the conference she wrote:

> I never think now of the contamination of the house . . . I do however wash my hands perhaps more than I need – often for hygienic reasons and sometimes not. When the devil tempts me I pull myself up and resist the temptation, or try to. I know I must fight this weakness . . .

Both these women see the problem now in terms of self-discipline, a matter of the will, the one who picks spots viewing it as 'lack of self-control now rather than a deep-rooted thing'. Mary Pytches recognises difficulties in ministering to those with 'obsessive or compulsive behaviour problems' and gives little advice on this area except to say that 'a measure of help' has come to 'many people' through the experience of 'resting in the Spirit'.[30] This happened to the woman who picks spots, which she viewed as a 'confirmation' of being released from a dislike of herself: nevertheless the habit has persisted even if it has decreased.

Masturbation is another area in which all informants claim there has been some decrease. Although such claims may be influenced by the social acceptability of the answer, three of these could quantify it and the fourth said he has control for a while until his feelings build up 'like a tidal wave'. For the one man who could give a very clear testimony in this area, it is closely linked with both self-discipline and his decision to tithe his time. His account was quoted at length in order to encourage others who may have problems in this area.

Infatuation and adultery

A married woman described how she received counselling and inner healing from a group of three people in her church, one of whom, a minister, I shall call F. She said:

> I had three or four counselling sessions. After the first one so much was brought out that I fell in love with F. I said to [my husband] I couldn't understand it – I had a crush on F. . . . I felt quite moved when he came in the room . . . I told [my husband and F.'s wife]; I didn't want to get it out of perspective. [F.'s wife] said that when the crush has passed off and I get to feeling normal I'll probably feel silly . . .

Mary Pytches warns against the emotional involvement which can easily result from one-to-one counselling with the opposite sex,[31] but the case cited above shows that infatuations can occur even when other people are present. This woman was honest about her feelings and expressed them to both of the other spouses involved, thereby helping to avoid the infatuation leading into other forms of personal involvement. Such honesty can be more difficult for those who fear hurting others' feelings or arousing jealousy or resentment. Mary Pytches sums up the problems involved in such confession when she writes:

> A husband may have committed adultery and in confessing it to his partner cause her to suffer a loss of value and feelings of rejection. It may well be right for him to confess such a sin to his wife, but first he must be sure God is prompting him and that it is not just a desire to dump his burden on another unnecessarily. It may be better to confess the sin to a counsellor and not to the partner concerned.[32]

There is a wide gap between infatuation and adultery, and the degree of public acknowledgement appropriate for one case may not be appropriate for another. Certainly a recurrent problem I encountered in my interviews centred not so much on the guilt of an extramarital affair as on the effects on the wife or husband who found out about it. He or she may feel deeply hurt by feelings of rejection and a wife may wonder what was lacking in her that her husband should look elsewhere. Feelings of jealousy or resentment towards the other woman may also arise.

One woman who in her questionnaire reported 'a little' healing in the area of 'forgiveness', supplying no further details, was reluctant to discuss the matter further during the subsequent interview. Her husband was present at the time. Later he admitted that there was a time in the recent past when he had been 'enticed', but was reluctant to go into further details except to say it concerned another woman in the church. I suspect that this may be what his wife was alluding to earlier in the interview when she said she had been 'able to discuss events and situations' with 'certain people' which she 'wouldn't have been able to do before'.[33]

The man quoted earlier who felt he had to confess to his wife about an adulterous affair in the past said that his wife's reaction was

> not very good at first. We had to talk and pray it through. It had to be worked through but it did improve our relationship quite tremendously . . . Also she realised she was partly to blame in the lack of communication at the time in our relationship which went through a rough patch . . .

His wife had not received any kind of 'inner healing' prayer regarding her reaction to her husband's infidelity, but the possible need for such ministry to deep areas of the mind is indicated by the next account:

> We'd been Christians for many years but had slipped well away, in a very dead church situation. We were separated and talking about divorce. At this time my wife was baptised in the Holy Spirit. (I was involved with someone else.) I went to talk with the people who had helped her, as a last

resort before divorce. I had a significant experience with them and was baptised in the Spirit. We laid ourselves open to God and what he wanted to do.

Two or three months after that, she was laid flat on the floor . . . Two or three team members came and prayed with her. One of them said to me, 'I don't know what's happening here.' He came back and said something to do with adultery – wham on the button, very impressive.

There were no recognisable effects. We decided it was something so deep down, a slight throwback to what had been happening, and she needed to get it out of her system. It hadn't manifested that we had seen. She was not aware of it and I was not aware but just some spring cleaning needed doing, the last cleaning out of what had happened in the past being sorted out.[34]

A similar lack of realisation about unconsciously borne feelings is mentioned in the following account from a woman who through a 'word of knowledge' discovered her former pastor's adulterous involvements:

I did receive inner healing . . . in particular . . . [for] release of any guilt I felt for exposing the past of our pastor . . . I'd had a few phone calls and letters from the pastor's wife because she couldn't understand why we did not go to her first. (We just prayed about the way the Lord led.) I was released from them: the power of the Holy Spirit came on me, I sobbed it out. Then I felt a complete peace about the whole situation. But between the 1985 and 1986 meetings I hadn't realised I was carrying the burden for it – obviously it was very deeply buried.

This is not the only case recounted to me of a pastor being involved in adultery or having problems in similar areas. Ministers are likely to be particularly prone to temptation in this area because their work allows them to visit women at home at almost any time of day and because they are likely to counsel people about intimate areas of their personal lives. If the pastor's own marriage has problems, or if he has just had an argument with his wife, he might look for companionship elsewhere. Such companionship might not at first involve any sexual element, but where a close friendship does develop between two people of different sexes it can easily develop into a form of erotic love too.[35]

A social situation conducive to infidelity can be further aggravated by spiritual attack in so far as one person attributed temptations in this area to the work of a witch coven praying for the breakdown of Christian marriages. He cited cases in their church of long, stable marriages under attack through sexual attractions and 'petty jealousies', all in a period of six to twelve months during which the church was involved in three missions in their own and neighbouring areas.

This church had at the same time been experiencing renewal, my informant commenting, 'Clearly, when you get renewal you also get Satanic forces.' Accompanying such renewal is often a greater freedom of physical expression through hugs or kisses. We are told to 'Greet one another with a holy kiss' (2 Corinthians 13:12) or a 'kiss of love' (1 Peter 5:14), but I wonder to what extent attractive young women in our churches receive more than their fair share of such kisses?[36] At a subconscious level our motivations are sometimes mixed, even when our overt intentions are pure, and such gestures can be misunderstood both by those concerned and by their spouses.[37]

Homosexuality

One woman I interviewed told me how she had received ministry on an occasion prior to the Harrogate conference regarding her homosexual relationship with another woman. She said that she had entered into the relationship not because of such tendencies in herself but because of the existing friendship which she already had with the person concerned. 'I knew it was wrong, but because you don't get out of it your conscience goes dead on you,' she said.[38] When at a John Wimber conference the Holy Spirit touched this area of her life, she wept in deep remorse: 'I've never cried like it in my life.' Later she received inner healing to help her forgive the other woman and to heal her emotional 'sense of upset' at the fact that the woman had subsequently married. Now, she says, 'all that has changed – we're still close friends and her husband doesn't know anything about it. I know the husband, they're going to have a child and I'm thrilled about it. All the old has passed over. Equally she's received the healing she needed.'

Independently of my random sample I also followed up by telephone two other women who at Harrogate received prayer about their homosexual relationship. During the few months prior to the conference they had both had consider-able amounts of free time and had engaged in sexual activities together frequently: it was a 'very heavy relationship'. At Harrogate they 'needed to confess this':

It had been awkward in our church to share it but at Harrogate there was more freedom to go forward and confess it. That was the turning-point – brilliant to make a stand for God. There were two setbacks from November to February but since February we've made a stand for God and are walking his path.

It's been very painful on occasions because you feel like you're bereaved. You almost feel like the person has died because you can't have the person in the way you'd wanted. There's no sexual relationship now – I couldn't have [sub-sequently] moved in [with the other woman] otherwise because we would have ended up . . . Since then our relationship has been glorifying to God . . . It's not been difficult sexually, that wasn't difficult, but rather that you couldn't have that particular depth of relationship that you wanted. I couldn't ever marry her – it was like the death of that person. That had to die: I had to grieve over the depth of the relationship we couldn't have – laying aside some-thing very special . . . and can't have that sort of rela-tionship again, . . . the depth of communication. Though we have a good friendship anyway, it's not the same.

Both these accounts of female homosexual relationships focus more on the feelings towards the former partner. The pain in that area seems to be more difficult to bear than the guilt feelings connected with the sexual involvements. It is a pattern not dissimilar to the pain felt by a wife when she discovers her husband's adultery. In all these areas inner healing would seem to be incomplete if it merely ministers to the sinner's guilt without also ministering to the painful feelings produced in others affected by that relationship.

Psychological well-being

Studies elsewhere in both Britain and the USA have consistently shown a significant correlation between high frequencies of spiritual experience and higher than average levels of psychological well-being. Such people also express greater than average satisfaction with their lives on a scale of 'happiness'.[39] Moreover, the American sociologists Greeley and McCready found that these results were attributable to the disproportionately high scores of those whose descriptions of spiritual experiences displayed certain consistent features which these sociologists called the 'twice-born factor'.[40]

There is also some evidence that the reverse effect can occur, whereby those with a relatively deep exposure to the occult display decreased levels of psychological well-being and 'happiness'. In 1986 I interviewed a random sample of 108 nurses in Leeds about their spiritual experiences and found that those who at some time in their lives had been involved with spiritualism ranked lower than average on these scales, whereas those whose principal spiritual experience was the presence of God ranked higher than average.[41]

For comparative purposes I also included these questions in my follow-up interviews, finding that the mean (average) scores for the hundred people as a whole were high in comparison with my nurses' study.[42] However, the two men who rank lowest in the scale of psychological well-being (at points 1 and 2) are both those who are known to have had marital problems.[43] Three others with such problems are among the twelve who are found at points 3 and 4 on the scale. Of these five with known marital problems, two also rank lowest on the 'happiness' or 'satisfaction with life' scale; all the other three also have scores below the average for the group as a whole. By contrast, those who had received inner healing at Harrogate for problems not directly related to marital relationships tended to have scores nearer to the average for the whole group.

What this means is that the extent to which there is a noticeable psychological difference as a result of spiritual experiences and/or inner healing also depends in part on the presence or absence of continuing stress factors. This is most noticeable in the case of marital problems, but there is some indication that other forms of stress also contribute to decreased levels of psychological well-being.[44] The focus of most inner healing is upon the individual's psychological adjustment to stress factors, either through forgiveness or by a realisation that Jesus is with the person in the situation. Less attention tends to be paid to possible ways of reducing continuing sources of stress. Sometimes those factors are felt to be beyond the control of those ministering, such as in those cases where a Christian is living with a non-Christian spouse or parents. In such cases the believer may need to put up with the stress with as positive an attitude as possible (cf. 1 Corinthians 7:12–17; 1 Peter 3:1–2). In other cases, however, the Christian community might have a responsibility to give practical help to those in need. James 2:15–16 might be paraphrased as, 'Suppose a brother or sister is without clothes and daily food. If one of you says to him, "Let me pray for your inner healing," but does nothing about his physical needs, what good is it?'[45]

Demonisation

It is appropriate to include a section in this chapter on deliverance from evil spirits because sometimes the hurts caused by others or personal experiences requiring some form

of 'inner healing' can become channels through which demonic forces might influence a person. This is certainly one of
the more controversial areas of John Wimber's ministry and I
would suggest that those who are unfamiliar with his
teachings on demonisation should refer to chapter 6 of his book
Power Healing. Here I can do no more than summarise a few
main points and add some other comments of my own.

The gospels and Acts frequently refer to 'dirty' spirits, but
there is no systematic teaching provided about their origin
and nature. Traditionally they are referred to as 'evil' spirits,
a usage followed by the New International Version which in
its footnotes states 'Greek *unclean*'. Revelation 12:7–9; 2
Peter 2:4 and Jude 6 refer to 'angels' which serve Satan or
have sinned and which as a result have been cast out of heaven
or bound in chains awaiting judgement. Wimber cites Origen
as one of the early church fathers who thought that the 'dirty'
spirits mentioned in the gospels and Acts can be equated with
these fallen angels. It is assumed, however, that the more
dangerous ones were locked up while others were allowed
some freedom on this planet, at least for a while.

Traditionally the English words 'possessed' and 'possession' have been used to translate the Greek term used to
describe the activities of these spirits in affecting a person.
However, Wimber points out that the term *daimonizomai*
commonly used in the Greek New Testament is better rendered as 'demonised' because it refers to a wide range of
influences from, and *activities* by, the dirty spirits which affect
the person who is 'demonised'. Even in the most extreme case
of demonisation, that of Legion in Mark 5:1–20, there is still
some degree of voluntary action possible by the so-called
'possessed' person, who in this case could run up to Jesus and
fall on his knees in front of him, interpreted as a sign of
desiring help. In the case of the 'demonised' man in Mark 1:23
there is no description of any aberrant behaviour or 'mental
illness'; rather, he seems to have been a 'respectable' (dare
one say 'middle-class'?) synagogue-goer.

'Demonisation' in the New Testament can also produce
physical illness (*e.g.* Matthew 12:22; Luke 13:11) although

there is no record of any dialogue between Jesus and the spirits causing these afflictions. Distinctions have sometimes been drawn between spirits being 'on' versus 'in' a person, or between spiritual 'oppression' versus 'possession', but these are sub-classifications made by modern Christians to demarcate areas of 'mild' versus 'severe' forms of 'demonisation'. The New Testament gives the general category but provides no finer analysis or typology. Some contemporary examples from the questionnaires filled in at Harrogate might provide an overview of some of the different ailments which at the conference were attributed by my informants to demonic causes:

'. . . a word of knowledge about a swelling or blockage in the left side of the throat below the jaw. It was an afflicting spirit of anger which was prayed about last year but hadn't fully gone. It now has' (from a twenty-three year old man);

'A woman saw a superimposition of a spirit on me' (from a twenty-five year old man; from the questionnaire it was not clear whether this was at the same or a different time from his receiving prayer for inner healing (guilt) or physical healing (dislocating jaw and bad tendons in knees and ankles), and whether or not there was thought to be a link between these different areas. He nevertheless reported total healing of his problems);

'Delivery from transvestism which held my body in bondage for many years, for which I now feel forgiven' (from a forty-two year old man);

'Release of anger, revenge or vengeance in relation to sexual abuse. Healing of impressions of Father God imposed through the behaviour of my own father – sexual abuse as a child' (from a forty-six year old woman);[46]

'Deliverance from guilt of past homosexual activities and masturbation resulting from a feeling of being physically unloved' (from a fifty-seven year old man);

'Afflicting spirit in my own throat' (from a twenty-one year old man who reported total healing of his throat problem; the diagnosis had come via a word of knowledge from another person while the informant was receiving prayer for physical healing of his throat and chest).

On pages 136–137 of *Power Healing* Wimber provides 'an incomplete list of symptoms' which may help to identify the presence of demons, but he stresses that 'the presence of one or more of these symptoms indicates the possibility though not the necessity that the person is demonised'. This is circumstantial evidence of the likelihood of demonic influence, but more direct confirmation comes from the manifestation of physical writhing or distortions in more severely demonised people (pp. 229, 240–241). Other evidence comes from revelations via spiritual gifts.[47]

On pages 130–132 of *Power Healing* John Wimber mentions a number of common avenues through which demons can gain access to a person's life. Some kinds of sin, including sexual sins, hatred and alcohol or drug abuse, often make a person susceptible to demonic influence. Occult involvements are particularly likely to lead to demonisation. From my experience of Japanese shrines and temples I would emphasise the need to pray for spiritual protection when entering such places, even as a tourist.[48] Tourists in Africa, Asia and elsewhere are often unaware of the spiritual dimensions of objects traditionally used in pagan cults. Even these can provide avenues for demonic activity, as illustrated by a friend of mine who was not delivered until he had got rid of some cult objects sold as 'souvenirs' in New Guinea but during the manufacture of which traditional curses had been pronounced. Deuteronomy 7:25–26 commands the destruction of images used in idolatry and forbids the people of God from bringing any 'detestable thing' into their homes. These are the demonic counterparts to the cloths which can be used to convey divine healing at times (Luke 8:44; Acts 19:11–12).

Sometimes demonisation can occur as a result of the sins of parents or ancestors. One woman wrote on her questionnaire that she had received 'deliverance and inner healing regarding incest with parents – release of hurt, and inner healing surrounding that, and deliverance from linked demons –

incest, mockery, sodomy, lust'. Some forms of demonic influence can be passed down a family line, particularly if an ancestor has been involved in the occult.[49] An example of this comes from a woman who wrote on her questionnaire, 'Setting free from father being a Freemason, mother having a crystal ball.' When prayed with, she emitted 'some kind of continuous vocal sound' after which she spoke in a different tongue to the one she had previously received. Another woman reported total healing for a pain in her back 'caused by a spirit of affliction connected to continued illness experienced by my father'. In January 1988 she wrote to me, stating:

> The pain in my back actually continued on and off for the next week . . . I didn't find this disappointing . . . but kept 'claiming' my healing and restating that Satan now had no hold over this area of my life . . . The pain in my back has gone. I still get back aches, but these are *easily* attributable to awkward movements or overwork, whereas before they sprung up totally irrationally . . .
>   . . . We have had confirmation of the spirit of affliction/ illness (or whatever!) while praying for [my father]. But as yet he has not been released from this.

There is scriptural support for the possibility that some back problems may be due to afflicting spirits (Luke 13:10–13). Other physical conditions which can have demonic origins include epilepsy (Matthew 17:15–18), dumbness (Matthew 9:32–33), blindness (Matthew 12:22) and deafness (Mark 9:25), though at least some of these can be healed without the expulsion of demons (Mark 7:31–35; 10:46–52). If a hereditary demon also causes a physical illness such as asthma, a doctor might recognise the hereditary nature of the illness without perceiving its spiritual cause.[50]

Some people find it difficult to accept that demons are to be found relatively commonly in this kind of ministry. This is largely a product of our Western worldview, whereby accounts of demonisation in the Bible have tended to be reclassified as referring to mental illness.[51] One of the very real difficulties in this area is knowing to what extent mental illness may be attributable to demonisation as distinct from other possible causes, including social factors, nutrition and viral agencies.[52]

Another problem is simply that of terminology. If we can give a medical name to something, we think it is therefore 'natural' and not caused by demons. However, it may turn out to be merely an alternative name, as, for instance, in the so-called 'Arctic hysteria' among some Siberian tribes which contains symptoms often suggestive of demonisation.[53] The fact that schizophrenia is found more commonly in developed than in underdeveloped countries might even be attributable to the lack of other categories in our culture for symptoms which elsewhere may be classified as the work of spirits. 'Schizophrenia' actually is a rather loose term which embraces a variety of symptoms, not all of which are necessarily present in any one case. Two different people might both be classified as 'schizophrenic' and yet have no symptoms at all in common with each other. Actually, most of the symptoms which may be indicative of schizophrenia are to be found in most 'ordinary' people but to a lesser degree: 'normal' people are 'schizotypic', meaning that they exhibit a few mild attributes of 'schizophrenia', but extreme cases exhibiting more symptoms may be classified as 'schizophrenic' in our culture.[54]

Among the diversity of schizotypic or schizophrenic symptoms are included those in which the person reports voices in the head or an awareness of unseen presences. Their identity may be interpreted in a variety of ways but not uncommonly they are regarded as guiding spirits. The person may even feel helped by them. In my research among nurses I came across examples of apparently normal individuals in positions of responsibility who spoke of having such guiding spirits. A few nurses identified the spirits as those of their grandparents who 'comforted', advised or encouraged them. One of these first became aware of the presence of her dead grandfather when she started having an adulterous affair, which led to the break-up of the former marriages of both herself and her lover. In other cases the spiritual presence is felt to be 'around' but is not necessarily identified as someone who has died.

Others report dream conversations with people who have died or they may feel an awareness that a particular dead person is still 'somewhere around'. Some nurses report seeing apparitions of dead patients or of their own dead relatives. The fact that nurses have a close involvement with life and death situations might make such experiences relatively more common among nurses; 36% of them reported such experiences. This is double the frequency among the general British public as shown by a Gallup Poll conducted during the same year, while earlier studies in two British cities have yielded frequencies of 7% and 13%.[55] Whatever the proportion may be, it is clear that a substantial segment of the public report experiences of what they interpret as the presence of the dead.

The question then arises whether or not these 'presences' are to be equated with the 'dirty' spirits which are commonly referred to in the New Testament.[56] I found a statistically significant link between reports of the presence of the dead and involvements with spiritualism or Ouija boards at some point in one's life.[57] Spiritualist mediums who believe themselves to be in contact with departed spirits exhibit manifestations such as changes in voice or appearance identical to that regarded as diagnostic of demonisation in Christian circles. Moreover, I have heard of several cases in which a medium has been subsequently delivered from unclean spirits (i.e. demons). This is consistent with the biblical condemnation of anyone who is a 'medium or spiritist or who consults the dead' because 'anyone who does these things is detestable to the Lord' (Deuteronomy 18:11–12).

'Demons, demons, everywhere', writes Peter Masters in criticising the high incidence of deliverance associated with John Wimber's ministry.[58] Those who feel that the frequent diagnosis of demonisation among Christians is rather 'over the top' should stop to consider the fact that 55% of my random sample of nurses had been involved in the occult in some form or other, that over a third of the sample reported experiences of the presence of the dead and that other studies have also shown such experiences to be not uncommon. These are among those who are even aware of such a 'presence': many people who are delivered from afflicting spirits do not report any such awareness.

A caveat is in order here. Although I suggest that most experiences of the 'presence of the dead' arc indicative of demonic activity – as supported by their close association with occult involvements – I also recognise that there are rarer instances in which this might not be the case. The appearance of Moses and Elijah during Christ's transfiguration might be classified as one of the 'presence of the dead', but in this case it was divinely initiated. In our own century the Russian Christian 'Vanya' also claimed to have been in the presence of the apostle John, Moses, David and Daniel.[59] There is also the passage in Matthew 27:52–53 which reports, 'the bodies of many holy people who had died were raised to life . . . and appeared to many people'. Such experiences were *unsought* and unexpected, in contrast to the *deliberate attempts* by mediums to establish contact with the dead in a way which is prohibited in the Bible (1 Samuel 28; Deuteronomy 18:10–12). However, a problem is raised for evangelicals by St Paul's repeated rhetorical question in 1 Corinthians 15:29, '. . . if there is no resurrection, what will those do who are baptised for the dead? If the dead are not raised at all, why are people baptised for them?' This is a dimension of Christianity obviously much closer to Catholicism, perhaps explaining why some practising Catholics report experiences of both the presence of God and the presence of the dead.[60] Those who then jump to the conclusion that these Catholics must be demonised should first find a satisfactory interpretation for 1 Corinthians 15:29.[61] All too often thc verse is relegated to reflecting an early Christian fallacy which we have now 'grown out of' – exactly the same kind of thinking which reinterprets demonisation as nothing more than psychopathology.

Cases in which people report experiences both of the presence of God and of the presence of the dead do seem to be rare, howevcr. For the most part the two kinds of experience are quite distinct and appear to have opposite effects on measurements of psychological well-being at the time of being interviewed. Sociologically, the two kinds of experience are also distributed differently. Experiences of the presence of God tend to be concentrated more among better-educated, middle-class people while those reporting the presence of the dead are much more often from lesser-educated or working-class backgrounds.[62] Probably this reflects the middle-class nature of most English churches, as a result of which many Christians may not realise how widespread cases of demonisation might actually be among the general population.

Deliverance

If the Old Testament prohibitions against trying to communicate with the dead have the prophylactic intention of averting demonisation, then the New Testament teaching on deliverance is the therapeutic, active counterpart to the 'preventative medicine' prescribed by Moses. There are no cases at all of deliverance recorded in the Old Testament, not even in the ministry of Elisha, whose 'signs and wonders' ministry is the closest Old Testament parallel to that of Jesus.[63] For the most part – with a few notable exceptions – the Old Testament prophets spoke God's *words* but did not do the *works* of the kingdom such as healing from leprosy or raising the dead. That is why Jesus pointed to his *works* when asked by John the Baptist's disciples if he were 'the one who was to come', and, I suggest, why the least of those who in the kingdom of heaven do the *works* of the Father are greater than John. However, John heralded a new, active phase in which the kingdom of heaven no longer relies only on 'preventative medicine' to deal with demons but is 'forcefully advancing' against them (Matthew 11:1–15).

Of those who filled in questionnaires at Harrogate, 104 people (6%) reported receiving some kind of a deliverance ministry. It is significantly more common among women than men, perhaps for the same reasons as inner healing is more often received by women.[64] Inner hurts are not infrequently the pathways through which demonic influences can gain

access. There are also indications that the need for deliverance is greater among those from lower social classes, a
finding consistent with those cited above that experiences of
the presence of the dead are more commonly reported by
these social groups.[65]

The degree of healing reported from deliverance is higher
than that for inner healing, which in turn is greater than for
physical healing. These comparisons are summarised in Table
2.3.

Table 2.3   Comparisons of subjective assessments of amounts of
healing received in different categories of healing

Degree of healing	Low	Medium	High
Physical healing	42.0%	26.0%	32.0%
Inner healing	21.5%	28.0%	50.5%
Deliverance	14.5%	17.5%	68.0%

Further analysis of the degree of healing felt to have been
received shows no significant difference at all according to a
person's sex, social class, marital status or education: all alike
report similarly high results. The only significant difference
which could be found is that those in their teens and twenties
are much more likely to report high degrees of healing than
those aged fifty or over.[66] This might be because older people
are more cautious in assessing their degrees of healing than
younger people. If so, why are they more cautious in their
assessments of deliverance and of physical healing but not of
inner healing, which shows no significant difference in the
degree of healing according to age? When it comes to raising
the dead, there are biblical precedents for a divine bias
towards younger people, and this might be generalised to
physical healing of other kinds. For deliverance, however,
there is no clear biblical precedent for a divine bias to the
young because there is usually no indication of the ages of the
people delivered. There is evidence in Mark 9:14–29, however, that the longer an unclean spirit has been in a person the
harder it is to drive it out.[67] If this is the case for a younger
person, is the problem intensified in an older person?

Among the hundred people followed up in my random sample, there were five who mentioned receiving some kind of deliverance ministry at Harrogate. One of these was the woman quoted earlier (in the section on 'sense of rejection') who reported having a spirit of fear cast out. Another woman described how she was praying for someone else when

> at the end I had my hands on him and I ended up just *weeping* . . . a weeping for someone else, a physical thing, not emotional. Then they realised the anointing was on *me* . . . and they prayed for me.
>
> Once or twice when I've been prayed for I got really scared and frightened, I don't know why . . . That time my face was twitching all over, a very strange sensation, the first time it's happened. I asked to lie down. They prayed against a spirit of affliction. I screamed out, 'I don't want you, I don't want you.' Some kind of deliverance was going on – I was feeling I was getting released from something. I kept getting a pain in my stomach and I kept getting a coughing, and I felt as if I was being choked . . .

Both of these women received other forms of ministry for inner healing during the same few days, either at the conference or at one of the team visits to other centres during the weekend after the conference. The extent to which they received benefit from such deliverance ministries, as distinct from other areas of ministry, is therefore almost impossible to quantify.[68] The next case, however, is more amenable to assessments of this nature:

> [About the spirit of insomnia], I was amazed, having been a Christian for twenty years you don't think you can get these things, especially having done a bit of deliverance myself. I can't remember having a decent night's sleep since being married and my mother said I didn't sleep well as a child. But I noticed that since my spiritual awakening two years ago it got worse and really bad particularly when something spiritual was going to happen. Before the mission, night after night I couldn't sleep a wink. Or if I was going to pray for somebody I couldn't sleep a wink.

I suspected something but didn't know about demons [*etc.*]: every time they prayed it got worse. In the workshop, on the day they did about spirits of affliction, by the time it got to the coffee break I just knew inside. After the break they had a long ministry session for people who felt they had spirits of affliction . . .

I was very weepy – I don't remember a lot about it. I was standing and weeping and a girl came to pray for me. I don't know what she prayed. I was in a very bad way – for me – and swaying all over the place. She grabbed my sweatshirt to keep me from falling, saying 'Stay with us, honey'; that's all I remember. There was a lot of weeping and wailing going on. When it was all over I was a bit shaky round the gills . . . I just burst into tears.

I went to bed that night and I just zonked out, just went to sleep. I just don't remember being awake but went straight to sleep. I woke up with the alarm in the morning and couldn't believe it. (Normally I take a long time getting to sleep and often wake up.) It's really brilliant – when you've not slept for all those years and you suddenly discover what sleeping's like . . . I used to take sleeping pills and they never worked – I went to get some once a year. In fact when I went to Harrogate I had been taking them but couldn't sleep. I didn't take one that night after prayer and I've never done so since.

This case shows a marked improvement from the time of the deliverance onwards. There was a slight recurrence for a period of a week or two about two or three months prior to the interview which 'was not as bad as it used to be – but that could have been anything, anxiety or whatever'. Overall the change appears to be highly significant.

The details about the problem intensifying prior to spiritual activities such as a mission or praying with someone have parallels elsewhere. I have heard of a spirit of asthma which kept somebody from attending church until it was cast out – after which other spirits began to manifest instead. Others also mentioned problems which seemed to recur at particular times, especially prior to Christian ministry of some kind but which were not at the time recognised as being from demonic sources.

Other aspects of what are attributed to demonic sources come very close to areas of inner healing, as in the following two cases:

Two of the team came and could see the Holy Spirit on me. I had some inner healing then – forgiveness about my divorce twenty years ago. They knew all about it: I was a battered wife; one had a picture of me being beaten. There was a spirit of deceit on me. We talked and these things came out, about how I'd not been completely truthful in court at the divorce, because of a fear that they wouldn't grant the divorce. It always bothered me about what I'd said in court. I was not a Christian at the time but I had sworn on the Bible. After I became a Christian I was still bothered by it – and it all came out . . . at Harrogate. I felt it was all dealt with then – it's not bothered me since then.

[About the spirit of insecurity] I wanted to find out my role: as an elder's wife I knew my main role was to support [my husband] in the eldership. They did pray with me and said that they knew the Lord would use me in the body of the church, but honestly I don't see any special ministries I've got apart from being a little lady who will sit and listen – but that's important too . . .

They said it was a spirit of insecurity. Four of them prayed. I think I fell down, I can't remember now. Although you don't realise it's happened, looking back I have got more confidence and I don't worry about things like I used to do.

These two cases also indicate long-term positive effects as far as the person is concerned, even though they are not as objectively measurable as is the case for the spirit of insomnia. Nevertheless these do conform to a general pattern whereby subjectively assessed results after deliverance prayer consistently tend to report relatively high levels of perceived positive change.

3

WORDS OF KNOWLEDGE

Issues to be considered:

How accurate are 'words of knowledge' in reality?
Can they be given any plausible natural explanation?
What kinds of people are most likely to receive them?
How does their accuracy relate to their associated healings?

The charismatic movement in many denominations has tended to focus on gifts such as speaking in tongues, the interpretation of tongues and prophecy, but 'words of knowledge' as used by John Wimber and his colleagues are relatively new and have therefore attracted considerable attention – and controversy.

In 1 Corinthians 12:8 Paul refers to the 'message of knowledge' (NIV) or 'word of knowledge' (AV) as a gift of the Holy Spirit. He finds it necessary in 1 Corinthians 14 to elaborate on the gifts of prophecy and tongues, but nowhere does he give any fuller exposition about the 'message of knowledge'. It would therefore appear to be a commonplace or well-understood spiritual gift about which no serious problems arose requiring further explanation from the apostle.[1]

Wimber interprets a number of biblical passages as illustrating the practice of this gift in the ministries of Jesus and his disciples. A clear example is in John 4:16–19, where Jesus reveals his knowledge of a woman's personal life. Wimber also sees the same gift in operation when Jesus calls

Zacchaeus by name (Luke 19:5); he says there is no evidence that Jesus knew previously who Zacchaeus was and the tax collector's sudden change of heart is probably attributable to his being supernaturally singled out by name.[2] In the early church a similar kind of gift is indicated by Peter's knowledge of secret facts about Ananias and Sapphira (Acts 5:1–11), who 'lied to the Holy Spirit' (v.3) or 'to God' (v.4). These examples seem to illustrate the work of the Holy Spirit who convicts with regard to sin, righteousness and judgement (John 16:8), resulting in the situation described in 1 Corinthians 14:24–25 whereby an unbeliever 'will be convinced . . . that he is a sinner and . . . the secrets of his heart will be laid bare'.[3]

Of an apparently different nature are accounts of information received about another person (who may or may not be present at the time) relating to the person's state of health or other matters not necessarily involving any conviction of sin. Some precedents for this might be seen in the ministry of Elisha (2 Kings 6:9–10, 32), who imparted factual information about the behaviour of both the king of Aram and the king of Israel.[4] New Testament examples might include the supernatural knowledge which Jesus displayed concerning Nathanael (John 1:48–51) or the woman with menorrhagia (Luke 8:43–48). In the latter case it seems that Jesus did not know exactly who it was who touched him until the woman identified herself – the closest New Testament precedent available for the formula often used in Wimber-type meetings which says, 'There is somebody here with a . . .'

Robert Baldwin, a Consultant Psychiatrist at Manchester Royal Infirmary, describes his observations of contemporary 'words of knowledge' in the following terms:

Sometimes the 'knowledge' may be quite specific, but usually it is general and nearly always aimed at areas of ill-health. Recurring examples I have encountered include various forms of pain originating from the skeletal system (commonly the back), stiff muscles, fallen arches, prolapses, infertility, and common emotional difficulties such as depression and anxiety . . . Recently, a young man came forward . . . and said sheepishly that he wasn't sure whether he should have come because a 'word' had been given for someone with low back pain, whereas his was in the upper part of the back![5]

Dr Baldwin's observations are supported by my questionnaire data from Harrogate. There were 504 people (27% of the sample) who felt that a 'word of knowledge' at the conference had applied to them. My next question asked them to specify what was said in the 'word of knowledge' and I then attempted to classify these according to levels of specificity. Many of these were either definitely or probably (as far as could be judged from the questionnaire) received during one-to-one ministry on a private basis. Obviously a 'word of knowledge' given in such circumstances is rather more specific than one given out publicly. In very many cases the person receiving a 'private' word feels that the person giving it could not have known such details about the recipient's personal life and therefore regards it as highly specific. However, I have tended to take a more rigorous view of the level of specificity in classifying as 'low specific' words given on a personal basis such as 'problems I have had with anger because of hurts in the past'. What I would regard as more highly specific personal messages include details such as the age at which an event happened or pictures of the scene, as illustrated by a twenty-three year old woman who wrote, 'Rejection as a child, useless; ragdoll thrown away. Little girl of four.' A number of people felt that more than one 'word of knowledge' applied to them at different times during the conference, some of which were more specific than others, but an overall impression of their general levels of specificity can be gained from the following table:

Table 3.1   Levels of specificity of words of knowledge received

	Public			Private		
	Low	Medium	High	Low	Medium	High
Number of cases	206	71	17	255	51	10

The public 'words' of low or medium specificity were often responded to by a number of people, so these figures are considerably greater than the actual number of such messages given out. Many of these messages were given out by John Wimber or his team members, but during some of the workshops or some times of individual ministry other words of knowledge were conveyed by 'ordinary' participants attending the conference. The specificity of their messages also tended to be low, as shown by Table 3.2:

Table 3.2   *Levels of specificity of words of knowledge conveyed by non-team members*

	Public			Private		
	Low	Medium	High	Low	Medium	High
Number of cases	12	13	13	480	120	19

These figures give indications of overall trends, but it is not always possible to match up those giving and receiving particular words of knowledge because almost a quarter of those registered for the conference failed to complete a questionnaire. Nevertheless it can be seen that the more specific examples tend to be relatively rare.

Statistical analysis of a detailed 'word of knowledge'

As an example of a highly specific case, consider the following public message given out at Harrogate by John Wimber:

There's a woman named Janet who at eleven years of age had a minor accident that's proven to be a problem throughout her adult life. It had something to do with an injury to her tailbone but now it's caused other kinds of problems and so there's radiating pain that comes down over her – er – lower back and down over her backside and down her legs. It has something to do with damage to a nerve but it also has to do with some sort of a functional problem with the – um – I think it's called the sacro-iliac.

For the same reasons as I gave in my report on the Sheffield conference, it is highly unlikely that these details could have been ascertained in advance.[6] They were nevertheless so specific that Janet soon identified herself, but as she was in the overflow hall (connected with the main auditorium by a closed circuit television relay) two of Wimber's team prayed for her there. A little later she spoke over a microphone from the other hall saying, 'The Holy Spirit touched me on my back complaint and is healing it.'[7]

The above 'word of knowledge' can be analysed in terms of the statistical probability of having this combination of elements through chance alone. To do this, the different elements need first be identified, their frequency of occurrence in the general population ascertained or closely estimated, and their theoretical permutations calculated. I shall err on the conservative side in order to obtain a minimum probability value, but the true one may well be considerably greater than the value obtained by these conservative figures.

The different elements can be isolated as follows:

a) Female: One of two possibilities.
b) Janet: As a conservative estimate let us assume there are a hundred possible female names to choose from.
c) Eleven years: As the majority of those at the conference were aged between twenty and sixty (but some were as young as sixteen and others were over sixty), let us assume a mean age of forty for the overall group. Taking a more conservative figure, let us assume that there are thirty possible ages at which this accident could have happened. (Note that Wimber mentions that Janet is an adult.)
d) Tailbone: This is considerably more specific than the mention of 'throat' in an example which I discussed in my report on the Sheffield conference. There I took a very conservative

figure of thirty organs in the body, but a more realistic estimate would be several hundred. Nevertheless I shall retain a very conservative estimate but shall take the figure of fifty rather than thirty because the specification of 'tailbone' is rather more specific than that of a general area like 'throat'.

e) Sacro-iliac: The sacro-iliac joint is at the top of the buttocks about three inches from the mid-line and extends downwards into the buttock itself. Because damage to the tailbone had already been specified, I shall take a very conservative estimate of one in ten such injuries resulting in a secondary problem with the sacro-iliac joint.

f) Radiating pain . . . down her legs: This also relates to the feature about 'damage to a nerve'. There is both nerve damage and a functional problem with the sacro-iliac joint, but because the nerve damage was caused by the injury to her tailbone and the sacro-iliac has been mentioned in (e) above, I shall not attempt to quantify the frequency of occurrence of these details but shall ignore them in my calculation. The effect of this is to reduce even further the final figure I shall arrive at, so it should be borne in mind that the 'real' figure will be considerably in excess of the figure I obtain by this means.

To calculate the statistical probability of obtaining this particular combination of features among all the possible permutations of elements, the numbers isolated above in (a) to (e) need to be multiplied together as follows:

$$2 \times 100 \times 30 \times 50 \times 10 = 3 \text{ million.}$$

This means that using the above relatively conservative figures there is a three million to one chance of obtaining all these features together by chance alone. If more realistic figures for some items were to be used, the probability estimate would be much greater than three million. For example, if we said there were a hundred organs in the body – still a very conservative figure – in item (d), then the probability estimate would double to six million to one. In the same way, any assignment of a value to the description of 'radiating pain . . . down her legs' in (f), a detail which was not quantified in the above example, would multiply the original three million by the value assigned to (f). Even if (f) had a value of only five, the overall probability rises to fifteen million where there are only fifty organs in the body and to thirty million if we take a figure of a hundred organs for (d).[8]

For now let us remain with the original conservative estimate of a three million to one chance against this combination of elements being due to chance alone. We now need to divide this by the number of people at the conference (about 2400). Rounding this up to 2500 and dividing 3,000,000 by 2500 we find that the crowd would have to have been 1200 times larger than it actually was for just one person to have had this combination of features through chance alone.

Statisticians usually express such probabilities in decimal terms, so that a probable occurrence of five out of a hundred would be written as 0.05. They would regard an occurrence of which the probability, assuming chance alone, is greater than 0.05 as having no statistical significance. If the probability is less than 0.05 it is regarded as significant and not likely to be due to chance alone. In the above calculation, 2500 divided by 3,000,000 produces a probability of 0.000833, which is therefore highly significant.[9]

In taking the example of Janet, I chose a detailed example, but this was the first one of a total of nine different ones given out on the Tuesday night of the conference. That evening John Wimber felt that God wanted to demonstrate the way in which his team prayed for people, and in order to do so he recognised he would need very specific words of knowledge; otherwise the stage would be crowded out by people coming up for a condition like backache. Examples of some of the other words of knowledge given out that evening are as follows:

I think that there's a young man named Laurence or Larry, and I don't know whether you've actually drunk this or whether you've breathed it in but you have some sort of chemical burn in the oesophagus that's produced an inflamed – or some sort of a problem in the whole upper bronchial area of your body and you've been treated for this. I guess it was September but I don't know if it was September last year or September this year. I don't know how recent it is but the word 'September' comes to me. And you've been having problems with it ever since, so the Lord wants to touch you.

A woman that's twenty-two years old that has a, has just discovered a lump in the left breast and, um, she hasn't even told her husband about it, and she's frightened. She's not sure what it is, she's of course frightened that it could be cancer and, um, if you'll come the Lord wants to touch you and heal you. You just discovered this recently. It was in the morning, I think Tuesday morning.

What's a fibula? It's in the leg – the lower leg? Is it the front part or the back part? Side? Inside, outside? It's the outside? Right, OK.

Someone has injured their fibula, and I believe it's the right leg, and, um, I don't know, I think I'm seeing that in reverse, no, it's the right leg, someone that's injured your fibula and the Lord wants to touch you.

Laurence, like Janet, soon identified himself, but he too was in the overflow hall down the road. This is significant because it refutes Baldwin's suggestion that 'when the

Wimber team members gaze into the audience to receive a "word", what they are unconsciously doing is reading the silent, potent cues of body language – the depressed faces, the anxious manner, *etc.*, which point to need'.[10] This idea is also far-fetched when it comes to a knowledge of specific details such as a person's name. That evening there was actually a quicker response from individuals in the overflow hall than there was from some of those in the main auditorium who for one reason or another were reluctant to come forward publicly, even though they identified themselves in private later.

The examples quoted above come from large conference situations in which a relatively high degree of specificity is necessary in order to single out individuals. The numbers present in an audience can cause variations in the degree of specificity of at least some 'words of knowledge'. In a large crowd a generalised 'word of knowledge' about a fairly common kind of problem has a low specificity because a number of people are likely to respond to it. However, in a house group of a dozen or so people the same statement may be relatively high in specificity. An intermediate situation is that of a church congregation with up to a few hundred people, where some sorts of messages may be specific enough but others too vague. This might be a problem with the attitude that house groups are useful training grounds for developing these gifts – which they certainly can be – if 'words' sufficient for a house-group situation are then spoken in larger meetings where they lose their credibility.

Receiving the gift

The 'knowledge' can be received in a variety of ways, the most common of which are as follows (I indicate also their relative frequencies among those who reported conveying words of knowledge at Harrogate[11]):

Table 3.3   *Ways in which words of knowledge are received*

Type of word	Frequency of report
Strong intuition	440
Mental picture	175
Pain in a part of the body	57
Seeing words written	38
Spontaneous utterance	97

A further thirty-one people wrote in 'other' descriptions such as 'hearing very clearly the voice of the Lord' or 'word in mind', which they felt to be different from a 'strong intuition'. Another way of receiving information, reported by fifteen people, involves feeling a tingling in their arms or a shaking in their hands over the affected area of a person being prayed for. (This awareness of physical changes in one's own body is perhaps to some extent a variant of the 'word of knowledge' in which one feels a pain, sometimes heat, in one's own body corresponding to the location of someone else's medical problem.) Three people thought they had received a 'word of knowledge' but did not convey it, either because of lack of confidence or lack of opportunity. A miscellaneous group (fourteen cases in all) received 'words of knowledge' in other ways.[12] Sometimes it involves a kind of empathy or sharing of the emotions of the other person, an example of which is described on pp. 270–271 of *Power Healing*.[13]

One particularly interesting manner in which 'words of knowledge' sometimes come to one informant is through 'the interpretation of spontaneous mime'. An example he gave is:

> I was busy praying for a particular person and realised I couldn't separate my hands. I opened my eyes and looked and saw I was holding on to my left ring finger. As soon as I started to pray for the marriage relationship of the person, I could move my hands.

It is significant that this man used to be a drama teacher. Just as prophecies in the Old Testament communicate divine messages in styles appropriate to the individual prophets, even making use of personal experiences such as Hosea's marriage, in the same way contemporary messages through words of knowledge utilise symbols readily understood in our own culture. 'Seeing words written' would be as inappropriate for a non-literate culture as it would be for most of us to see the same message written in Chinese characters.[14] Both in dreams and in words of knowledge, as also in prophecy, there are many different symbols available to the Holy Spirit in order to communicate God's messages to us.

Although the information may seem to be channelled through one or more of the 'ordinary' senses, it is conveyed in an 'extra-ordinary' manner. Seeing in the 'mind's eye' a picture or words written utilises a form of vision; feeling another's pain utilises a form of the sense of touch. For strong intuition or empathy, however, it is as if the 'ordinary' senses are circumvented – unless it is a kind of 'inner hearing' analogous to the 'inner eye' which 'sees' words or pictures invisible to others. In a rather different category is the experience of saying something spontaneously and hardly realising what is being said until it is verbalised, apparently involving a transcending of normal speech processes. A few examples may help to clarify how these are conveyed in practice:

'A picture of a ship, followed by a moonlit calm sea. The person admitted to a fear of water' (from a thirty-four year old man; mental picture);

'"Adultery" – in MacDonald's burger bar in town! When I sat down on a table with a local resident – It was true! (of her *ex*-husband) and I was able to tell her about the Lord and his healing' (from a twenty-eight year old man; mental picture [of words written?]);

'A word concerning ministry in Egypt – the Lord promised to bless' (from a forty year old man; spontaneous utterance);

'I explained a picture by using an illustration of how my eleven year old child responds to the Spirit. The age of eleven was the "key"' (from a thirty-two year old woman; linked mental picture and spontaneous utterance);

'I received a mental picture of a chemical formula in fluorescent numbers as on ticker tape concerning a man we were praying for with diabetes' (from a thirty-nine year old man; both mental picture and seeing words written);[15]

'I had a vision of a man's face with the left hand bottom side blotted out. I then felt I had to *walk round the Hall* to find him. I kind of felt the Lord telling me *to walk on*. I asked one man but he was the wrong one. However the second one I asked was the right one. Great blessings by my praying for him' (from a fifty-seven year old woman; mental picture);

'I saw in my mind's eye the word "ANGER" on the body of a woman seated next to me. I explained this to her and she admitted feeling very angry about relationships in her church with others and the lack of a husband as she approached middle age. We prayed about this together' (from a thirty-six year old man; seeing a word written);

(a) 'About someone – grandmother or aunt – called Emma or Anna in South Africa' (strong intuition),

(b) 'Also a word – "married"' (seeing word written),

(c) 'An impression of a black strong-box containing treasure' (felt box as in hands) (all from a thirty-seven year old woman: presumably (c) also involved some other channel besides touch because of the details of 'black' and 'treasure');

'From a mental picture of a heart surrounded by a cave. Lock broken on first door, open – series of other doors one after another' (from a forty-two year old woman; mental picture).

Comparisons with spiritualism and ESP

In my report on the Sheffield conference I compared these words of knowledge with apparently similar phenomena such as telepathy or the utterances of spiritualist mediums. I found that the level of specificity or accuracy in the words of knowledge was considerably higher than those reported from scientific studies of either ESP or mediumship. Furthermore, the quality or nature of occurrence is very different from the kind of telepathy alleged to occur between close friends or relatives, and is also very different from that which occurs in a mediumistic seance through the use of so-called 'inductors' (physical objects associated with a person) by means of which a medium seeks to ascertain knowledge about such a person.

By contrast, the 'words of knowledge' given out by Wimber and his colleagues at conferences in Britain occur between people having no prior relationship with each other, without the use of 'inductors' and with an accuracy level which comes close to 100%. This contrasts with, for example, statistically significant scores such as 1839 correct guesses out of a total of 6800 or 279 out of 1000 trials in some tests for telepathy.[16] Similarly, Boerenkamp's study of fourteen mediums and psychics concluded that about 10% of their utterances met the criteria of 'no logical explanation' but of these only one out of ten met the criteria of 'sufficient degree of correspondence' between statement and reality. This 1% incidence of 'unexplained' and 'true' statements was sufficiently low to be explicable in terms of chance alone.[17]

Nevertheless, there remains a real theological question about the similarities between the modes of communication as found in spiritualism and in the Christian examples discussed here. As I see it, there are three possible Christian positions: (1) all these psychic gifts are from demonic sources, irrespective of the context in which they occur, and Christians should have nothing to do with them; (2) the psychic information can come from either divine or demonic sources but the channel utilised by these is in itself neutral; (3) God created man with a capacity to receive communications from him through a variety of channels but at least some of these channels have been usurped frequently by demonic agencies.[18]

To at least some extent, one's choice among these perspectives depends on one's starting-point. If one begins with a consideration of spiritualism, for example, and emphasises some apparent similarities with the outward forms of charismatic gifts then one tends to be drawn to the first conclusion.[19] Those who start from a consideration of ESP and attempts at scientific investigation of it tend to categorise both occult and Christian varieties under the same heading.[20] Christians influenced strongly by the contemporary charismatic movement are probably more inclined to the third perspective.

If all creation, including man, was originally viewed by God as 'very good' (Genesis 1:31), this presumably applies also to the human capacity for spiritual awareness. Man would have been given channels for communication with his Maker but, like a radio set, these might be tuned in to other sources too. Just as physical eyes can be directed to read either the New Testament or pornography, so also our spiritual 'eyes' may be directed in various directions. However, it is not the eye which is to blame for any pornographic input but rather the will which has chosen to direct the eye that way. In the same way the 'eyes' of our hearts (Ephesians 1:18) are in themselves neutral; though created for good, they can be used to serve both pure and impure purposes.

For this reason it is important to distinguish between the *channel* of a communication and its *source*. Mental pictures, intuitions and so on are merely the channels, but it is the *source* which determines the *content*. The content reflects the character of its origin (Luke 6:43–45). This is why New Testament guidelines for testing the source of a revelation focus upon the content and the character of that revelation (1 John 4:1–3; 1 Corinthians 12:3).

'In one's right mind'

Words of knowledge are the most democratic of the common charismatic gifts. What I mean by this is that all the other common gifts are closely associated with the sociological variables of age or sex – but words of knowledge are not. For example, among those who had exercised the gift of prophecy at some time in their lives prior to the conference, there are statistically significant links both with age and marital status. There is a peak among those in their thirties and a steady decline both sides of this peak; single or married people are much more likely to report it than those who are widowed or divorced. It also tends to be rather more common among men than women, possibly accounting for the links with marital status.[21] By contrast, women are significantly more likely than men to report receiving pictures during prayer, but this gift has no significant link with marital status.[22] I speculate that in many churches there may be certain social factors operating in the recognition of some of these gifts, especially the more public ones like prophecy, producing a stereotype of the kind of person who is likely to be recognised as having such gifts. The significant links between younger age groups and gifts such as speaking in tongues or the interpretation of them are probably to be accounted for by the apparently greater degree of receptivity among younger generations to the charismatic movement. These suggested interpretations must, however, remain speculative.[23]

Even though there are no significant links between words of knowledge and age or sex, there does appear to be a very close connection between musical or artistic talents and the development of this gift. For instance, in 2 Kings 3:15 Elisha asks for a harpist and receives a revelation from God while the music is playing (vv. 16–19, 20). Considering that John Wimber used to be a professional musician, might it be that a sensitivity to music or to other forms of artistic expression is conducive to a sensitivity to words of knowledge too?

For this reason I inserted an additional question into my interviews and discovered that there is indeed a highly significant link between receptivity to words of knowledge and the development of musical or artistic abilities.[24] This relationship is indicated in Table 3.4.

What I here count as a 'musical or artistic pursuit' means, for example, playing a musical instrument relatively frequently as contrasted with listening to music or having learned to play

Table 3.4   Relationships between words of knowledge and
             musical or artistic abilities

	People receiving words of knowledge relatively frequently	People receiving words of knowledge relatively rarely	People reporting no experiences of receiving words of knowledge
People reporting current musical or artistic pursuits	30	10	8
People reporting no current musical or artistic pursuits	11	16	25

an instrument in the past but not keeping it up subsequently. Its degree of development is positively linked with the degree to which there is a development of words of knowledge; similarly, the absence of current musical or artistic pursuits tends to be correlated with a lessened development of words of knowledge.

This finding raises a number of complex theoretical questions which I shall attempt to outline briefly.

1   To what extent are musical or artistic abilities produced by heredity and to what extent by social environmental factors? There is some evidence for both hereditary and environmental factors, and in practice it is virtually impossible to quantify the relative importance of either element.[25] The same *might* apply to a receptivity to 'words of knowledge' – but for these I feel the social environment has a very important part to play in terms of the social acceptability of this gift. Individuals having any sensitivity to this dimension of experience are likely to repress it in a hostile social environment.

2   To what extent do these abilities relate to brain hemisphere dominance? In contemporary Western culture most

people tend to have the left hemisphere of their brains 'dominant' over the right hemisphere. The left hemisphere is generally associated with logical, analytical or 'lineal' thinking whereas the right hemisphere tends to be associated with more intuitive, holistic or three-dimensional modes of thought. They complement each other as different types of thinking, each important in its own way. Whereas the left hemisphere is associated with mathematics, for example, the right is associated with art.[26]

However (despite the use of the term 'dominance') neither way of thinking is inherently superior to the other. We need them both. Left-handed people (who are assumed to have dominant right brain hemispheres) tend to make very good architects, tennis players and archers because of their enhanced perception of spatial relationships (*cf*. Judges 20:16). Perhaps the links between right brain hemispheres and 'intuitive' thinking predisposes them to a receptivity to words of knowledge in the same way as dreams might be mediated through the right hemisphere. If – and it remains 'if' – the right halves of our brains are to some extent connected with a receptivity to divine communications (via media such as dreams or words of knowledge), then those receiving words of knowledge might be said to be literally 'in their right minds'!

3   If there is any possible link with brain hemisphere dominance, does this mean that divine revelation is limited by biology, with some being genetically more receptive than others? This is by no means necessarily the case, because our brains are complete entities and none of us is entirely governed by one half or the other. Studies of the characteristics of brain hemispheres are largely derived from a few cases of brains divided surgically for various reasons, but we know relatively little about how the two hemispheres actually interrelate in ordinary, normally joined brains. The right hemisphere controls movements in the left half of the body, and conversely for the left hemisphere and the right half of the body, but in walking or seeing we use both legs or eyes together in a complementary manner.

I suspect that a large part of the diversity among us in artistic or musical ability can be attributed not to genetics but to social environment – although I am aware that some individuals do seem to be particularly gifted in a way which might be due to hereditary factors. For most of us, however, it seems highly likely that social and educational factors may inhibit the development of talents which are potentially within us all. In a society where the men need to go out hunting for food, there is an advantage in developing the 'right hemisphere' capacities for three-dimensional spatial perception. In contemporary Western society, however, children have 'right hemisphere' artistic creativity stimulated in kindergartens and primary schools but as they progress through secondary schools the emphasis tends to shift more to the analytical and logical forms of thought characteristic of the left hemisphere. When I asked informants about artistic, creative or musical interests they not infrequently mentioned such pursuits in the past but for one reason or another they had neglected them later. I therefore suspect that the stifling of 'right hemisphere' modes of thought may be a social or cultural phenomenon for most of us, perhaps analogous to stunted physical growth through malnutrition: whatever growth potential is there through heredity can be considerably enhanced or stunted by nutrition or other environmental factors. Probably most of us – and perhaps all of us – have the *potential* for developing these dimensions of sensitivity or awareness but this potential also depends on favourable environmental factors.

Developing the gift

Some evidence that a potential receptivity to words of knowledge may be inherent in most of us comes from my finding that all but seven of the hundred people in my random sample replied 'yes' to a question on whether or not they had ever felt a strong conviction that they should visit someone or do something at a particular time. All of these seven are among those who say they have never received a word of knowledge.[27] There seems to be a continuum between these different areas of receptivity or sensitivity. The promptings to action can be rather less tangible than words of knowledge, but in terms of listening to God they appear to be part of the same spectrum.

As illustrative examples of these 'promptings' I shall quote from two individuals who do *not* report receiving words of knowledge:

'Just before Christmas, about November time, I had an urgent feeling I must get to A. (another village): I couldn't drive fast enough. I rang [our vicar's] bell twice but I didn't go round the back. That was about the time [the vicar and his wife] had their house broken into. They feel the burglars were disturbed because they only half searched the house, and they think I was the one who disturbed them. The burglars broke in at the back' (from a sixty-two year old woman);

'I was saving up to buy a house but I felt the Lord was saying I should give the majority of my savings to a missionary . . . I decided on a figure of £1400. I wondered why not, for example, £1401 and then felt a "Yes" about it, an incredibly strong "Yes" within, but as it seemed a silly amount to send I just sent £1400. It later turned out that the missionary's shortfall that year had been £1401' (from a twenty-seven year old man).[28]

Another not uncommon experience involves feelings that one is being warned in advance about something which is going to happen. Such feelings were reported by 43% of my random sample but there is no significant correlation between these warnings and receiving words of knowledge.[29] Some people reported that the 'warnings' had come through dreams, an area of spiritual experience often mentioned in the Bible but which tends not to be accorded very much significance in our own culture. This again points to social or cultural factors which can inhibit the recognition of different ways in which God might speak.

Most people interviewed about words of knowledge said that usually the information comes to them in one particular way, but some mentioned a variety of ways. For example:

'I sat watching Blaine [Cook] and suddenly my brain was clicking in – coming to me the same as Blaine's before he gave them. "Injured right ankle in a football accident": Blaine gave that out later – a specific one and I got it too. God . . . taught me . . . to grab on to what was coming in at the periphery of my thoughts too. Like "amnesia" – I grabbed it and hauled it in and God made it clearer . . . taught me to trust also little bits and pieces going on behind my mind.'[30]

'Most frequently it is a picture followed by a word, such as a picture of an elbow on a white dot with "left elbow" in writing underneath: that was for a woman with her left elbow frozen; she was healed on her way up to the front without receiving prayer . . . The picture thing developed strongly: . . . shortly after Harrogate I got a picture of a massive big ear with a cork stuck in it and underneath the word "right ear". A woman near to me put her hand up. People prayed for her. My wife sat next to the woman who told her that she'd been healed of deafness in her right ear . . . If there's more time, normally a picture comes. If it's an impression, I ask, "What is this?" and a picture comes. If there's less time there's just an impression.'

'In all sorts of ways. I often get names of people and a particular concern about an illness or something wrong with them . . . such as "Brian" plus something else, I've forgotten what. We've got two Brians that I knew of and knew both quite well. I tried to put it out of my mind but it came back very clearly. I had to excuse myself because I knew the two people – but it applied to a third Brian I didn't know about.'

'Basically, in a small group. The Lord gives me a very clear picture and then tells me what it is.'

'Feeling a sensation of pain which is "not mine"; having an idea or word come into my mind "out of the blue" while praying.'

'Thoughts come into my mind, an impression, written word in my mind's eye, or pictures. Once I was in a meeting (at John Wimber's conference in Frankfurt, Germany) and we were encouraged to receive words of knowledge. First I saw a written word, which was the name of the train station, with the impression that someone had fallen at the station and hurt her hip . . . When I spoke this word out, nobody responded at first. I had told the Lord just before that I wanted to grow in this and was willing to fail and maybe look foolish, so I felt at peace when there was no response. Later, though, I was told that after the meeting two people responded to this word and both got healed. This encouraged me so much and showed me once again that faith is spelled r-i-s-k!'

Many more examples could be given, but the above quotations illustrate both the diversity of methods and also some of the variation in specificity. It appears as if some of the more specific items of information concerning names of people or places tend to occur in conference or church settings but are rarer in small group situations. Does this indicate a kind of 'divine economy' whereby enough information is given as is necessary? Alternatively, does it reflect the degree to which individuals are sensitive to this area or willing to take risks? I suspect that both processes may be operative.

In my report on the Sheffield conference I noted (*Power Healing*, p. 261) that the more specific information was imparted by those with more experience in this area, which as a generalisation is probably still valid in so far as there may well be links between specificity and one's degree of confidence. However, from my own experience I now recognise that relatively specific information can come also to those with little or no prior development of this gift.[31] The same was true of Samuel's first experience of hearing very specific information from God at a time when 'the word of the Lord was rare' (1 Samuel 3:1). For Samuel the information about what would happen to the house of Eli might be seen as a 'prophecy' rather than a 'message of knowledge', but both involve receiving from God information about others and may utilise similar channels such as visions or pictures.[32] We too, like Samuel, may at first mistake the voice of God for a 'natural' or human communication.

Verifying the gift

Some of the examples quoted above mention individuals who responded to words of knowledge and confirmed their accuracy. However, this does not always happen. A few informants felt that their words of knowledge had been accurate most or all of the time, but others recognised that up to about a third of their messages had not been responded to. They rationalise these results either by recognising their own lack of sensitivity to the voice of God or by assuming the message had been accurate but the recipient had been unwilling to respond in public. Cases were sometimes cited involving intervals of weeks or months before the accuracy of a word of knowledge was verified. Such a situation could lead to a lack of confidence in words of knowledge among some people. It might be the person who gave out the information or it might be others in the church, including perhaps some of the leadership, whose confidence can decrease when there is no public response to certain messages.

Several of my informants said that for them the most significant part of the Harrogate conference was the Tuesday night when John Wimber gave out nine different words of knowledge, of which only a few were responded to that night. Some of these were highly specific, including those about Janet and Laurence quoted earlier. Both of these were in the overflow hall, whereas in the main auditorium virtually nobody came forward. Wimber admitted that this was a most unusual situation for him and after a while it was suggested that they ask God why this was so. There was then a prophecy to the effect that God had allowed his servant to be made to look foolish because those present had begun to treat John Wimber as if he were an idol.

In the questionnaires at the end of the conference several people remarked on how they felt this prophecy had applied to their own attitudes, even though on the following night Wimber said he did not feel like an idol and questioned the divine origin of that prophecy. Several of those interviewed referred back to that evening as a time when their respect for Wimber increased greatly because of his willingness to stand on what he believed God had told him. It was also an encouragement to them to see that it is not always easy, even for a well-known figure like John Wimber, to undertake this kind of a ministry. One man put the focus more on Wimber's reaction, or lack of it, to the prophecy:

The non-prophecy: . . . because it was not dealt with at once a lot of people were saying they'd got to take it as true until the leadership team took it otherwise. It put a damper or depression over the conference. It's the first time I've known something like that happen at a John Wimber conference . . . so there's a need for a team of discernment to be present to deal with the problem quickly. A non-prophecy which might be true is by no means easy to detect. It made me think on: (a) the risk of cult mania – having studied church history I can recognise the dangers. A lot of people started off well and have gone off the rails. Because it was allowed to stand, it left a lot of people with hanging doubts. The noticeable thing about John Wimber is that he tends to get into the background as much as possible. (b) There's something of value in looking at this, to watch out for future situations, not necessarily for this [kind].

Whatever position one takes on this issue, it highlights the need for verification of words of knowledge as well as for discernment in relation to other gifts of the Spirit. It opens up questions about developing feedback mechanisms in meetings so that others can verify the accuracy of the information. This can be an encouragement to those giving out words of knowledge in public as well as facilitating an acceptance of the gift within the church. A problem of confidentiality arises, however, where the message concerns embarrassing or private matters. In such cases people may be reluctant to identify themselves in public and may prefer to do so in private later. Any information afterwards conveyed to others should in such cases be of a general nature to the effect that the word of knowledge was confirmed, without specifying the person involved.

'Inaccurate' words of knowledge

Another problem can arise if the word of knowledge is felt to be only partially accurate. Then the hearer can be in doubt about whether it is intended for him or her. An example is a woman who because of confusion did not go forward in response to a word of knowledge that

> There's a young woman that has just had a miscarriage, and as part of the treatment – I think they call it D and C, where you've had your womb scraped – and in so doing you've . . . um – there's been an injury that the physicians have said possibly will cause you to not be able to get pregnant again, and the Lord wants you to come and he's going to heal you tonight so that you can have a baby.

Although the details of 'young woman' and probably 'miscarriage' were not applicable to this fifty-five year old woman, the other details were sufficiently close for her to write: 'I have had a D and C (dilatation and curettage), received an injury. Also bladder repair in which some stitches burst causing the "sling" to partly come adrift. My prayer was that my bladder would be OK. I wondered if somehow the message was misinterpreted and was in fact for me.'

When the word of knowledge is rather less specific, more than one person may respond to it. Some may respond because it is only partially applicable, such as if the message specifies a hearing loss of 60% but theirs is 90%. However, somebody for whom the description is more accurate may then be inhibited from going forward if he or she sees someone else responding first to the same word of knowledge.

It is therefore virtually impossible to prove any inaccuracy in words of knowledge, but efforts should be made to verify their accuracy as far as possible.

One effect of such verification can be that certain individuals become recognised as having the gift. A side-effect is that others may then leave all the words of knowledge to the 'specialists' and not expect to receive the gift themselves. The leadership in some churches may require that words of knowledge, prophecies and the like be given out only by those known to the leaders, not by visitors. They might also want to vet the messages before they are given out. To some extent this may become a form of censorship even if the intention is to separate the wheat from the chaff and to follow the biblical instruction to 'weigh carefully what is said' (1 Corinthians 14:29). One informant visited a church where visitors were not allowed to give out revelations purporting to be from God, but there she received a word of knowledge about persistent nosebleeds. She then prayed, 'Please, God, give it to someone else,' after which a woman from that church gave out exactly the same words. On occasions where two or more people receive identical or very similar words of knowledge, one may complement the other, as illustrated by a man who experienced an 'incredible pain' in his stomach when someone else called out the word 'cancer' as a word of knowledge. He then went up and said he thought the message was for stomach cancer. If there is no obvious public response to complementary words of knowledge received by two or more people then that mutual complementarity might be interpreted as confirming a divine source of the messages. For this reason it may be important also to develop feedback mechanisms for ascertaining such complementary messages which might not have been given out during the public meeting.

The opportunities afforded for giving out words of knowledge can affect their delivery too. Sometimes there is little or no time allowed for such messages during a service, or else hostile attitudes to them may inhibit their delivery. In some churches words of knowledge are written down for leaders to read out (if judged to be appropriate) while in other churches the messages may be delivered verbally to all. Sometimes there is an expectation that divine revelations will come during a particular time while the congregation is quiet, but I know of cases in which words of knowledge have been received well in advance of a service or at other unexpected times during it. Prior expectations about words of knowledge also affect their content, because many people have seen them used only to refer to cases of physical healing. They therefore become receptive to information of that kind but perhaps less receptive to divine revelation about the sins of others. However, it is this latter kind of revelation which is better documented in biblical examples of words of knowledge, not only in the New Testament but also in the Old (*cf.* 1 Samuel 15:10–11; 1 Kings 21:17–19).

Words of knowledge and healing

In practice, however, words of knowledge about areas of personal sin do occur frequently during ministry on a one-to-one basis. This keeps the information confidential as well as allowing ministry to be conducted in an environment where the person may feel able to talk about such matters. For this reason public words of knowledge usually relate to physical healing but private messages to areas of 'inner healing' or sin. In the afternoon workshops on inner healing or demonisation fairly general categories are normally spoken publicly, such as 'incest' or 'rape'.[33] Both victims and perpetrators of such sins may be asked to respond, sometimes along with others mentioned in different categories, so that, in general, anonymity is preserved in public. The explicit details are revealed only in the individual ministry sessions with one or two others. On rare occasions there may be a public word of knowledge about someone's sin, an example of which I have quoted on p. 252 of *Power Healing*. These may be specific enough for the person concerned to recognise his or her own sin (and hopefully repent of it) but are not usually so detailed that others would recognise who it is. In other cases words of knowledge about physical problems may bring forward for ministry people requiring prayer about areas of personal sin who would not have responded to words of knowledge about such areas – as exemplified by two women at Harrogate who were thereby helped to bring their homosexual relationship to an end.

During the ministry times words of knowledge may also inform those praying how they should pray. They may need discernment about whether to pray for physical or inner healing or even for deliverance. In some cases relatively unusual methods of ministry may be discerned, as in these examples from a thirty-three year old housewife:

'To pray for healing of sight, to place heel of hand on left eye.'
'To heal someone's foot, it would happen tomorrow. And the way – to kiss them.'

A similar case comes from a twenty-nine year old woman who received the words 'Sleeping Beauty' while praying for a woman who was lying on the floor under the power of the Holy Spirit. After thinking about the story of Sleeping Beauty, she leaned over and kissed the woman, who then woke up.

These examples of words of knowledge in personal ministry sessions differ from the type which are given out in public and are thought to isolate those individuals whom it is believed God wants to heal at a particular time. This interpretation applies more to the specific than the general words of knowledge, however, in so far as the actual degree of reported healing for the general ones ranges from little or no healing through to a great deal or total healing. An example of this occurred on the Tuesday morning at Harrogate when during his talk John Wimber received various mental pictures of hands, limbs or skeletal problems. He accordingly gave out a very general call for anyone with skeletal problems to step into the aisles where his team members would pray for them. Many people did so. The variation in their reported degrees of healing by the end of the conference can be seen from the following examples:

Little or no healing reported for 'back pain', 'back – damaged disc', 'pain at the base of the spine caused by stepping off the pavement', 'slipped disc – bad back for five years' or 'backbone – inability to touch toes';

'A fair amount' of healing reported for 'severe spinal pain' or 'cervical spondylosis';

'A great deal' of healing reported for 'pain and stiffness in cervical lumbar spine, rib and scapula' (from a registered physiotherapist), 'cervical spondylosis (in neck)', 'pain in back', 'painful shoulder' (from an occupational therapist), 'pain (recurrent) in lower back' or 'spine bent at top' (from a fifty-two year old woman who added, 'A lot of pain on day prayed for – felt heat and pain went. I have felt continuing straightening since');

'Total healing' of the particular problem reported for 'undiagnosed pain of left elbow – two months duration. Pain in right knee as result of fall – eighteen months duration', 'stiffness in left knee joint' (but the left sprained ankle was healed only 'a little') or 'healing of back condition – deliverance from an afflicting spirit'.

Public words of knowledge with a medium range of specificity are associated with a fairly even spread of reported degrees of healing. For example, in one of the afternoon workshops there was a word of knowledge about a bruised or damaged 'left instep' to which two different people responded. Both of them claimed a 'fair amount' of healing by the end of the conference.

By contrast, where the word of knowledge is more highly specific, people are more likely to report either a 'great deal' or 'total' healing. Whereas 62.5% of those responding to a highly specific word of knowledge reported high degrees of healing, the rates fall to 30% and 45% for messages of medium and low specificity respectively.[34] The more specific words of knowledge tend to raise the levels of faith both of those receiving prayer and of those giving it, probably an important contributory factor in facilitating their apparently greater 'success rate'.[35] This relationship is brought out by considering the following examples.

1   Janet, aged thirty-six, the woman who responded to the word of knowledge analysed in detail earlier, wrote in a letter dated 20 January 1988, 'My back appears healed and I am not receiving any discomfort from it.' By contrast, a woman of a different name reported no healing at all for an 'area of inflammation around the lumbar vertebrae and sacro-iliac joint causing much pain in the lumbar region and down the right leg'. This forty-three year old woman, who has nursing training, did not receive prayer in response to a word of knowledge.

2   A twenty-three year old woman responded to a word of knowledge that 'there is someone here who suffered damage to the eyes through some kind of vapour or fumes, something hot'. She had been experiencing intermittent pain behind her eyes caused by gas fumes from a stove top. On a questionnaire filled in a year later she wrote that she had no recurrence of this condition since the conference and also since then had not worn her glasses which previously she had used for close work.[36] This contrasts with the case of a thirty-one year old man who made no reference at all to the above word of knowledge and who reports no healing at all for an eye condition caused by chemical damage from an aerosol spray can. The detail of 'something hot' in the word of knowledge is applicable to fumes from a stove top but not to those from an aerosol can. That particular message was conveyed during an afternoon workshop, so it was quite highly specific because only about a quarter of those attending the conference were at each of the four workshops held simultaneously.

Contrasts such as these raise theological questions about the kind of God who seems to differentiate among his children in an apparently arbitrary manner, as if playing a kind of lottery in which people have to wait for their particular numbers to come up. This might be the case if there were no pattern to these specific words of knowledge, but in fact there is a statistically significant link with the age of the person identified. When public words of knowledge for physical healing are analysed, it is found that those aged under forty constitute 85% of those responding to highly specific words of knowledge, the percentage dropping to 60% and 46% respectively for messages of medium and low specificity.[37] This trend is consistent with the pattern noted in chapter 1, whereby younger people report significantly much greater degrees of healing than older people, and is also consistent with biblical accounts of raising the dead. What appears to be a divine bias has a consistency behind it.

I would speculate also that in some cases God might choose to display his compassion through physical healing to those who are about to undergo difficult circumstances in other areas of their lives. For example, Janet wrote of having 'suffered physically and emotionally at various times through-out the year', mentioning difficulties experienced by her husband and sons 'in sickness and with unemployment *etc.*'. She went on to describe other problems, and towards the end of her letter wrote:

> . . . although financially the situation is not apparently secure, we are both experiencing what we can only describe as supernatural peace and security. This we recognise as being from God. There have been many moments during the last year when we have been perplexed and confused as to why things were happening the way they were, and many times we've both cried real tears and prayed that we were unable to stand any more pressure . . .

Compare this with the next account, from a woman who also responded to a specific public word of knowledge. On her questionnaire she wrote:

> Blaine Cook said there was a lady with a spinal problem at the bone that was the third from the bottom of the spine – it was at an angle. *I knew it was me* because in July I'd had a 'petit mal' epileptic fit where I didn't lose consciousness for more than a split second but in that time I fell backwards off a step on to a concrete path. Later I was shown the X-Ray

and at the third bone of my coccyx it was fractured and out of line.

In a letter a year later she wrote:

I think that this last year – 1987 – has been about the most difficult year of my life, and yet it has also been a year of much growth in the Lord. Many difficult things have been happening at our Church Fellowship . . . At home too there have been many problems as my husband has been made redundant for about the eighth time in the last twelve years, and we don't find that very easy. I eventually got so low that by the end of the summer I was wondering how long my nerves would last before I had a nervous breakdown. However, at the same time I knew that there was no need for me to have a total breakdown because (a) deep down I knew God was in charge and (b) I felt it just wasn't 'ME' (if that makes sense to you) . . .[38]

These two accounts are very similar in the details of (1) a very specific public word of knowledge, (2) long-term healings of painful areas at the base of the spine and (3) a subsequent year of difficulty, financial hardship and also problems with other areas of ill-health.[39] Moreover, they both report substantial spiritual growth and development at the same time, despite the problems. The pattern is consistent enough to raise questions about biblical precedents for this, but these are hard to find because often we know nothing about the subsequent histories of those who had been healed. Among those healed as 'signs' (in John's account) there was certainly subsequent interrogation and increasing opposition from the authorities in Jerusalem (John 5:9–15; 9:8–34; 12:10–11). The church in Smyrna (modern Izmir) was not far from Ephesus, where 'God did extraordinary miracles through Paul' (Acts 19:11–12), but later there were 'afflictions and . . . poverty' at Smyrna and a warning that 'the devil will put some of you in prison to test you, and you will suffer persecution' (Revelation 2:9–10). The Shunammite woman whose son was restored to life through Elisha's ministry was warned of a coming famine and had to live for seven years among the Philistines (2 Kings 8:1–6). God does not promise an easy life afterwards to those who have experienced his healing.

It is noticeable that at least one case of total healing cited earlier (for a 'back condition') was attributed to deliverance from an afflicting spirit. There is an example of such a healing (or deliverance) during the ministry of Jesus (Luke 13:10–13). Considering that reported degrees of healing are greater for cases of deliverance than for inner or physical healing, it is possible that at least some of the highly specific words of knowledge pinpoint people with afflicting spirits. (I know of at least one case in which this was so and I suspect it for one or two others.) I raise this question because there was one case of a highly specific word of knowledge at Harrogate for which the person in question received no prayer during the conference. As it is an important exception to my generalisation that higher degrees of healing are associated with more specific words of knowledge, I shall conclude this chapter by detailing the case and letting the reader judge the evidence.

A woman from Holland wrote on the questionnaire that during the conference she received a word of knowledge for the first time. It consisted of seeing a man's name and at the same time the words 'curvature of the spine' came to her mind. She wrote:

> I didn't express it in the meeting, as it had never happened to me before – I checked my guidance first to see if the man was actually there. (He was.) Then I tried to contact him and told the staff of the conference, receiving his address, and I hope to write to him.

I later wrote to the man in question and received from him the following account (written in October 1987):

> In youth I suffered from osteo-condritis. This normally produces arthritis of the spine in middle age. I have been seldom free from back trouble for forty years and more but it had been getting worse, aggravated by damage to the

top of the spine in November 1985 . . . I had some time in hospital in adolescence but there was no effective treatment . . .

At the first meeting John Wimber asked those with back trouble to stand for prayer. I was eager to do so. During the prayers I cried quite a bit but there was no sensation of warmth or anything like that and no healing seemed to take place.

During one of the evening meetings when I was in the main hall a lady from Holland (in the old theatre) saw in a vision some sort of banner or scroll with my name and title printed on it and a note about curvature of the spine. (Kyphosis accompanied the childhood complaint and has remained.) She tried to get in touch with me at the conference but failed. In due course she wrote from the Netherlands. We continued to pray locally but improvement was not convincing.

Next scene. Follow-up meeting in Sheffield sometime that winter. David Pytches asked congregation for words of knowledge. First one was 'sharp pain in middle of the spine'. When the time came I went forward and was ministered to. Experienced curious twisting sensations of whole body . . . Tried to find whatever might be causing hold-up in healing. Forgave everyone most thoroughly *etc*. Went home happy but uncured.

Gradually, however, over the year there has been great improvement. I have been able to play keyboard, lift things, go swimming a bit, *etc*. Still not wholly right and have to take care how I sit and sleep but expectation of being crippled has quite gone, Praise God . . .

It . . . has got gradually better. Since that general improvement, there have been relapses . . . notably on occasions when it would be tiresome. Once before a meeting with a group I lead who had been praying regularly for me. Most recently during the night before this questionnaire arrived in the morning.

4

PHYSICAL AND SPIRITUAL PHENOMENA

Issues to be considered:

Is it possible to explain the behaviour associated with healing by theories of:
1) Mass hysteria?
2) Learned behaviour?
3) Suggestion?
Are there experiences which it is difficult or impossible to account for by known psychological processes?

Possibly the most controversial aspect of John Wimber's ministry (and of those who follow his example) concerns the place of behaviour such as people falling over, screaming, shouting, or laughing. Some find their hands or legs shaking, while other less dramatic kinds of behaviour include tingling hands or fluttering eyelids.

Although some (perhaps all) of these phenomena had been seen in Pentecostal churches before the advent of John Wimber's ministry, they have become so closely associated with Wimber in the minds of many people that I have even heard them referred to as the 'Wimber wobbles'! Shaking hands are sometimes experienced by those praying for other people, one idiosyncrasy of Wimber's methods being the practice of laying hands *above* as well as on those receiving prayer for healing. Apparently this practice evolved in the hot and sticky conditions of a school gymnasium without air conditioning in California, when only one person on a healing team would actually 'lay on hands'.[1] Their example, however, has been imitated by others elsewhere, even in the cooler British environment, which Wimber himself recognises to be a humorous side-effect of his ministry.[2]

Second-hand observations

Any assessment of these phenomena needs to be based on first-hand reports from participants as well as observers. However, all too often opinions on such phenomena are derived from second-hand reports which quote the impressions of observers who do not take the trouble to interview participants about their own perceptions of their experiences. For example, on 15 November 1986 a conference in London was addressed by Professor Verna Wright, FRCS, Professor of Rheumatology at Leeds University. These credentials give an air of authority to his views, but when he provides 'a medical evaluation of a Wimber meeting' it is clear that he himself has never actually attended such a meeting. This probably accounts for the factual errors when he states, 'Recently [actually, it was over a year previously] John Wimber [actually, some of his team] was in Leeds where he conducted in St. George's Church one of his evening meetings . . .'[3]

Wright is in fact referring to the series of meetings held by some of Wimber's team from the Friday evening to the Sunday afternoon following the Sheffield conference in 1985. The following year, after the Harrogate conference, another team visited Leeds and held meetings in the Grammar School. Wright later mentions the conference held in Harrogate and even admits that he had one of the delegates to that conference staying in his own home (which is in Harrogate too). There was ample opportunity for Wright to have witnessed John Wimber's ministry for himself or at least to have attended personally his team's visit to Leeds Grammar School. But what was presented to a conference as 'a medical evaluation of a Wimber meeting' is based on second-hand opinions from five unnamed Christian doctors. Their description is entirely 'external', meaning that they describe events as they perceived them without any attempt to interview participants afterwards in order to obtain the informants' own perceptions of what was happening to them.

Even the 'external' events might be described differently by other observers. For example, the account quoted by Wright states, 'There was an hour's repetitious chorus singing which began the proceedings.'[4] By contrast, my wife Ruth, who also attended these meetings at St George's Church, recalls that not once but twice during the same evening the worship was interrupted as the congregation was encouraged to introduce themselves to their neighbours or to talk among themselves. It is possible that she is remembering a different meeting to the one described by Wright's colleagues and that later meetings were toned down in the light of criticisms raised by two of Wright's colleagues on the Saturday afternoon. Their views, as reported by Wright, were that the meetings generated a state of suggestibility through human manipulation. How that is done is detailed by Robert Baldwin, a Consultant Psychiatrist in Manchester who appears to have witnessed either a team visit or else attempts to implement these models in his own church; he gives no indication that he himself has attended one of John Wimber's conferences. Baldwin's comments focus on apparent similarities with voodoo ceremonies and other rituals in which 'a preparatory excitatory stage, most commonly repetitive, rhythmic music led to a state of extreme suggestibility in which normal reasoning powers were, to a greater or lesser degree, suspended. In some cases this would amount to a trance state . . .'[5]

At the conferences which I attended in Sheffield and Harrogate any emotional build-up from the initial worship was very largely dissipated during the next hour or so while listening to the teaching given by Wimber or one of his colleagues. After this there was almost always a break for refreshments and using the toilet. A Baptist minister whom I interviewed remarked on this, saying, 'I was also very struck by his casualness, not at all hyped up. Who would have a coffee break half way through a sermon? He just started again without a deep long prayer . . .' After this refreshment break the audience would reassemble for the 'ministry time', without any further 'repetitious chorus singing' of the type referred to by Wright's colleagues.

A considerable number of those from the Leeds area who had attended the Sheffield conference also went to the meetings that weekend at St George's Church. The rest of the congregation at St George's were people who had little or no prior exposure to this kind of ministry. In other words, half (or whatever proportion it might have been) came to the team meetings 'hot', with high expectations after their four days at Sheffield, while the other half came in 'cold', with little or no teaching on this topic. At Sheffield there appeared to be an increase over the four days in the levels of expectation of many people. The 'clinics' began relatively quietly and gradually became more 'dramatic' as the conference went on and as people were taught more about these matters. I suspect that the differences between my assessment of the Sheffield conference and Wright's colleagues' views of one meeting in Leeds are largely attributable to the fact that they perceived a relatively artificial situation in which half the group were 'hyped up' and the other half (including themselves) came in 'cold'.[6]

It appears as if some of the critics of Wimber's teams would require (1) a greater depth of teaching provided on any biblical precedents for such phenomena as well as on healing in general, and (2) no prior mention of any of these phenomena in order that they could not be attributed to suggestion.[7] This is easier said than done. Obviously, the teaching on these phenomena cannot precede the ministry time because then the second requirement would not be fulfilled. At Sheffield there was no formal teaching on these phenomena until the third day except for some reassurance by Wimber *after* some people had screamed that such screaming is often the expression of deep emotional hurts rather than being indicative of demonisation.

A number of those present at the very first ministry time at

Sheffield did manifest various 'phenomena', one of whom I described on p. 264 of *Power Healing*. There I wrote that 'In subsequent sessions there may have been more expectancy of seeing such behaviour and so the element of psychological suggestion cannot be ruled out for later meetings even if it is difficult to account for phenomena at the first "clinic" by such a theory.' The problem now is that reports about these phenomena have become so closely associated with John Wimber in the minds of many people that it is almost impossible to quantify the extent to which people may or may not be responding to suggestion. However, in my interviews I came across two cases where such phenomena were reported without any prior suggestion having been communicated. One of these involved a fifty-seven year old woman who a year before the conference had begun to experience the hand shaking phenomenon but had attributed it to her age until at Harrogate she discovered it to be a manifestation of the Holy Spirit. The other involved a lady whose body began to shake while being prayed for *before* either she or those praying for her had had any contact at all with John Wimber's ministry. Such anecdotes indicate that some of these phenomena can occur spontaneously, but they do not answer the questions about John Wimber's particular ministry. A more scientific approach is necessary.

Testing for mass hysteria

Those who assert that these phenomena are due to suggestion assume that among the audience there will be some people who are 'more suggestible' than others and who will respond sooner. Others may then follow the precedent as the new kind of behaviour is learned and imitated.

The problem with this hypothesis is that we need a good quantitative measurement of hypnotic suggestibility. However, to do this would involve my attempting to hypnotise those I interviewed in order to find out if they were 'suggestible' or not – a procedure which I am sure would be unacceptable to most of those I interviewed as well as to myself. In any case it would not tell us very much about their degree of suggestibility to Wimber's ministry. Suggestibility is often context-specific and is highly influenced by the respect accorded to the person making the suggestions and the person's openness to such ideas. (I am sure that many people would respond more positively to suggestions made by John Wimber than by myself!)

A less direct but probably more meaningful test comes from comparisons with a study conducted by two doctors named Moss and McEvedy who investigated a case of mass hysteria among schoolgirls. The girls had attended a ceremony in the town's cathedral where 'a considerable number had either fainted or felt faint', but the next day eighty-five girls were admitted to hospital exhibiting 'swooning, moaning, chattering of teeth, hyperpnoea and tetany – the general picture of gross emotional upset'. Twenty of them were still in hospital three days later 'and were continuing to faint or overbreathe to the point of tetany'.[8] Tests for organic causes of their conditions all proved negative and the psychiatric opinion was that most of the girls were hysterical.

The main area of overlap between these symptoms and the 'Wimber phenomena' concerns hyperventilation or overbreathing apparently induced by psychological causes. While 'swooning' might have some resemblances to the Wimber-style falling phenomenon, there are no clear parallels to phenomena such as shaking limbs, screaming or shouting.[9] What is important about this study for comparative purposes, however, is that Moss and McEvedy carried out subsequent psychological tests which confirmed not only the diagnosis of mass hysteria but also the hypothesis of Professor Eysenck, who predicted that *more hysterical individuals would rank high in both extroversion and neuroticism*.

Moss and McEvedy conducted retrospective tests upon the schoolgirls which showed that most of those reacting with these symptoms did have high scores in both extroversion and neuroticism, using the Eysenck Personality Inventory to measure these scales. This contains about a hundred items, which if asked in an interview situation would have taken up so much time that I would have had little time left for asking about healing, words of knowledge, physical phenomena and so on.[10] However, Eysenck elsewhere presents a much shorter personality inventory (the 'short version of the MPI') consisting of twelve of the most diagnostic questions. A factor analysis of these items produces what Eysenck calls 'a good approximation to simple structure' in which 'all the items are in the predicted positions'.[11] In other words, it gives an adequate preliminary indication of rankings on the extroversion and neuroticism scales sufficient for gaining a general overview of personality trends in these two dimensions.

Results of this shorter test among the hundred people in the random sample are as follows:

Fig. 1

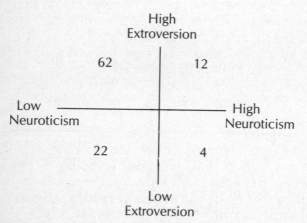

This shows that most people rank high on extroversion and low on neuroticism, and of the remainder over half rank low on both scales. Only 12% rank high on both scales.

The above diagram assigns people to one of the four quadrants, depending on whether they rank above or below the half-way line on each scale.[12] This conceals the scattering of replies actually obtained, which for the quadrant in which we are particularly interested (high extroversion plus high neuroticism) is as follows:

Fig. 2

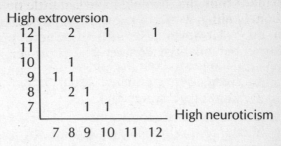

This shows that only two people rank above point 8 (*i.e.* two-thirds up the scale) on both the extroversion and neuroticism scales together, the others being just one or two points over the dividing line on at least one of these scales. The two who do rank high on both scales are both mature, married men and the only common link I can perceive between them is that they are both relatively 'young' Christians, having come to faith during the few years prior to the conference.[13]

In terms of the different physical phenomena, neither of these men reported the more 'extreme' kinds of behaviour such as screaming, shouting, or falling over during the Harrogate conference, although both had experienced the 'falling phenomenon' earlier in their Christian lives and one of them did report 'behaviour resembling drunkenness' both at Harrogate and previously. However, these kinds of behaviour are found also among people belonging to other psychological 'types', as shown by Fig. 3 below. In this I tabulate the kinds of physical phenomena reported both at Harrogate and previously by the hundred people followed up in my random sample. The physical phenomena are classified by the index letters used in the questionnaire, which asked respondents to indicate which of the following phenomena they had experienced (1) in the past and (2) at the conference:

a) Tingling in your hands
b) Hand or arm shaking
c) Stiffening of your body
d) Weeping
e) Laughing

f) Fluttering of your eyelids
g) Falling over
h) Screaming or shouting
i) Hot areas on your body
j) Changes in your breathing
k) Behaviour resembling 'drunkenness'
l) Other (please specify)

Fig. 3

High Extroversion

(62 informants)				(12 informants)		
	Past	*Conference*			*Past*	*Conference*
a)	32	35	a)		8	7
b)	28	31	b)		5	6
c)	6	5	c)		1	1
d)	43	28	d)		8	6
e)	21	15	e)		3	2
f)	16	13	f)		3	3
g)	23	10	g)		6	2
h)	3	2	h)		0	1
i)	22	22	i)		3	7
j)	28	28	j)		6	5
k)	11	8	k)		4	4
l)	7	8	l)		2	4

Low Neuroticism ————————————————————— High Neuroticism

(22 informants)				(4 informants)		
	Past	*Conference*			*Past*	*Conference*
a)	10	4	a)		3	3
b)	10	9	b)		1	1
c)	4	4	c)		1	1
d)	14	7	d)		3	3
e)	9	5	e)		1	2
f)	3	5	f)		0	0
g)	11	6	g)		1	0
h)	1	0	h)		0	0
i)	9	10	i)		1	2
j)	9	7	j)		2	1
k)	3	1	k)		1	1
l)	1	1	l)		0	0

Low Extroversion

What is immediately clear from these figures is that reports of these phenomena are spread across all the different categories of people and are by no means confined to those high on both the extroversion and neuroticism scales. This argues against a theory that these phenomena are due largely to a form of mass hysteria.[14] Only three individuals in my random sample left this question blank, presumably indicating that they had never had any such experiences; these three are all in the 'high extroversion, low neuroticism' category.

Taking those reporting these phenomena at the Harrogate conference (as a group for which the social environment can be assumed to be relatively constant) it is found that among those ranking high on the extroversion scale there is no significant difference between the 'low neuroticism' and the 'high neuroticism' groups in the proportions reporting these phenomena. Similarly, comparing those in the 'low extroversion' groups with those in the 'high extroversion' groups there is again no statistically significant difference according to the degree of extroversion.[15] In other words, there is no particular psychological 'type' which is more prone to these kinds of experiences than others.

Learned behaviour

The rich variety of human cultures is due largely to the human ability to learn different ways of behaving. It is easier for a child to be socialised into a culture from birth than for an adult to learn new rules of behaviour when living in an unfamiliar culture. At some point or other most adults who go to live in such a culture for a prolonged period undergo a phase in their 'culture shock' when they react against certain irritating features of the new environment – but after living there for a while they find themselves behaving as if naturally, in many culturally appropriate ways.

The same is probably true of reactions to the physical phenomena associated with John Wimber's ministry. Some people converted within such a setting regard these as natural elements of their 'spiritual culture', whereas others brought up in different traditions either react against these elements of a 'foreign culture' or else after a while find that they have been socialised into new ways of behaving. They might not even be conscious of the degree to which they have adapted: in technical jargon, the new behaviour has become 'internalised'.

There is a substantial body of opinion which feels that at least some of these physical phenomena result from such a process of learning a particular kind of reaction or form of behaviour. John Richards, for example, quotes the opinions of Cardinal Suenens and of the evangelist Don Double (who also has a healing ministry in which these phenomena occur), who both agree that in at least some cases the 'falling phenomenon' (referred to by a variety of terms) can be psychologically induced.[16] Don Double considers that the evidence of whether or not it is divinely induced comes from whether or not the person experiences a definite resultant change in his or her life. One of my informants related how on three different occasions she had experienced either healing (her leg reportedly growing two and a half inches) or a meaningful message believed to be from God while she was lying on the floor after falling.[17] She went on to say:

> This [being] 'slain in the Spirit' has happened at other times, but I think it was my subconscious allowing me to do it as nothing really actually happened to me, so I think it was spurious. It quite often happens because I think prob-ably I'm quite suggestible in some ways – I do things because they're expected. Not that I deliberately do it, but it just happens and so I'm dubious about claiming it is from God unless I can see definite proof.

What applies to the 'falling phenomenon' probably applies to other phenomena too. 'By their fruits you shall know them.' In the fellowship attended by one of my informants there is (I am told) someone who very easily manifests hand shaking and who is regarded as a 'spiritual barometer', alert-ing the fellowship to the Spirit's presence. Without having met or observed this person myself, I am not in a position to give an opinion on whether or not this behaviour is psychologically or divinely induced. This is a pastoral problem of discernment for which almost the only guideline is the test of results.

Statistically, there is obviously a clear connection between experiencing a phenomenon in the past and then again at the Harrogate conference. For each of the phenomena, a sizeable proportion of those who have previously experienced it report the same experience again at Harrogate. However, there is a very real problem in knowing how to interpret these figures.

For example, those reporting the experience of falling over can be tabulated in the following way:

Table 4.1 Reports of falling over in the past and at Harrogate

| | | Have you fallen over during the Harrogate Conference? | | |
		No	Yes	Row Totals
Have you fallen	No	1036	129	1165
over in the past?	Yes	499	226	725

This table could be interpreted as showing that of those who had fallen over in the past, 69% (499 out of 725) did not repeat the behaviour at the conference. Therefore it could be argued that it was not 'learned behaviour'. On the other hand, 31% did fall over again. Is this to be regarded as 'learned behaviour', or is it that they were receiving further genuine ministry from God which necessitated being 'laid out'? We might say that probably no more than a third of those who have done this in the past will repeat the behaviour simply out of responding to a psychological 'habit', but we are unable to say whether those who do so out of 'habit' constitute as few as 1% or as many as 30%.

On the other hand, 11% of the 1165 people who had not fallen in the past did so for the first time at Harrogate. This constitutes about 7% of the total questionnaire sample. Are these people learning a new form of behaviour or are they receiving a much-needed ministry from the Holy Spirit? Statistics alone are unable to answer this question, and it has to be resolved by recourse to individual questioning. All I am able to say is that in my random sample only one person (quoted above) admitted to a recognition that the falling phenomenon in her own experience can be at times psychologically induced. Others who described such experiences spoke of them positively as having been of significant benefit in their personal lives.

In my report on the Sheffield conference (*Power Healing*, p. 266) I noted that there appears to be a progression over time from the more dramatic to less dramatic phenomena in the experience of certain individuals. This appears to be linked with a belief that various problem areas have been sorted out during the more 'dramatic' sessions. The 'milder' phenomena such as tingling or shaking hands are associated not so much with receiving healing as with ministering healing

Table 4.2   *Percentages of those re-experiencing various phenomena during the Harrogate conference*

Phenomenon	Percentage repeating the experience	Number repeating the experience	Percentage of total sample of 1890 people
Tingling of hands	68%	648	34%
Hand or arm shaking	65%	502	26%
Weeping	65%	781	41%
Changes in breathing	58%	480	25%
Hot areas on the body	57%	390	21%
Fluttering of the eyelids	50%	227	12%
Stiffening of the body	42%	82	4%
Laughing	41%	273	14%
Falling over	31%	226	12%
Screaming or shouting	30%	34	2%
Behaviour resembling 'drunkenness'	29%	98	5%

to others. Therefore it is not surprising that the frequency of re-experiencing phenomena is higher for the 'milder' than for the 'stronger' forms, as illustrated by Table 4.2.

It can be seen from this that not only are the more 'extreme' phenomena less likely to be repeated but also their proportion of the total sample generally tends to decrease too. Conversely, among those who have not experienced various phenomena previously, higher proportions report the 'milder' than the 'stronger' ones as occurring for the first time to them at Harrogate:

Table 4.3 *Proportions of those not experiencing particular phenomena previously who do so for the first time*

Phenomenon	Proportion experiencing it for the first time	Number involved	Percentage of total sample of 1890
Tingling of hands	37%	340	18%
Hand or arm shaking	31%	344	18%
Weeping	28%	196	10%
Hot areas on the body	28%	333	18%
Changes in breathing	26%	272	14%
Laughing	20%	243	13%
Falling over	11%	129	7%
Fluttering of the eyelids	8%	112	6%
Stiffening of the body	7%	124	7%
Behaviour resembling 'drunkenness'	7%	107	6%
Screaming or shouting	3%	47	2%

To some extent these figures could be interpreted in terms of social acceptability: it is more desirable to be known as someone who often has tingling hands (seen as indicating an 'anointing' for healing) than as someone who is likely to scream or shout. However, the problem with this interpretation is that it does not explain why some people scream or shout in the first place. Another interpretation, which is more consistent with the data, views the more 'extreme' phenomena as occurring usually while a person is receiving ministry and tending not to recur except in cases requiring further ministry. The 'milder' phenomena tend to be associated more with the process of ministering to others and are therefore very likely to recur. Changes in one's breathing, hot areas on one's body and weeping are usually (but not entirely) associated with receiving ministry but are 'milder' forms of behaviour than falling over, screaming, shouting or appearing as if drunk. Sometimes the 'milder' forms may occur first, followed by 'stronger' forms as ministry continues with certain people, a process which may also account for the higher proportions of people reporting the 'milder' forms of behaviour.

Finally, it may be asked whether or not certain personality 'types' are more or less likely to repeat such behaviour again. Fig. 4 shows the proportions of those at the Harrogate conference (in the second columns of Fig. 3) who also reported having had the same experiences previously.

These figures actually tell us very little overall because of the low numbers involved. In many cases the actual number of cases is fewer than five, producing a variation in percentages of over 20% for each case. It is virtually meaningless to say that 50% or 100% out of a 'group' of just one or two individuals behaved in a particular way. The low numbers in many categories also mean that for statistical purposes it is necessary to combine different categories. Doing this allows us to compare in general terms between those ranking high and low in scales of extroversion or neuroticism but it produces almost no significant results. For most categories there are no significant differences according to personality types. The only major exception is that those ranking *low* on the neuroticism scale repeat the 'falling phenomenon' much more often than do those ranking high on the neuroticism scale. This is the opposite effect to that which is to be expected from a comparison with the hysterical reactions of schoolgirls studied by Moss and McEvedy. Moreover, extroversion appears to have little (if any) influence on this behaviour, because the difference between 83% and 100% among those

Fig. 4

High
Extroversion

a)	23 = 66%	a)	4 = 57%
b)	17 = 55%	b)	4 = 67%
c)	2 = 40%	c)	1 = 100%
d)	24 = 86%	d)	4 = 67%
e)	10 = 67%	e)	0 = 0%
f)	7 = 54%	f)	1 = 67%
g)	10 = 100%	g)	0 = 0%
h)	0 = 0%	h)	0 = 0%
i)	13 = 59%	i)	1 = 14%
j)	18 = 64%	j)	3 = 60%
k)	5 = 63%	k)	2 = 50%

Low   High
Neuroticism   Neuroticism

a)	4 = 100%	a)	2 = 67%
b)	7 = 78%	b)	1 = 100%
c)	1 = 25%	c)	1 = 100%
d)	6 = 86%	d)	3 = 100%
e)	2 = 40%	e)	1 = 50%
f)	3 = 60%	f)	0 = 0%
g)	5 = 83%	g)	0 = 0%
h)	0 = 0%	h)	0 = 0%
i)	7 = 70%	i)	1 = 50%
j)	5 = 71%	j)	1 = 100%
k)	1 = 100%	k)	1 = 100%

Low
Extroversion

ranking low on neuroticism is produced by a variation in only one person. However, it must be pointed out that nineteen other people ranking low on the neuroticism scale had fallen over in the past but did not repeat the behaviour at Harrogate. Therefore personality is for the most part a relatively poor predictor of who is likely to exhibit these kinds of phenomena as a result of 'learned behaviour', because for almost all these phenomena there are no clear links with personality types. Irrespective of personalities, there are some behaviours (such as screaming or shouting) which are almost never repeated, and other behaviours (such as hands tingling or shaking) which are frequently repeated. These patterns are consistent with the pattern whereby phenomena associated with being ministered to are rarely repeated whereas those associated with ministry to others often recur.

Sociological variables

What appear to be more important associations with these phenomena are links with age and sex. Several of these kinds of behaviour are more commonly reported by those in their teens, twenties or thirties than by those aged forty or over. The phenomena are by no means absent from the older age groups but are merely less commonly reported. Some statistically significant examples are presented in Table 4.4.

Table 4.4   Examples of links between physical phenomena and age

Age groups	Hand or arm shaking	Stiffening of the body	Fluttering of the eyelids	Hot areas	Changes in breathing
Teens	56%	15%	30%	37%	44%
Twenties	50%	16%	26%	43%	46%
Thirties	48%	12%	21%	41%	44%
Forties	39%	10%	13%	38%	35%
Fifties	42%	6%	11%	29%	36%
Sixty and over	37%	1%	3%	29%	23%

Such statistically significant links do not necessarily mean that age in itself is responsible for causing these effects: some other social factor linked with age (such as marital status, social status, perhaps even income) might actually be responsible. The same may be true of differences by sex or marital status, the latter also being associated with age differences. Nevertheless, it is pertinent to note those phenomena which do have significant links with these sociological variables, as shown in Table 4.5.

Table 4.5   Sociological links with physical phenomena[18]

	Links with age	Links with sex	Links with marital status
Tingling of hands	—	—	—
Hand or arm shaking	* Y	—	* S, D
Stiffening of the body	** Y	—	* S
Weeping	—	** F	* D, W
Laughing	—	* F	** D, S
Fluttering of the eyelids	* Y	** F	—
Falling over	—	** F	—
Screaming or shouting	—	* F	—
Hot areas on the body	* Y	* F	—
Changes in breathing	** Y	** F	—
Behaviour resembling 'drunkenness'	—	—	** W, S, D

KEY: *   = Statistically significant association
       ** = Highly significant association
       Y   = Younger age groups
       F   = Female
       S   = Single
       D   = Divorced
       W   = Widowed

In compiling this table I have used only the data on phenomena at the Harrogate conference itself: reports of such events occurring some time prior to that conference do not furnish details of age or marital status at the time of the occurrence. To some extent these statistics from Harrogate confirm my impression at the Sheffield conference that 'some of the more extreme emotional feelings were experienced by women more than men' (*Power Healing*, p. 267), but my impression that younger people exhibit these kinds of behaviour more than older ones is not so statistically significant. This can be taken as a warning against making superficial judgements about these phenomena on the basis of attendance at merely one or two meetings (as has been done by some of Wimber's critics).

The *interpretation* of these sociological statistics is another matter. Do we say that women are more hysterical than men? Or that they have more emotional needs which may need deep ministry, which is often accompanied by these phenomena? It *might* be the case that women do tend to be more 'emotional' and expressive in our culture and that when they experience ministry they tend to demonstrate emotional symptoms. However, even if this applies to some behaviour, it does not apply to all, because there is little or no statistically significant difference between the sexes for phenomena such as hand tingling, shaking arms or stiffening of the body. On the whole, it seems that those kinds of behaviours more associated with *receiving* ministry are those found more among women and would seem to be consistent with their receiving a higher proportion of the prayers for inner healing and deliverance.

The links with marital status are more problematic. Why do married people appear to display some forms of behaviour significantly less than others? Do they find within marriage and family life the kind of ministry to their emotional and social needs which some single people might lack? This suggestion is unconvincing to a consultant psychiatrist, who informs me that, if his psychiatric practice is anything to go by, married people seem to need more rather than less help.[19] Might it be that Christian marriages are somehow 'happier' than non-Christian ones? Much as we might like to believe this to be the case, it is very difficult to find sensitive enough measurements of 'marital happiness' which could compare Christian and non-Christian samples. The usual indices such as divorce rates are too crude, being affected not only by official dogma (both among Catholics and Protestants) but also by social constraints of acceptability in some religious circles. It might even be that social acceptability influences my findings that married people are less likely to exhibit some of the physical phenomena discussed in this chapter if in at least some cases the presence of a spouse inhibits the other spouse from manifesting such behaviours.

To a certain extent links with age might reflect life-cycle stages – including singlehood, marriage and widowhood for many people. The kinds of personal problems requiring ministry also tend to change during one's lifetime. Physiological changes over time might also lead to less pronounced physical reactions among older people.[20]

Although the incidence of some physical reactions might be linked with the likelihood of certain categories of people receiving prayer for inner healing or deliverance, there are no obvious links with prayers for physical healing. On the whole, it would seem that the physical reactions are physiological barometers which indicate that changes are occurring within an individual.

Trance-like states

To many people, the word 'trance' has connotations either of hypnotism or of spiritualist mediums. It is possible for Christians to overlook the significance of biblical references to Peter or Paul falling into trances (Acts 10:10; 22:17). These were associated with visions or revelations, just as John's vision of Christ produced the physical response of falling 'as though dead' (Revelation 1:17). A very different cause – the expulsion of an unclean spirit – led to an apparently very similar result in the boy who 'looked so much like a corpse that many said, "He's dead"' (Mark 9:26).[21] The physical appearances of this boy and of John on Patmos told outsiders next to nothing about the spiritual causes of their physical conditions.

It is the same with trance or trance-like states. I prefer the term 'altered states of consciousness', instead of terms such as 'trance' or 'trance-like states', in order to dissociate from our minds the connotations of hypnotism or spiritualism. Other 'altered states of consciousness' which might be compared with the trance include meditation, sleep, coma and perhaps even prayer. The comparison with sleep is particularly relevant because often in the Bible it is the context in which God gives a significant revelation using the channel of a dream. John Sanford has shown how biblical accounts of dreams, visions, revelations from angels and even being 'in the Spirit' all overlap considerably with one another, as when an *angel* appears in a *dream* (Matthew 1:20; 2:13,19).[22] Later in this chapter I shall quote accounts of visions of angels or experiences of being in a 'heavenly' place while the person's physical body was laid out on the floor during a meeting. These 'altered states of consciousness' shade into one another, as do their concomitant physical states.

I am told that somewhere C. S. Lewis compares the physical or physiological level of experience to the narrowest layer of an inverted pyramid.[23] At the physiological level it is almost impossible to distinguish the emotions of 'love' and 'fear' in terms of bodily reactions such as increased heartbeat, respiration or adrenalin secretion. The 'cause' lies outside the physiological level altogether, and these reactions are explicable only by reference to the next higher and wider level, that of the mind and/or emotions. The 'spiritual' level is higher and wider still. The same is true of states such as 'trance', dreams and even glossolalia ('speaking in tongues'). An analysis of the surface phenomenon tells us next to nothing about its source. If we believe that God intended these to be channels for communication with him, then we know also that those same channels can be taken over and used for the wrong ends by unclean spirits. If our prior experience of trance has been associated with one of the 'corrupted' sources of communication – the channel itself being neutral – then we assume that this is always the case; we do not expect a channel previously carrying dirty water suddenly to bring clean water. In a society where everyone tells lies, a person who speaks the truth will be assumed to be lying too.

Testing for 'suggestion'

'Suggestion' in a Christian healing context is almost a dirty word. People react against it, fearing lest they be labelled 'suggestible'. They seem to feel that it has connotations of being less intelligent, foolish or inferior in some other way.

'Suggestion', however, may actually be a very helpful and positive force in our interactions with one another. Few parents may be aware of the extent to which they use their powers of suggestion in influencing their children, whether for good or ill, and it is likely that a certain 'suggestibility' plays a very important part in the socialisation process. Among adults too, as advertisers well know, the power of suggestion remains strong and can be manipulated both for good and ill effect. Much of it is suggested through symbolism rather than directly through words. In a religious context – our present concern – religious symbols can evoke deep and powerful sentiments.

Why is man like this? Presumably there is some positive purpose in man's having this capacity for suggestibility. Christians are likely to assume that God created man this way, implying that it was part of God's good and perfect intention for mankind. Presumably like other divine gifts it is liable to corruption through being used for the wrong ends. Even if one were to argue from an evolutionary rather than a creationist point of view, it can still be asserted that the human capacity for suggestibility must have some adaptive function.

'Suggestibility' is actually closely akin to 'faith'. Both involve putting one's trust in the authority of another. There are passages in the New Testament which show that *faith* is the quality God is looking for in man, not 'suggestibility'. It can be presumed that it was for this purpose that God created in man the capacity for faith. The miraculous signs recorded in John's gospel were 'written that you may believe that Jesus is the Christ, the Son of God, and that believing you may have life in his name' (John 20:30–31). Similarly, in Matthew's gospel it is clear that Jesus was looking for *faith* when he healed people.[24]

'Suggestibility', however, connotes human manipulation.[25] In terms of Wimber's kind of ministry, it connotes a view that the various physical phenomena are predicted in advance and that certain 'suggestible' people respond accordingly. Such a view is advocated by Professor Wright and the doctors quoted by him. How plausible is this?

On the third day of the Sheffield conference participants were provided with a list of 'phenomenological responses' to the work of the Holy Spirit. Assuming that these common phenomena were therefore known about by most of those attending the Harrogate conference, their occurrence might therefore be attributable to 'suggestion'. In my questionnaire I listed these items, asking respondents to tick the appropriate boxes if they had experienced any of these.[26] At the bottom of the list I included a box for 'Other (please specify)'.

When I later tried to classify the responses to this 'other' category, I was very surprised to find that I needed *over two hundred* different classifications.

Some of these are obviously variants on the 'standard list', a good example being those who mentioned a shaking or quivering in their legs or on the back of their legs. One man in my random sample described his experience as:

I felt the back of my calf shaking in a way one can't do oneself. Everything that couldn't shake was shaking. I felt it coming up my back and shaking everywhere, but particularly noticed it in places where I wouldn't normally shake – muscular spasms which I've not had before or since.

Certain descriptions of phenomena in this miscellaneous 'other' category tend to cluster around a number of common elements in the accounts. For example, there are those who mention something like 'electricity' or 'power' but who describe it in a variety of ways, such as:

'Very strong "electric current" through arms, with fingers turning in';
    'Electricity feeling over head';
    ' "Electric shock" during the presence of the Holy Spirit';
    'Envelope of "energy"? – difficult to describe. "Cone" of power/energy descended on me';
    'Aura of tremendous power around lower arms and hands';
    'Electricity in legs';

'Force field coming over me like rain running down from head to toe. It was like something out of *Star Wars*.'

Despite the variations in vocabulary, there is obviously a common nucleus of some kind in all these descriptions. The fact that phenomena of this kind are not among the 'standard list' of predicted responses tends to go against the view that these experiences are due to suggestion alone.[27]

This is further borne out by other kinds of experiences reported. Some people, for instance, reported feeling *cold*, not heat, describing 'waves of cold', 'severe chilling', 'cold hands' or 'cold sensations over body'. Coldness is the direct opposite of what is likely to be expected on the basis of suggestions about heat or hot areas connected with the work of the Holy Spirit. This raises the question of whether or not coldness is actually a sign of demonic activity in or around a person, but I have insufficient evidence at present to pass an opinion.[28]

Another phenomenon mentioned by at least a dozen respondents concerned what is variously described as a shaking jaw, chattering teeth, or (the opposite) stiffness or numbness in the mouth or jaw, paralysis of the jaw muscles, dryness in the mouth, a stiffening of the neck and face, or similar reactions. A medical doctor who reported paralysis of jaw muscles occurring when the Holy Spirit was invited to come wrote that he 'was prayed for as a result of spasmodic jaw paralysis said to represent some repressed problem – What?' He claimed no healing at all. His physical reaction is not one of the well-known phenomena attributed to the presence of the Holy Spirit, but it does have features in common with the reports of others. It does not seem to be equivalent to the 'slurred speech' of those who appear as if drunk.[29] My personal suspicion is that it could reflect the physiology of those being prayed for, analogous to the shaking of whichever hand one writes with, although I would not rule out the possibility quoted above that a reaction like this is connected with 'some repressed problem'.[30]

Another kind of experience reminiscent of the stigmata of

some Catholic mystics describes a 'pain in both hands about the size of a thumb print in the centre of the palms'. Two such cases are reported – one by an Anglican minister and the other by an Anglican layman who was baptised in the Roman Catholic Church. Others reported a 'burning' in the hands, but in at least one such case it referred to very hot palms while laying hands on others.

A few others reported pain or discomfort elsewhere, such as a 'violent pain in neck' or 'burning in area of the heart and of the wrists'. If these are areas of their bodies receiving healing, then the pain may be an indication of activity in those areas. Just as pleasant warmth is communicated to the brain by the nerves but an 'overstimulation' of those nerves through exposure to excessive heat is translated as 'pain', so in the same way the experience of 'hot areas' on the body may become 'pain' when activity of an intense nature is taking place. In two cases reported to me the pain seemed to be associated with the 'burning out' of a lump or a growth of some kind.

Further unusual experiences referred to feeling (unseen) physical objects. Their nature may be unspecified ('object in hands') or else described in detail as 'like a wide belt being put round my wrists' or 'feeling of ring placed on index finger of right hand'. One lady in the question on charismatic gifts wrote, 'receiving objects. Felt gifts in hand: *e.g.* rod . . . and sandals.'[31]

Perhaps related to these kinds of experience are the more commonly reported ones described in terms such as 'weight on arms', 'heaviness in the arms', 'a great weight pressing down on arms and head', 'pressure on palms of hands', 'weight coming down upon shoulders causing me to bend over' or 'a weight placed across my outstretched arms and shoulders – it felt as if I was straining my head forward, with a gentle pressure on my forehead'. To some extent these might be regarded as side-effects of prolonged lifting of one's arms in worship were it not for other similar accounts which speak of a weight or heaviness on one's body. Examples include '*extreme* heaviness of both arms and chest', 'feeling of pressure over front of body' or a 'heavy, magnetic force which is over-powering'. Others seemed to refer to not dissimilar phenomena in terms of 'head being gently pushed backwards – extending my neck', 'gentle but firm pressure on chest and stomach', '"nice" heaviness or weight on head' and even perhaps 'bending backwards till the head is at the height of the waist'.

In my report on the Sheffield conference (*Power Healing*, p. 267) I discussed such reports and argued that the mention of 'weight' could not be attributed to suggestion because it had not been mentioned from the platform. In a footnote I noted that the Hebrew word for God's glory (*kābôd*) has a primary meaning of 'weight' or 'substance'. Subsequent investigations have led me to go further than this and to suggest that what is here described could actually be the same kind of phenomenon as that experienced by the ancient Israelites. What has led me to this conclusion has been the mention of a 'cloud' or 'mist' by a couple of other people in connection with their experiences at either Harrogate or at the subsequent team visit to Leeds. An even more dramatic case occurred while Jill (the girl described in chapter 2) was receiving her visions of Jesus. One night her pastor noticed a transparent mist in the same room, but two nights later his wife saw

> a grey mist that came up . . . arched up along one wall of the room. I knew it covered half a chair, blotted out the dressing table and just a bit of the mirror was poking out of the mist. I looked round the rest of the room and looked back and it gradually went from the top. This was while Jill was worshipping the Lord and his presence was powerful there. So real . . . I couldn't see the furniture through it.

She and her husband concluded that this was equivalent to the biblical descriptions of the presence or glory of God which is often perceived as a 'cloud'. A close link between this phenomenon – the Shekinah – and what might be interpreted as the 'falling phenomenon' (especially with reference to the idea of 'weight' as being at the root of the Hebrew word for 'glory') comes in 2 Chronicles 5:13–14, which reads ' . . . the house of the Lord was filled with a cloud, so that the priests could not stand to minister because of the cloud; for the glory of the Lord filled the house of God' (RSV).

Other spiritual phenomena

While many experiences reported in the 'other' section of my questionnaire referred to physical sensations of the body, some seemed to refer to visions or other matters of a more 'spiritual' nature. A few gave vague comments such as 'certain visual phenomena' or brief descriptions like 'with eyes closed a vision of a burning "bush" and sense of tremendous power/energy'.[32]

One person described an experience 'like strong electric shocks. Dancing flashes of light above my head. Flickering? Tongues of fire', which to me is reminiscent of the account of the coming of the Holy Spirit in Acts 2:3. The previous verse mentions 'a sound . . . like the blowing of a violent wind', and it is well known that the Greek word *pneuma* means both 'wind' and 'spirit' as well as 'breath' (*cf*. John 3:6–8). For this reason it is of relevance to note that a number of descriptions of experiences at Harrogate referred to a 'breeze on head', 'cool wind over face and hands', 'sense of wind blowing', 'cool wind all round me' or 'wind over (left) hand'. A fuller description comes from a woman who wrote:

> My hands were raised and I was wearing a long-sleeved blouse. Then it seemed as if my arms were bare and a wind was rushing up my forearms from elbow to wrist. My arms became weightless and at the same time I had a mental picture of this wind, as waves curling up my arms. I cannot say how long this sensation lasted, probably only a minute or two, but I was left feeling complete peace inside.

In the conditions of the Harrogate conference centre it is impossible to attribute these experiences to any 'ordinary' draught from doors or windows. Neither was this a phenomenon predicted from the stage or in the literature. Although the biblical references to the Spirit being like a wind are well-known, those who report these experiences do not seem to have expected them. Instead, it would appear that both the biblical accounts and the Harrogate experiences have a common origin.[33]

At one session during the conference Wimber did refer to 'passing on the mantle', meaning that it was time now for the British Christians to take over this kind of ministry.[34] Through the power of suggestion it is possible that these comments might have given rise to accounts of: 'feeling as though a heavy coat had been put on my shoulders', 'experience like a blanket falling over me', 'mantle' or 'felt as if a heavy sheepskin coat had been draped over shoulders'. However, the fact that only one of these four used the vocabulary of 'mantle', the others searching for other words to describe their experiences, would seem to indicate that the concept of a 'mantle' was not necessarily in the forefront of their minds at the time. I have no way of knowing from the questionnaires if these experiences took place before or after Wimber's mention of a 'mantle' concept because in the end I decided that a questionnaire asking people to differentiate between the days of the conference would be too cumbersome.[35]

A similar kind of experience which is less easily attributable to suggestion speaks of a 'gentle pulling on my jumper at the back (more like a magnetic pull)'. In addition, the forty year old man mentioned above who felt something like 'a heavy sheepskin coat' over his shoulders specified that at the time he was wearing a light pullover, commenting: 'I even felt behind me to see if someone was pulling on my clothes, but no one was anywhere near.'

Two people reported smelling fragrances at the conference, one of them specifying it was a 'fragrant smell of flowers'. I wrote to her for further details and received the following reply:

When I smelt the sweet fragrance of flowers, it was during my workshop in the main Conference Hall. Next to me sat a young German man. After the session finished . . . I asked him if he had smelt the flowers. He just said 'No.' I asked if he felt anything, and reluctantly he told me he 'had walked in the garden with the Lord'![36]

'Out of the body experiences'

'I was sat at the bottom right hand [corner] of the auditorium. When the Spirit was called down, I could see right from the back of the auditorium and the Lord spoke to me.'

This account was written on the questionnaire in the section for 'other' experiences relating to physical phenomena and seems to describe the woman's spirit being drawn temporarily out of her body. Another woman who gave no indication on her questionnaire of having had an experience of this nature gave the following account during an interview with her:

At Harrogate when I was prayed for . . . I went out cold on the floor. From what I was told, I was out for a good twenty minutes. After a time – I don't know how long – I was up somewhere looking down at what was happening. I was watching Blaine Cook. We were in the upper part [of the auditorium] and he was near the stage, praying for people. I'd had it in my mind I'd like to get down there and watch what he was doing and hear what he was doing. He said the best way to learn is to get stuck in. My body was on the floor but I felt I was taken down and I was overhead watching. He was praying for a woman at the time and she had a pink blouse on. It was tremendous. I was up there looking down and could see J. and C. praying over my body and I wasn't there. I was looking at them. It took me a long time to get this into perspective – no basis or other experience to back it up or explain why, just that it did . . .

I saw Blaine, then J. and C., also saw other people around. I remember seeing one of the team coming along, putting his hand out over me, praying in tongues and then stepping over me and walking on. That was a confirmation to me I was meant to be out on the floor. John Wimber had said that for some people stand them up but others are supposed to be on the floor. So I knew I was OK and supposed to be on the floor and the Lord was doing something. Afterwards I felt turned inside out and scrubbed so clean it was unbelicvable.

This account has been quoted at length because there is no way in which it can be attributed to suggestion.[37] My informant claimed that at the time she 'went out cold' she did not know who was praying for her but that later J. and C. confirmed they had been doing so. Her lucid recollections of pertinent details about the woman in the pink blouse or the team member who stepped over her can be paralleled in other accounts of 'out of the body experiences' in which there is an accurate recall of details which the person could not have known at the time and could not deduce from anything heard.[38]

The fact that some people do spontaneously find their centres of consciousness to be outside of their physical bodies cannot easily be doubted from an examination of the evidence presented by competent researchers such as Celia Green or Michael Sabom. David Hay came across 'one or two' such accounts among a random sample of 172 people interviewed in Nottingham.[39] In my own random sample of 108 nurses in Leeds, three reported such experiences, of which two occurred in the context of receiving an operation (so might be the initial stages of near-death experiences). Both of these also described meaningful experiences of the presence of God, whereas the individual who found herself looking down at herself while sitting in her own bedroom is a generally non-religious person.

Compared to these studies which show that only a small percentage of the population report such experiences, it seems highly significant that among those interviewcd in my random sample as many as 18% described experiences in which they felt themselves to be leaving or to have left their physical bodies. Of these I would classify five as 'marginal', describing perhaps the initial stages but without a clear separation of the centre of consciousness from the body. Of the remaining accounts, three occurred while the person was ill in hospital and may be classified as near-death experiences, in two cases being the initial stages in which one's own body is sometimes perceived. Another three interviewed described experiences at Wimber's conferences, of which one has been quoted already. Another is worth quoting quite fully because it illustrates the differing reactions of those involved:

At Sheffield . . . John was preaching on the feeding of the five thousand. My mother and sister next to me thought I'd fallen asleep but I could remember all John had said but couldn't move physically. The strange thing was it didn't bother me – I felt at peace with the situation.

At the coffee break they tried to wake me up and were worried when they couldn't. Then they felt a peace that it was really the Holy Spirit at work and began to pray for me where I was. Then an American paramedic, one of the team, came up and was dubious about what was happening. He did tests to see if I was conscious and could feel pain. Though the tests were OK he was still quite worried. They actually called for an ambulance and I was taken to the . . . General Hospital . . .

It was frustrating because a friend on the balcony at the time felt he'd had a message from the Lord for me but I'd gone. On the way I consciously heard all my mother and her friend were saying to me but I was unable to respond. They laid me on a trolley. Then things came together gradually and I began to cry and everything was alright.

All I can say is it seemed looking back that the Lord had separated part of me from my body – a lot of inner healing was taking place there, equipping me for leadership. I had the feeling at the time that he was ministering in such a way that if it hadn't been so unusual I suppose humanly speaking I'd have tried to stop what he was doing . . .

It was strange that though my eyes weren't open I could see things around, like I could visualise me being carried out as though I had my eyes open. I could see the ceiling and I remember them laying me out in the entrance hall while waiting for the ambulance. I remember looking into the face of [our] curate there even though my eyes were closed. He was just talking to me, about anything really . . . I didn't see John Wimber while he was talking: I was lying down on the chair next to me, but I can remember as much of what he said that night as I can of other nights. I can remember my mother and her friend talking in the ambulance but I'm not so sure of whether I could see them or not.

The third person reporting an 'out of the body experience' while receiving prayer at one of Wimber's conferences said:

I felt I was stepping out of my own body and having a look round. It seemed to be all swirly colours as if I was able to look round the meeting but I had my eyes closed at the time. I felt I was being picked up. I could identify seeing heads like people worshipping and praying with their hands up in the air . . . no one that I felt I recognised . . . I felt God was cleansing me and saying over and over again that he was forgiving me . . .

All but one of the remaining accounts of out of the body experiences also took place in the context of prayer. Two of these were regarded as the occasions of an initial 'baptism' in the Holy Spirit, and it is significant that both of these used the vocabulary of cleansing to describe their feelings afterwards: 'I felt every part of me was taken apart, washed and put in clean again,' or 'I felt *really clean*.'

Three of these eighteen described experiences that occurred while they were involved in prayer groups, finding themselves detached from their bodies. Two of these could see their own bodies and those of their friends while looking down from above, one of them perceiving one or more extra persons in the group than there should have been. He then told the group about his experience and they interpreted it as 'a confirmation of the presence of the Lord. But at that time we were also very conscious of the reality of angels.' The third case involved no perception of the individual or of the group, but instead 'a sense of being outside my body but I don't know where . . . I came to myself when the minister was asking if I was alright and his wife said my face was glowing, like an angel.'[40]

Two others described 'heavenly' types of impressions, both of these occurring in their own churches while they were 'resting in the Spirit' (as the 'falling phenomenon' is sometimes termed):

> I felt I was in the seventh heaven. I felt loved in a way I had never done before and felt God's arms round me . . . I felt I was on a cloud. (People around said they could tell by my face I was not really there.) . . . I saw what I think were angels – some kind of heavenly being – in white and glowing. (No wings! – Normal but wearing white and glowing.)

> While she prayed, I had a most wonderful feeling of being bathed in warmth and light – a golden feeling really . . . For a week afterwards I was on a different level, on cloud nine. I didn't want it to go – for that short time I was in the presence of God, an experience of heaven on earth.

Interpretations

Do such experiences sound as if they are of demonic origin? If 'by their fruits you shall know them', I find it impossible to attribute such accounts to any source other than God. However, I have to raise this question because Roy Livesey, a Christian author who has written on topics such as 'deception', has assured me that 'out of the body experiences' are definitely of occult origin.[41] In conversation with him, it turned out that he had become a Christian a few years previously after himself dabbling in a number of occult areas. It is understandable that from such a background one is likely to react strongly, perhaps even to over-react, to anything which has resemblances to the occult – just as those who have already been exposed to tuberculosis exhibit a clear skin reaction when inoculated against it.

Dr Richard Turner, a consultant psychiatrist, informs me that out of the body experiences (what he calls 'depersonalisation') are not uncommon phenomena 'which can occur when an individual is experiencing a good deal of emotion. In some ways it can be seen as protective to the individual.' He would therefore hesitate to suggest that such experiences were either demonic or particularly Christian, but instead 'one has to analyse them in the context in which they are experienced'.

It is true that there is a considerable literature on 'out of the body experiences' in occult circles, including some on techniques designed to induce experiences in which one's consciousness becomes separated from one's body. (As far as I am aware these do not include the 'heavenly' type of experiences described at the end of the previous section.) What is not so well known, however, is the fact that similar experiences can also occur in a Christian context. Beardsworth quotes several examples of them occurring during prayer, preaching or even while leading the coffin bearers down the aisle when taking a funeral service.[42]

A problem for some Christians is that the Bible makes scant reference to such experiences. Paul writes of being 'caught up to paradise' and hearing 'inexpressible things . . . that man is not permitted to tell', but does not know if this occurred in the body or out of the body (2 Corinthians 12:3–4). John was 'in the Spirit' when he had the visions described in the book of Revelation, but again it is not clear whether or not he was outside his physical body (Revelation 1:10).[43] Perhaps he did not know himself. It appears, however, that the Russian Christian 'Vanya' (Ivan Moiseyev) was transported in his physical body to a place where he could glimpse the heavenly city.[44] Ezekiel (3:14–15) speaks of the Spirit lifting him up and taking him to the exiles near the Kebar river (which might have been a physical transportation like that of Philip in Acts 8:39–40), whereas Daniel (8:2) saw himself *in a vision* beside the Ulai Canal. During the vision he himself falls prostrate and is addressed personally (v.17), and at the end of it he was physically exhausted and 'lay ill for several days' (v.27) – reminiscent of those who have visions during illness or while close to death. Whether Elisha's ability to tell the king of Israel the very words spoken by the king of Aram in his bedroom (2 Kings 6:8–23) came as a result of his being there in a disincarnate form or from direct revelations as 'words of knowledge' is an open question.

From the evidence available, however, I would suggest that the experience of finding oneself out of one's physical body is in itself *neutral*. In itself it does not tell us whether the event is of a 'positive' or 'negative' character. We must look for other clues to tell us that. In an 'occult' context where the experience is sought for its own end or for other self-interested motives then, as Roy Livesey suggests, it might be a spiritually unhealthy practice. On the other hand, if it occurs spontaneously in a context of prayer and is associated with a sense of the presence of God then I have to assume that God has allowed it for a definite purpose. A final, more neutral category involves those people who unexpectedly find themselves out of their bodies without being engaged in either occult or Christian practices at the time. I can only assume that such experiences are allowed by God in order to point out to them that there is more to life than merely the material plane of existence.

Demonic phenomena?

Some of the physical phenomena at Wimber's meetings are attributed to a 'power encounter' when the Holy Spirit encounters resistance from either sin or demonic influence. Indications of a 'power encounter' may include stiffening of the body, screaming or shouting – although these might also be attributable to the release of inner hurts. These kinds of reactions are seen as resulting from both positive and negative influences in conflict.

Other reactions appear to be much more associated with

positive feelings or influences, examples being experiences of 'intense joy', 'ecstasy', 'dancing in the Spirit', 'arms *pulled* up in adoration' or 'gentle moving outwards of my arms to receive – it was not my doing'. Contrasting with these are reports of negative experiences such as 'feeling of blackness and being choked/strangled at neck', 'shivering and choking' or 'sick and retching'. These might be attributable to strong reactions from a negative source.[45] Other phenomena often attributed to demonic sources include eyes rolling upwards, speaking with a voice of the opposite sex or knowledge of previously unknown foreign languages while the spirit has 'manifested'.[46]

Another category of experience may be open to a different kind of interpretation. Some individuals reported the following:

> 'Noise of jet engine in head when first introduced to the Holy Spirit';
> 'Pinned to the ground and buzzing all over – *i.e.* anointing accompanied by visions and the Lord giving revelation of ministry';
> 'Sound of wind on eardrums – similar to the pressure when swimming underwater.'

Other auditory experiences such as 'hearing [an] audible voice saying my name' might be attributable to human factors – perhaps someone was actually speaking the name – but these accounts of a 'buzzing' noise compared to a 'wind' or a 'jet engine' seem to have no such natural explanation. They are reminiscent of Acts 2:2, where the coming of the Holy Spirit is accompanied by 'a sound like the blowing of a violent wind'. Similar words are used to describe a 'tremendous rushing sound . . . the sound of a tornado, a tremendously gushing wind', a 'buzzing . . . just a "zzzz"' or a sound 'like a swish . . . like mist going by' which is sometimes heard by those having near-death experiences. All of those who report these phenomena also experienced being outside of their physical bodies, and a ringing or buzzing sound can sometimes signal the onset of an out of the body experience.[47] I suggest therefore that these experiences might be related to the initial stages of leaving one's physical body. Others reported feeling 'weightlessness', a 'feeling of being lifted up' or being 'legless', which might also be related to the same phenomenon. Before attributing such experiences either to God or to the devil it is necessary to evaluate them for what they might be in themselves. Interpretations can follow later.

Visions of angels

A thirty-nine year old man whom I interviewed told me:

> At least twice I was laid out in the Spirit [at Harrogate]. I think he was just relaxing me. One time when I was in the centre of the hall, when I went down I was aware of a whole lot of angelic activity in the room – it was very soothing and very beautiful. As if a lot of angels – I couldn't actually see their form but I could see the effect, like wind stirring up leaves. Like a whirlwind of angelic activity going up to the ceiling and then coming down to people, and I could hear the faint hum of angelic harmony as they went, in praise – I felt that's what it was. Like leaves spiralling up and down again in the wind . . .

The other time he was 'laid out' he had no such vision, merely a feeling of peace.

Because angels are not part of the common experience of many Christians, it may be appropriate to include here accounts by two other people interviewed even though they are referring to events at their own churches, not a John Wimber conference. The first comes from the wife of a Baptist pastor:

> Last year, at the beginning of June, I glanced round in church and saw people tiered up to the ceiling, the building full from floor to ceiling. I looked back forward and just accepted it. I glanced a couple of times and it was there; I looked over a period of a minute. Then ten to fifteen minutes later it was gone. I just saw it was full. The daft

thing about it was I didn't question what they were sitting on. I was in a room full from floor to ceiling (in a small hall) and a number of people commented on the singing that it seemed as if more people were there than really were – that it was powerful.[48]

A Pentecostal minister gave the following account of events at his previous church:

During a meeting some in the congregation saw an angel above D. and myself on the platform preaching. There was a period of two weeks when the church was stood on its head, a lot of supernatural phenomena.

A Church of England man came to the church and was struggling to understand the phenomena he was seeing. He was right at the back of the church and four or five of us saw a shaft of light fall on him. He fell and as he fell said, 'The Lord bless thee and keep thee' – as he was C. of E. He was on the floor for fifteen minutes and came up speaking in tongues. That dissolved a lot of his intellectual problems – he didn't oppose the things seen but didn't understand.

There was a meeting where visitors from the USA, Australia and Israel all arrived at the same time, all with the same prophecy for us . . .

A lady went to a home and a masculine angel dressed in a blue robe appeared to her . . . – things that we never commented on in church. The two of us as ministers never saw them so [we] just said they were interesting . . . My main intellectual problem was that there must be some fruit at the end of the day to authenticate it as being of value . . .

In the middle of all this, a gypsy came to the church and said his sister was dying of cancer, had been given three weeks to live. 'I believe your church believes in divine healing,' he said. My wife and I went to pray for her. As we did so she sat bolt upright in bed and smiled. We led her to the Lord, left her jubilant – we just put it down to her being saved. On the Sunday all the gypsies came to church and filled one side because they saw the change and she had improved significantly. She lived another six weeks but died a Christian; it was not a complete healing, but it led up to forty gypsies being converted. We baptised twenty-eight in water and over a two-week period forty came to the Lord, most of whom were filled with the Holy Spirit. We kept in touch with some of them – a lot of ministry on tape for them. We heard tremendous reports of the influence they have had . . .

This account seems to put some of these 'supernatural' experiences into perspective: they each happened for a purpose, even if that purpose was not necessarily clear at the time. It was during the period of heightened faith and expectancy as a result of the angelic and other visitations that the church also saw significant 'fruit . . . to authenticate it as being of value'. The same is probably true of angelic visitations in the Bible: sometimes God's purposes are revealed very soon afterwards (*e.g.* Genesis 19:1–29; Luke 2:13–20; Acts 8:26–39), but in other cases there may be a long period of waiting or of difficulty before the fulfilment is seen. Then the angelic promises provide reassurance that, despite the problems, God's promises will be fulfilled (*e.g.* Genesis 16:7–12; 1 Kings 19:5–18; Luke 1:11–20, 26–38; Acts 27:21–26).

The importance of physical phenomena

On p. 224 of *Power Healing* Wimber denies that the physical manifestations are 'a necessary means or necessary accompaniment of the Holy Spirit's action'. Instead, they 'often accompany what the Holy Spirit is doing' and tend to accompany 'profound healings or spiritual renewals; they are not normally associated with healthy Christians' walks'. The general consensus among most of those I interviewed is that the presence or absence of these manifestations does not seem to be directly related to the observed degree of healing, although some assert that if there are manifestations then 'God has been doing *something*'.

If physical healing sometimes involves a speeding up of

ordinary healing processes in the body, it is not surprising that some heat should be noticed as a side product. This can even become pain in cases such as those where a growth of some kind disappears. Wimber also remarks, 'it should not be surprising that such physical phenomena accompany the healing of deep inner turmoil, the reception of forgiveness for grievous sin and the remembrance of painful experiences' (*ibid.*).

However, I feel we can go further than this and suggest that the physical symptoms: (1) act as *signs* that the source of the healing is supernatural, not natural; (2) identify the kind of source from which the healing is received.

If healing is often a *sign* of the presence of God's kingdom, then prayer accompanied by physical manifestations tends to convince people more dramatically that the healing was not due to conventional medicine or other explanations. Probably the most dramatic cases occur during deliverance from unclean spirits, but in other kinds of healing accompanied by physical manifestations it may be equally clear that something 'super-normal' is going on. This may be important both for the person receiving ministry and for those who witness it.[49]

Second, the physical sensations are often in themselves indicative of the nature of an unseen force. To illustrate this I shall quote two of those I interviewed who described experiences during their lives of an evil presence. From a fifty-eight year old man:

A friend who was a pastor . . . came to me and said a family had arrived, very distraught . . . They'd been involved with someone who said he could introduce them to a guiding spirit. Even the four year old saw it. They were very, very frightened so [they] came to church, not something they normally do. They accepted Jesus. Then we went to their house. I prayed but didn't feel anything. While there, the other man who started it all came and I felt a very unpleasant sensation. The hair on my head just bristled: I felt a fear and the presence of something not good for me, that it was not good to be here. He was into the occult a lot and we talked to him about Jesus and he had to get out.

From a thirty-three year old woman:

[At a steak bar where I used to work] one night we were in charge and had locked up, switched the lights off. It was a Saturday night and I'd gone up the stairs to the office – very narrow, almost spiral stairs and quite dark . . . I had to go up with the money and check it. For no reason the light went off. I felt cold and felt like someone was pushing me to the top of the stairs, a most horrible experience. I just screamed at the top of my lungs but it didn't seem very loud. I heard A. come into the building and the light came on. There was a story that a girl had hung herself there over some lover a long time ago . . .

These accounts illustrate the kind of physical phenomena associated with a sense of an evil presence. Symptoms include 'fear', 'a very unpleasant sensation', hair bristling, feeling cold and a sense of being pushed, with intent to harm or kill. All these contrast strongly with the feelings of well-being, joy, peace, contentment, acceptance and so on which are often associated with sensing the presence of God.

Beardsworth writes, 'How can one "feel" a "presence" without perceiving anything? By its emotional effects, evidently . . . This Other cannot be near without arousing the corresponding feelings, the appropriate response . . . like the magnet and the sentient bar of iron.'[50] These emotional effects and physical reactions in our physical bodies serve as indications of the nature of the unseen presence, enabling distinctions to be made between hostile and benign presences. If 'by their fruits you shall know them' can be applied to this sphere too, then these physical reactions in many cases constitute essential elements in recognising the divine source of healing processes.

5

'DOIN' THE STUFF'

Issues to be considered:

Are some types of people more likely than others to feel anointed by God for a healing ministry?
To what extent do people actually put into practice what they have learned at Wimber's conferences?
What results have they seen?
Can these be verified by doctors?

Some of the physical phenomena described in the questionnaire seem to be linked to a sense of 'anointing' for particular ministries. Examples include descriptions of 'tingling on top of head – feeling of oil pouring over', 'feeling similar to standing under a cold shower (but it was a pleasant experience)' or 'tingling at back of tongue as people . . . prayed for me to be released in singing'. Sensations described as a 'mantle', 'blanket' or 'heavy sheepskin coat' falling over a person were noted in the previous chapter. Others wrote vague comments like 'feeling anointed to minister' or 'various anointings'.

Some people quantified the degree to which they felt they had received anointings of this nature and I received comments from others that a question on this area ought to have been included. I had indeed considered including such a question but decided that whatever a person felt at the conference may be rather subjective and that a better test of such anointings was to ask about it six months later in the follow-up interviews. At the conference subjective feelings of 'anointings' are probably influenced considerably by the intensity of the associated physical sensations.

However, there is some unexpected evidence that these subjective evaluations of the degree of anointing received may in fact correspond to some kind of divine commissioning. The computer analysis of those who reported degrees of anointing showed a significant association with social class, in particular showing that in Social Class II there were a far higher proportion of people reporting a high degree of anointing than would have been expected.[1] On further analysis of the 108 people reporting degrees of anointing in Social Class II, it was found that *nurses* were reporting significantly higher amounts than others in that social class.[2] Analysing this group even further, it was discovered that the same high degree of anointing was reported also by others in health-related professions, such as physiotherapists or health visitors (who have initially trained as nurses anyway), and that almost all of them report high degrees of anointing.[3]

What is significant about this finding is that it is consistent with the existing vocations of these people who have relatively more contact with patients than do hospital doctors. By contrast, there is not such a distinctively high degree of anointing reported by doctors, many of whom report medium amounts. Neither do clergy and other Christian workers show any significant variation from expected values. Therefore there is a selectivity in the amount of anointing apparently bestowed on people, showing a bias not to professional clergy or doctors but instead to those who already have close contact with the sick on an ongoing day-to-day basis.

One pastoral implication of this finding relates to the selection of those who may be invited to join healing teams in churches. It is often assumed that the minister ought to be part of such a team and that Christian doctors ought at least to be considered for such ministries.[4] Nurses are more easily overlooked, especially if some of them are perceived as housewives. However, if they do receive significantly higher degrees of anointing for healing and related ministries, it is important for the church to recognise this fact and to allow such gifts to realise their potential within the life of the church.

In addition to healing, others felt they had received anointings for a variety of ministries, including intercession, evangelism, music or deliverance. The validity of these anointings can be tested only by subsequent developments, but the leadership of the church has an important role in allowing such people to exercise some of the more public ministries, thereby helping any gifts to develop.

Bestowal of charismatic gifts

Although these kinds of conferences focus on healing, many people also report benefits in the development of charismatic gifts. In my questionnaire I asked about such gifts which had been received (1) at any time in the past, and (2) for the first time during the conference. Some people ticked both boxes, adding a comment to the effect that the gift had further developed during the conference. Others, however, seemed to mean that they had used these gifts both previously and at the conference. Counting only those who ticked the box for 'first time', and excluding those who ticked both boxes, the numbers who entered into an initial experience of these gifts are as follows:

Table 5.1 Numbers experiencing the bestowal of various charismatic gifts for the first time at Harrogate

Speaking in tongues	35
Interpretation of tongues	7
Words of knowledge	130
Prophecy	23
Receiving pictures during prayer	80
Recognising the presence of spirits	71

Sometimes the development of a gift can be unexpected, as illustrated by the comment of a Norwegian lady who wrote on her questionnaire, 'In Brighton . . . I prayed for a lady in tongues. She heard the words in brilliant English!' The wife of one of those I interviewed told me how she overheard another woman at the conference expressing frustration and wondering what she was doing there. A conversation developed between the two of them for about five minutes until the other woman made a comment about understanding relatively little of what was going on because she spoke hardly any English. At that point both women realised that they had been understanding each other perfectly. They presumed they had either both been speaking in tongues or both been given a gift of interpretation, or else some combination of the two.

Participation at the conference

Although Wimber's team demonstrated how to pray for healing, they also emphasised a 'learning by doing', encouraging others to participate too. Many of those at Harrogate had also been to the Sheffield conference and so had some prior understanding of what to do. There are numerous examples of involvement in ministry during the conference, but I shall cite just one case in which I have reports both from those ministering and from the person receiving ministry. A married couple prayed for a friend and they reported seeing the friend's look of amazement as her leg grew. The woman's own account can be quoted as follows:

> I had suffered for some years with back problems. At the conference . . . I asked two friends . . . to pray for me because I had backache. They asked the Holy Spirit to come on me and just stood for a while; after a few minutes they asked me how I was feeling. I replied, 'I know it's a funny thing to say, but I feel as though I am standing uphill on one side!' They asked me if I had a short leg, and I said if I had I wasn't aware of it, only pain in my right hip and back. They told me to sit as far back in a chair as possible and she . . . knelt in front of me and I put my heels in her hands. To my amazement my right leg was approximately

half an inch to one inch shorter than my left. Following things through logically, I was run over by a Brewer's Dray when I was one year old and my pelvic bones were 'shifted' higher on the right than the left, so logically the whole leg must have been shorter, but since I have always been very active . . . and I also have what is known as a 'hyper-mobile back', I compensated for it. Anyway, they commanded my leg to grow in Jesus' name, and we waited, and suddenly my hip began to vibrate and I felt my trousers dragging on my tights! It seemed to go on for ever, and when I stood I felt as if I were being pushed over to my left! It felt weird and it took me about a week to get used to it. I have never had a backache since!

Those who prayed for her reported that this was the first time they had prayed for a leg to grow.

There are many more testimonies of involvement in healing during the conference, but it may be appropriate to quote one concerning evangelism. One man wrote on his questionnaire:

The Lord enabled me to lead a lady cleaner at the conference centre to the Lord. Her testimony was that she had sensed a power, a presence from when the VMI (Vineyard Ministries International) team arrived. She had felt a peace during the week and saw something different in the people. She was thirsting to know more. I linked her up with a local church.

An unusual form of ministry during the conference was reported by a woman who wrote on her questionnaire, 'For the first time when ministering wholeness and forgiveness to a girl, I felt that the Lord made up a little song for her, to minister to her, and I sang it to her.'

'Doin' the stuff'

John Wimber usually gives his personal testimony during a 'Signs and Wonders (Part I)' conference, such as the one in

Sheffield. In it he tells how, after reading the accounts in the New Testament of healing the sick, driving out demons and so on, he went along to a church where he expected such things to take place. After the end of the service he asked someone, 'When are they going to do the stuff?'[5] Since then the expression 'Doin' the stuff' (especially with an American accent!) has entered into Christian jargon (at least in some circles) to the extent that it is even printed on sweatshirts sold by Wimber's organisation! To British eyes this smacks of American commercialism, but it does put the emphasis on *practice* rather than thinking. This is the purpose of John Wimber's conferences – to train other Christians in 'doing the stuff' because he does not believe it is sufficient for Christians merely to gather information if it does not affect how they live out their lives in practice.[6]

There is an English expression that 'the proof of the pudding is in the eating', and I believe the same applies also to the stuffing! I therefore asked those I interviewed what they had done to put into practice the teachings they had received at these conferences. Again and again I was told about praying for relatively minor ailments such as headaches or colds, sometimes backaches, with varying degrees of reported 'success'. In many cases it was impossible to quantify the extent to which healing (if such there was) could be attributed to prayer because of the simultaneous action of drugs and natural processes of recovery. Those receiving such prayer were almost invariably other Christians belonging to the informant's own fellowship. Often prayers for 'inner' healing were reported to be commoner than those for physical healing.

Some people told me of what sounded like particularly dramatic cases of physical healing involving others in their churches. One pastor said:

We've seen some tremendous healings in the last six months . . . A woman's neck froze up and couldn't move. I and two others prayed for her. As each one prayed, the pain got worse. Then on Sunday morning she came for prayer and was instantly healed – lifted her arms.

A man had the base of his spine crumbling. He went into hospital and had the last five vertebrae fused. Then they found that a disc bone was growing inwards and would sever the spinal cord. He was told he had to have an operation to cut off the bone, but he had a fifty-fifty chance of paralysis by the operation because it was so close to the spinal cord. We prayed for him in a meeting before he was going to go to the hospital on the Wednesday. He had a steel cage round his chest, and crutches.

[After prayer] he was apparently out of pain and mobile. He went to the hospital and drove all the way . . . The doctors asked where the crutches were – they were in the car – and he had no steel cage on. They called the specialist in and found there was no need to operate. They released him to go home and come back in a month's time. Last week he's just been back and was told there was no need for an operation. The disc problem of bone growing in to cause the paralysis was no longer there, but there's still some curvature of the spine.

The consultant had a different story to tell, writing to me:

Sadly I think the account given in your letter by Mr . . . is from a medical point of view somewhat 'over the top'. The situation was that he had a deformed spine which following an injury became painful and we carried out a spinal fusion using screws and strengthening his spine. He subsequently developed leg pain and my clinical view was that as we had put him straight this had in some way compromised one of the nerves and produced his sciatic pain.

I therefore planned to readmit him and release the nerve surgically. He attended the Christian meeting ten days before admission for the second operation and dramatically improved.

Spontaneous improvement of sciatica is not uncommon and we have no objective evidence that there was any anatomical change produced by the religious experience.

I hasten to add that I believe that faith healing may have

quite a large role to play in the management of chronic back pain.[7]

There is no doubt that this patient did have a very real healing in terms of his sciatica. The clinical notes quoted in note 7 document the extent of his pain over a period of some six weeks and state that it 'dramatically improved' after attending a Christian meeting. Either he or his pastor, or both, may have misunderstood what the doctors told him about the 'central disc protrusion' which is referred to in his notes, leading to some exaggeration. This exaggerated account must be regarded as 'fantasy' (see p. 9), but that does not minimise the healing of the sciatica, which has to be regarded as fact.

Another case reported to me concerned a five year old girl with whooping cough. Her mother wrote to me that the child

had had whooping cough for five or six weeks before it was eventually diagnosed. She had been treated for a chest infection, then possible asthma, but it wasn't until [Dr N.] told me to record her coughing at night-time that he realised what it was. He immediately sent her up to the hospital for a chest X-Ray, which was on a Friday, either at the end of January or beginning of February . . . The following Monday I went to the doctor for the results. He told me that there were large shadows (particularly on one side) on her lungs, that these may take years to disappear or that she may even be left with permanent damage.

I came away devastated because my thoughts went immediately to a friend of mine, who, in her late thirties, still suffers because of shadows left permanently on her lungs as a result of whooping cough as a child.

I was told to take [my daughter] up to see Professor S. . . . By this time the church had been alerted to pray, some even fasted and prayed, and the Lord had given us Isaiah chapter 35 to encourage our faith.

. . . On the Wednesday, Professor S. had more X-Rays done there and then, and afterwards he showed them to me, together with the X-Rays she had had on the previous

Friday. He had a young trainee with him and directed his conversation more towards him than to me, explaining the X-Rays and speaking of her previous ones as if they had been taken at least a month beforehand.

With my own eyes I saw that the large shadows which had been causing concern on the previous X-Rays had completely disappeared just five days later. All that was left was a slight haziness which Professor S. said could be dealt with by physiotherapy.

You can imagine how wonderful all this was to us, but I must explain that neither Professor S. nor Dr N. saw God's hand in it . . .

This account sounds like a well-documented case of accelerated healing, but the Professor's version of the story is rather different. He wrote that the girl was referred to him in January 1986

with a history of cough and vomiting diagnosed as whooping cough. A chest X-Ray on 24 January showed complete collapse of the right middle lobe. A repeat X-Ray on 29 January showed some improvement. Chest physiotherapy was arranged. A further chest X-Ray on 26 February showed considerable improvement, although there was still some residual peribronchial disease in the right middle lobe. Thereafter she was not referred back by her GP and so I assumed that resolution proceeded normally. I enclose copies of the three X-Ray reports, which confirm . . . that the middle lobe collapse took a great deal longer than five days to resolve.

The X-Ray reports are as follows:

24.1.86.   CHEST: There is almost complete collapse of right middle lobe with associated consolidation and also extensive collapse/consolidation in the lingula.

29.1.86.   CHEST: Allowing for the slightly different projection, I doubt there has been much improvement since the previous examination of 24.1.86.

> There is still extensive disease in lingula and
> middle lobe.
> 26.2.86.   CHEST: There has been a great deal of improve-
> ment but there is still residual peribronchial
> disease in the right middle lobe. The lingula
> changes have improved also.

The telling phrase 'allowing for the slightly different projection' easily explains the mother's misinterpretation of what
she saw on the X-Ray. Though she was sincere in what she
believed, I have to classify her interpretation as 'fantasy' in
the sense in which I am using that word in this book (p. 9).

On the other hand, there are other cases referred to me
which do indicate definite healings following prayer. A
woman suffering considerable pain from a twisted neck
reported:

> I'd had trouble for a few weeks after the treatment and it
> was really getting me down. Someone asked me if I'd like to
> pray. I accepted. Three or four people prayed and laid
> hands on me. It's difficult to describe how I felt; I got a
> warm sensation . . . Before this, for quite a while I'd had
> pain. I'd been off work eight weeks and been having
> treatment . . . and traction, quite painful. The drugs didn't
> do any good at all . . . After I was prayed for the pain just
> seemed to go . . . Since then I've had no pain at all. I
> stopped taking all the tablets – painkillers – because they
> didn't agree with me. I've no bother now.

Her doctor could merely confirm the treatment prescribed,
describing the condition as 'pain in right trapezius and
torticollus; some pain at level of fifth vertebra of cervical
spine', for which the treatment had been 'non-steroidal anti-
inflammatory drugs initially, followed by physiotherapy
(traction, heat, collar) – not of great help. From 16.7.85 an
antidepressant for ? anxiety/depression. Gradual
improvement from this date.'[8]

The only discrepancy in the two accounts is that the doctor
describes the improvement as 'gradual' but the patient views

it as sudden and as dating from the time of her receiving prayer.

An Anglican minister told me of a woman whose hysterectomy was postponed because of her high blood pressure, which had been 180 over 120. He visited her in hospital when

> she had just had a bath and was wearing a nightdress with six inches of cleavage showing. She's a very loud woman and spoke in very familiar terms to me, also telling me about the problems of the other five women in the ward. I was so embarrassed . . . and thought, 'Let's pray and get this over as quickly as possible and get out.' But just after I prayed for her a nurse took her blood pressure and it was 120 over 80, so the next day she had her operation. (The Sister said she needs to get the vicar to come and pray for her blood pressure too!)

The same vicar also mentioned how he had prayed for a woman with a viral encephalitis whose prognosis was very poor and who was expected to die within three to six months. This was at the end of 1986, after John Wimber's conference in Harrogate. By the time I interviewed this vicar in August 1987 the woman was described as being '100% well', but in a case like this it is impossible to assess the degree to which her recovery was due to prayer rather than medical care.

A Baptist pastor (who had attended Wimber's Sheffield conference in October 1985) described the case of M., a thirteen year old boy from a working-class background whose family had faced numerous problems including losing their home owing to unemployment and being unable to meet the mortgage repayments. The boy had experienced

> more or less severe bouts of asthma all his life, but when they were rehoused . . . in a council house all the trauma of that set M. back a lot with his asthma. It was a prefab. with hot air vent heating. By December 1985 [the mother], doctor and headmaster were writing letters to the council about the situation at home. In the previous eight weeks he'd had only one full day at school. He didn't come to

church normally, but he came along to a baptismal service when we had a ministry time and his mother . . . asked me to pray for M. I went to him but he wouldn't stand up, a very embarrassed thirteen year old. I prayed for him and saw absolutely nothing and he felt absolutely nothing . . . But he was at school all that week and for approximately seventeen to eighteen months he was without any serious asthma attack. But two months ago he had a really nasty attack which landed him in hospital . . . I don't know why it recurred two months ago.

M.'s mother had previously come to faith in Christ, from a background in which she had no previous church contact, and her husband started to come to church sometimes too after witnessing M.'s prolonged freedom from asthma attacks. The family doctor merely supplied me with details of drugs which had been prescribed without giving any personal comment about the case.

Jill, the girl described in chapters 2 and 4, was described by her minister's wife as having

unusually shaped hands – two fingers were permanently bent. When she was eight years old she'd had an accident in the playground at school. The teacher hadn't paid attention to it but by the time they discovered she'd smashed her fingers it was too late . . . She'd been ten years like that. She was out in the Spirit and her fingers straightened [when prayed for] . . . When she came to, we said, 'Look at your hand.' She couldn't believe it . . .

An article in the local press quoted Jill as saying:

It was just like a blackout. I woke up and found my fingers straight. People in college just could not believe it. When I went to a surgeon for a check-up, he asked who had straightened my fingers and when I told him no one had operated, he could not believe it.

An Anglican minister told me that his church had seen relatively little healing among those who attended Wimber's conferences, but instead had seen some more dramatic cases within the church itself through repeated and persistent ministry to certain individuals. Wimber himself has emphasised the need for such ongoing ministry. At Sheffield he said that some measure of healing is reported by 30% of people after one session of prayer but the percentage rises with repeated sessions.[9] In a letter to me in June 1987 he wrote:

> . . . in Southern California . . . we have ongoing prayer teams praying for some people upwards of twenty to twenty-five times. We've seen a very, very high rate of healing in that kind of situation and we feel that it's much more effective than the seminar or conference kind of situation.

The need for persistence in prayer is taught in Luke 18:1–8, but we normally interpret this to refer to repeated sessions of prayer on different days. One man told me how in his fellowship most of the prayer for healing is done by the leadership, who may stop after a short while, but a sixteen year old girl persisted for half an hour in praying for a sixty year old woman with arthritis until she had her mobility restored.[10]

These cases of prayer for healing within the church family show varying degrees of resultant healing. They stand in contrast to the high rates of healing reported by a few people who furnished accounts of how they had prayed for non-Christians.

Power evangelism

In marked contrast to the relatively gradual or 'undramatic' cases of healing reported in many church situations (with a few exceptions), there are a few accounts of praying for non-Christians which seem to show rather *higher* degrees of healing. I shall quote some of them at length because they also illustrate the doubts and battles experienced by some of the Christians involved:

(a)   A child with croup – I went for a baptism visit to talk with the parents about what they were taking on in their promises. I said I'd pray for him and then felt really awful lest nothing should happen as they were not Christians. I laid hands on him and prayed; I went home worried but then thought no more about it. But six to seven years later I was visiting the grandfather of the child in hospital and thought I ought to visit but procrastinated and didn't. So I did the funeral visit to the mother. There was the son – the father of the child: I asked if he had any faith and he said, 'Oh, I know there's something, because you laid hands on our [son] and he's never had it again.' That began links with that family and [the child] began to come to Sunday School and has certainly made a decision. His mother has become a Christian and his father also later accepted Christ but the widowed grandmother has not moved at all yet.

(b) About Christmas 1985 a girl at work was healed. I'd talked with her about healing. On Wednesday night as I was reading the Bible I kept seeing verses about signs and wonders. The next morning I went into work. She was in quite a lot of pain because her back was very painful.She had a kidney infection which was causing problems. Someone mockingly said she ought to get me to pray for her. I then offered to do so. She said that the night before she'd been begging God to heal her. We arranged an appointment for lunchtime. She went back and told her whole department.

People had been jeering and making fun of her. We had come so far I realised it was all or nothing. The Lord had got to do something.

She then had cold feet about it. I said, 'All I'll do is simply pray for you: I'll be the one who looks stupid if nothing happens.' We got into a conference room where it was quiet. I prayed first that she'd have peace about it. I touched her on her shoulder and prayed for Jesus to send his Holy Spirit on her with healing power. I prayed for her kidneys. She said she felt something going through her body. I prayed again a similar kind of thing.

After I finished praying she said, 'You're not going to believe this . . . but it's gone.' She felt power going through her and she said it's gone completely. Later she was actually jumping around and there was no question she'd been healed . . . She went back to her department and everyone was stunned.

I was feeling like I was on holy ground. A guy who'd been mocking said, 'So it works then.' Someone else in her department just didn't want to talk with me! Another guy was an atheist and said he'd heard . . . The story went all round at work – even the security guards the next day asked, 'What's all this about?'

. . . Her illness didn't come back at all. Two months later she thought maybe it was coming back but still she had no problems . . . I did want to establish that she was definitely healed . . . and she had been definitely healed.

. . . She hasn't become a Christian but sometimes goes along to a bit of a dead church. Since then she has also asked me to pray for things like a problem at work when she feared she might lose her job . . .

(c) The first occasion was when I was hot from Harrogate. I just called on our neighbour across the road and found her child was off school sick. I offered to pray for him. The lad said, 'I'll be alright in the morning.' He got worse after I prayed – had bad glands. That was my first experience but I felt pretty stupid.

Then her aunt had a serious car accident and she came racing over: 'Would we pray?' We got daily bulletins about her aunt in intensive care. She felt it was definitely a miracle about getting her sight back and movement.

J. [the neighbour] said the thing that struck her was it was kind to pray for [her son] and we cared – therefore she came to us for something that really mattered. Her twin sister before used to say there's no God, but since we prayed for her aunt now she says she'll never say there's no God. Since then J. started coming to church a few times.

(d) On a Saturday afternoon, in [the] High Street. There were six lads, one very loud-mouthed. He told us to pray for a girl's knees. We did so and she said they were better. He had said if she were healed then he'd believe. Since he was a child he couldn't do sports or run because of his asthma. We prayed for him. Before, he could hear himself breathing and then all the noise had gone. Then he said, 'Thank you very much' and went.

On the Wednesday evening he came here with a friend. He said he'd run all the way home, two miles away, the first time he'd run in his life.[11]

(e) There was a woman at work with a migraine. I felt I had to pray for her, out of compassion. I leaned over her desk, put my hand on her forehead and commanded it to go in the name of Jesus. It went. I felt it was right to pray just like that. But she also has a severe backache, but God said I couldn't pray for it just like that. I told her it can't be a quick prayer: there's a lot more tied in, and she seems to recognise that herself. This morning I was talking with her and she was asking what it meant to be born again.

(f) The night before my second day at a job . . . I had a dream. I was in the doctor's sitting room, a blonde girl came in, sat down beside me and cried. She had pain in her stomach area. She was crying because she was worried sick what the pain was. The next day I was next to this same girl. I've never told her about the dream but the dream gave me confidence to tell her I'd pray for her. (Her sister had had a stomach operation and she was afraid she'd got the same thing as her sister.) The tests were negative.

(g) At college I was talking with someone about a friend and was told she was ill. I thought I'd go to see her. [This was after the Wimber visit to Sheffield.] She invited me in and we were talking. Before, I'd felt it right to visit her. During the course of the conversation I got a very strong feeling that God wanted to heal her, a surge of faith that I'd never felt before. I asked if I could pray with her. She was afraid a little, so I explained about it and she trusted me. I prayed with her and she was healed. She had laryngitis in her throat. We also got into some inner healing . . . it would have been helpful to have had a woman with me, to talk about it. I don't know if it was linked to the physical healing or not. I called the Holy Spirit down and she fell to her side. I prayed a little, sat her up and asked what was going on. She spoke a little, then cried . . . After we'd sorted some things out, her throat was OK. I asked what she wanted to do as a result; she said, 'Become a Christian.'

. . . A few of her friends came back and saw her and gasped. 'I thought you were ill,' said one . . .

(h) One woman who is a non-Christian at work – I prayed for her rheumatism in her shoulders and she was healed immediately, but there was no spiritual response. At the time she experienced tingling, heat and relief from her pain, but since then she's been off work with rheumatism elsewhere.

(i) When I came back from Sheffield all the scaffolding was round the house. I was so full of faith. A builder fell off the bottom two rungs of a stepladder outside my door and twisted his ankle on the step. He was in absolute agony and rolling around. They sat him on my doorstep and I said, 'Would you like me to ask Jesus to heal you?' He couldn't get his Wellie off because his foot was so painful, so I laid hands on his Wellie. I had an anointing in my hands, they were shaking, but nothing happened. He was taken to hospital but two hours later he walked back from the hospital. He said, 'Your prayers must have worked after all, because when I got there they said it was only badly sprained and I had to be careful on it.' He told his workmates and they all asked me questions about it.

(j)   On an outreach I was sitting at a table talking with a couple and I got an anointing like someone touching the top of my head, and I thought, 'What on earth is this for?' I knew the woman went to church and he didn't. All of a sudden the man went 'Ow', yelled out and held his head. His wife said he sometimes gets a very severe pain in his left temple. I asked, 'Would you like me to ask the Lord to heal it?' He half nodded, he was in a lot of pain. I sat him down on a park bench and prayed, rebuked the pain and said, 'I command you to go in the name of Jesus' – and it went. He said, 'The pain's gone,' but he didn't really acknowledge that God had touched him . . . [he] just said, 'We could do with you back home, because my sister's very ill with arthritis.'

(k)   I prayed for another chap, a lapsed Baptist . . . He'd had a stroke and was paralysed. He came into the café in a wheelchair, with his wife. I'd got an anointing and a couple of others had got anointings too. I said, 'Would you like us to pray?' We prayed for him for one and a half hours. (I was with three students – two were complete novices and one had prayed a little before.) He could feel sensations in his foot which he'd never felt before – he could feel warmth where it had been cold in his toes. The next day the same four of us prayed, but we also had with us a little girl, nine years old. She invited the Holy Spirit to come. She sat there and gazed into the man's face, and where she put her hands she could feel warmth. As we prayed for this man, who'd had no feeling in his left leg before, [another girl] felt sensations in her arm as if it was up his leg. She could feel the sensations coming up. By the time we'd finished he could lift his leg a little from the knee and his foot was beginning to go up and down; originally it had been completely paralysed. Before, all he could feel was cold, but at the end he could feel warmth and people touching him. But he never batted an eyelid about his relationship with God.

(l) . . . a young chap, an artist: one night his eyesight practically went. They took him into hospital and he'd lost 80% of his sight and all his motor . . . faculties started to go, his speech slurred. Some of us felt we should pray for him. At the time he was working on a crucifixion painting, but it turned out later that he had been involved in the occult. He was in hospital a week, but [he] came out for a painting exhibition where we wheeled him into the kitchen and prayed for him. He could feel a trembling in his body but put it down to his illness. Then he could feel something on top of his head, but nothing apparently happened then. We took him back to hospital. The next day he was much worse, but the day after that was dramatically better and released from hospital . . . He acknowledged God had done it but didn't acknowledge God. I didn't know at the time that he was into the occult.

(m) There was a woman whose jaw was out of alignment. A. prayed and it was with a great clicking and crunching that her jaw moved over so much that the woman now had a lisp because her tongue was not aligned. Two weeks later she brought along her husband with a pain in his shoulder. A. gave him to myself and someone else to pray with. I discovered he was not a Christian and she had a vague wishy-washy idea. I told them about the Lord and they made a commitment.

(n) We'd been doing a scheme of door-to-door visitation . . . The week before we should have done that street, but I started off on the wrong street. I knocked on the door and then realised that we'd already done that street – but in fact no one had visited that house. I explained who we were and asked if there was anything she needed. She then said, 'My baby's got cancer.'
     I went in to support T., the mother. I'd only been a Christian eight months, and it was a first in everything. I spoke to [my vicar] and he encouraged me to pray for the baby, L., too. I'd been to Harrogate with him – just for

the last day, and then I went to the team visit at the . . .
school – and he told me to do what I'd seen them doing.

I saw stage by stage, week by week, L.'s recovery . . .
In the first fortnight the tumour on his arm shrunk four
centimetres in length and four centimetres in diameter.
But then there was a long period when there was no
observable change in the tumour, but the protein count
was dropping. One day I couldn't actually go to T.'s; I
used to go for two and a half to three hours and prayed on
Thursday before her Friday visits to the hospital. (I think
this was in September.) That Thursday I prayed all
day . . . I couldn't get him out of my mind and felt
strongly that there was something wrong and needed
prayer. Even by bedtime I was still praying. I was about
to give up because I felt God wouldn't heal unless T.
made a commitment. The next day L. was pronounced
healed.

T. also on that Thursday felt frightened and on the
Friday felt very petrified going to the hospital. She felt
the doctors were going to tell her something was not
right. Then she was told L. was completely alright.

. . . The doctor said that in twenty-five years he'd
never seen it happen, for it to shrink so rapidly and
disappear. He went and got others on the Friday to look
at L. They couldn't understand why nothing was there.
T. was shouting they must make sure it's gone . . . There
was no muscle scarring or anything left, nothing whatsoever. His bone was perfect, no deformity at all . . .

T. isn't a Christian as yet. She accepts God healed
L . . . but as yet she's not come to church. But I believe
she will . . . T. got to the point where she used to pray
with me at the hospital, but the doctors just laughed and
that embarrassed her. They didn't accept it very well, the
fact that we were praying for him. We prayed for three
months before he was pronounced healed.

Technical discussion of case (n)

[*Summary*: The baby had a malignant tumour which had grown around the nerves and arteries and would have required amputation of the arm. The consultant attributed its disappearance to 'spontaneous remission', but in the medical literature such tumours have normally been cut out or the limb amputated.]

For case (n) I was able to obtain copies of the consultant's regular reports to the family GP. The first is dated 1 May 1987, when the baby (who was born at the end of February) was two months old. I quote the relevant details:

. . . this baby was referred to my paediatric surgical colleague . . . in mid March with the sudden appearance of a lump on the left forearm . . . In the following few weeks up to the beginning of April the lump appeared to increase in size and the decision was made to perform an excision biopsy. Unfortunately, when the lesion was explored it showed a large lesion infiltrating in and around nerves and arteries of the forearm and was non-excisable. The lesion was biopsied and subsequent histological examination has shown this to be an infantile fibrosarcoma . . .

. . . The management of this tumour is difficult to plan. Infantile fibrosarcoma is obviously a very rare tumour but nevertheless quite well described . . . In the past, therapy has centred around radical excision, which in L.'s case would mean above elbow amputation. There are other cases which have been treated with chemotherapy and appear to have responded successfully to this. Nevertheless in a baby of L.'s age this would offer particular difficulties in management as he would not be able to tolerate very high doses.

We have discussed L. with a number of experts from other centres, and many of them feel that there is justification in just watching and waiting as some patients are known in whom this tumour has undergone spontaneous regression. After much thought we have decided that this is probably the best approach to take with L. and have discussed this with his parents. They are obviously extremely anxious but appear to accept our advice . . .

[7 May 1987]   I reviewed L. in the clinic this week . . . I was pleased to note that on this occasion his tumour appeared to be a little softer and marginally smaller when measured . . .

[18 May 1987]   . . . we saw L. jointly in the clinic today. By objective measurement the tumour is a few millimetres larger but the other arm has also grown. Subjectively the tumour is not increasing in size but I think any apparent decrease is due to settling of post operative induration . . .

[29 May 1987]   I am fairly convinced that L.'s tumour is slightly smaller and he has been well. His preoperative Alpha Fetoprotein was 1120, which may be a useful tumour marker, so I have taken blood for a further assessment today . . .

[19 June 1987]   . . . There is no significant change in the swelling of the left arm. I have taken blood again today for Alpha Fetoprotein levels – his previous result on the 5th June was 128 KU/L, which represents a further fall . . .

[26 June 1987]   There is little doubt on subjective clinical assessment that L.'s tumour is smaller, although the left arm is still generally thicker than the right . . . His Alpha Fetoprotein's are gradually falling too, the level on the 12th June being 64. We will continue to monitor this.

[27 July 1987]   I reviewed L. on two occasions since the beginning of July. He is extremely well clinically and there is little doubt that his tumour is shrinking and has become softer. There is no evidence of metastatic disease [i.e. secondary tumours] . . .

[4 September 1987]   L. is very well indeed. His mother thinks that the forearm lesion is continuing to shrink.

On examination the maximum circumference of the forearm was 16.5 cms., which was unchanged from the previous measurements. His chest X-Ray remains clear . . .

[11 September 1987] I reviewed L. in the Oncology clinic today. He is very well and his mother thinks that the tumour has shrunk further.

On examination today there were no abnormal findings apart from the tumour on his left forearm which measures 2.7 cm. in length and 16.1 cm. maximum circumference. It feels softer and the edges are less distinct . . . I have taken blood for Alpha Fetoprotein, the last result of which was normal.

We will see him again in three weeks' time . . .

[5 October 1987] I am glad to say that L.'s forearm tumour is not clinically detectable. His Alpha Fetoprotein continues to fall slowly, being 18 KU/L on the last examination. He is being reviewed again in three weeks . . .

[28 October 1987] . . . The tumour in his left forearm is no longer palpable, although undoubtedly the forearm is larger than the right side.

There was no lymphadenopathy and chest X-Ray was clear . . . We will review him again . . .

[23 November 1987] L. remains extremely well, without any abnormal symptoms and without any real change in clinical findings.

[11 January 1988] L. was reviewed in clinic recently. He is very well. His left forearm now feels soft and, although it is still slightly larger than the right forearm, there is no sign of tumour. The rest of his physical examination was entirely normal . . .

From these reports we see that there was a sudden and dramatic disappearance of this baby's tumour between 11 September and 5 October. From being 2.7 cm. long on the forearm of a six and a half month old baby – occupying a substantial portion of the forearm – it could not be detected on examination at the clinic referred to in the letter written on Monday 5 October. Since the clinics were on Fridays, the previous one would have been on 2 October. *This is precisely the time when the Christian lady had been praying earnestly throughout most of one particular day for the baby's recovery.*[12] It should also be stressed that psychosomatic explanations (involving a form of auto-suggestion) are not normally considered applicable to a six month old baby.

This case reminds me of one quoted by Rex Gardner. A consultant paediatrician wrote to him about a child with measles encephalitis who made a rapid and complete recovery, which the consultant attributed to a 'spontaneous resolution'. Some eighteen months later he discovered that a church had arranged an all-night prayer meeting to pray for the child's recovery. The paediatrician wonders how many other cases of 'spontaneous resolution' are related to persevering intercessory prayer.[13]

The consultant involved in L.'s case wrote to me on 27 January 1988, enclosing copies of the correspondence quoted above. He noted that patients with congenital or infantile fibrosarcomas 'are usually treated by wide excision' [*i.e.* cutting out of the tumour], but 'a number of authors have reported success using chemotherapeutic regimes. Nevertheless anecdotal evidence has also suggested that these tumours regress spontaneously over a period of months and for this reason we have decided not to actively treat L.'s tumour but merely to watch and see what happens.'

In the same letter he stressed, 'I think it is important that you realise that this is a recognised situation with this tumour and suggest that you familiarise yourself with the literature,' after which he quoted from an article which mentioned that similar tumours 'may eventually regress spontaneously'.[14] Nevertheless, the same article concludes by stating, 'Surgery is generally the only effective way of treating the fibromatoses, but operations may sometimes cause more morbidity than the tumours.'[15]

One of my medical advisers, a highly respected consultant, very kindly conducted further research into this kind of tumour and supplied me with copies of the pertinent articles. He found that the authorities on it were very cautious about the possibility of spontaneous remission.

The article by Allen on 'the fibromatoses' which was quoted by L.'s consultant classifies L.'s type of tumour as 'congenital fibrosarcoma-like fibromatosis'. He records no cases at all of spontaneous remission of such tumours and writes, 'it will also be interesting to see if congenital fibrosarcoma-like fibromatosis is ever multifocal or undergoes spontaneous regression or growth arrest'.[16] Although he later states that the fibromatoses 'may eventually regress spontaneously', he classifies tumours of the type which L. had under the heading of 'fibromatoses' because he believes that they do not metastasise – that is, form 'secondaries' or change their location. He writes, 'only time will tell if this is correct'.[17] However, after his article was submitted for publication he read an article describing fifty-three cases of a tumour identical to the one he called 'congenital fibrosarcoma-like fibromatosis'; metastases occurred in five of these patients. As a result, Allen added a footnote to his article, stating he now believes 'the term "congenital fibrosarcoma-like fibromatosis" should be abandoned in favour of Chung and Enzinger's "infantile fibrosarcoma" and that the tumour should be classified as a fibrosarcoma, rather than a fibromatosis'; 'local excision, whenever surgically feasible, is still the treatment of choice'.[18] Therefore Allen's remark about the possibility of spontaneous remission of the 'fibromatoses', which L.'s consultant quoted in his letter to me, does not cover the type of tumour which L. actually had.

Chung and Enzinger's article is very revealing about the severity of infantile fibrosarcoma. I quote from their summary:

Of the 48 patients with follow-up data, 31 were alive and well with no evidence of recurrence, eight were alive with recurrence, and one was alive following lobectomy for metastatic tumor. Of the living patients, 12 were treated with amputation, nine with radical or wide local excision, and 15 with simple excision. In two cases surgery was followed by chemotherapy, and in one, by radiotherapy. Eight of the 48 patients with follow-up had died, four of metastatic tumor (8.3%) and four of miscellaneous causes. Wide local excision appears to be the treatment of choice unless the size of the tumor and its anatomic location require amputation.[19]

In view of these facts about infantile fibrosarcoma, I find it extremely remarkable that L.'s tumour should have disappeared completely without surgery or any other treatment, and that its sudden disappearance should have coincided so closely with the time when a Christian woman was repeatedly praying in earnest throughout one day for the baby's healing.[20]

Other forms of power evangelism

Because John Wimber's ministry is so often associated with healing, people sometimes forget that in his book *Power Evangelism* he gives examples of conversions resulting from words of knowledge alone. Biblical precedents for this might be found in Luke 19:1–10, John 4:4–42 and 1 Corinthians 14:24–25 (where the description of prophecy seems to incorporate words of knowledge through which the secrets of the unbeliever's heart are 'laid bare'). In Acts 2:1–41 the gift of tongues also led to conversions and in Acts 16:6–10 Paul was guided to his next place of ministry as a result of a vision received at night. I would like to mention two contemporary accounts of a similar nature.

A medical student visited Istanbul in the summer of 1988 and prayed one morning for God to enable her to witness through 'signs and wonders'. That night she witnessed at length to an Iranian man with limited English. After a while he remarked, 'I don't know if you are speaking in English or

Farsi, but I can understand everything you are saying.' The next morning their conversation reverted to its usual limited level punctuated by frequent repetitions or clarifications.

The need for a 'word of wisdom' in knowing how to act upon a 'word of knowledge', dream, prophecy or other revelation is illustrated by a case which came to my notice in the course of this research. A woman saw in a dream a map of an area she had not previously visited in a city about two hundred miles away. Accompanying this were details of a street name and house number. Subsequent examination of a map of that city confirmed that a street of that name was actually located in the area seen in her dream. Her response to this was to write an evangelistic letter to the occupants, followed later by other Christian literature. The occupants of the house never replied to her letter, so in my capacity as an independent researcher I contacted them to ask what their reactions had been. Through a Christian friend of theirs I learned that the family had been disturbed by the woman's correspondence because they feared lest they had been put on some mailing list without their consent.

Accidents and emergencies

There are a few reports of healings in emergency situations involving other Christians:

(a) One Sunday morning I was preaching about God providing opportunities to minister. As I went out the door, being the last to leave, I saw an accident across the road – a car was sandwiched and an old man was in the car sandwiched between two other cars. He had no outward sign of injury but I went to pray for him. He'd had three heart attacks in the last few months. He hyperventilated and his lady friend said he was going to die, but I said it's God at work. I knew that's what God had ordered and I was just following the script. The guy was a Christian; his heart was literally pumping and racing and on the surface it looked as if he was about to die. I sat in the car with him for half an hour. People were quite amazed because it looked as if he was going to die. I only had a sense of appointment that I had to do it – I don't feel called to stop at car accidents!

(b) Our older boy was hit by a car travelling at thirty miles an hour and he was carried along the road for fourteen metres. He was not breathing and was blue. A doctor was in the car behind and said it was serious. I said, 'In the name of Jesus, start breathing.' Immediately he coughed and spluttered and started to cry. I know at my command something happened. He was out of hospital in two days and there was no bone damage, nothing except cuts in his backside. The first day the doctors made him lie without moving because they said he had to have broken something, but they could find nothing in the X-Rays.

(c) Our son . . . four or five months ago fell off the climbing frame and his teeth went through his tongue. The cut was very wide and it was loose. My wife said we should take him to hospital but I was filled with rage because I felt it was something from the enemy and I rebuked it . . . Within five minutes it had closed.

Our daughter always seems to end up at the doctor's but with [our son] there are instances when it seems to be immediate. Like when he had mumps – he was suffering with the pain and asked me to pray for him. As I was praying, he said, 'Dad, it's gone.' In the same way as asking for an aspirin he came for prayer.[21]

It is noticeable that two of these three accounts involve children who are suffering, which is consistent with what was noted in chapter 1 about God seeming to have a bias for younger people in the area of physical healing. The exception in case (a) above involves a sense of divine appointment and in this is similar to some of those quoted above in the section on 'power evangelism'. Although the people concerned may not have had a specific 'word of knowledge' about praying for particular people, they nevertheless sensed that such prayer was in the will of God.

Some of those I interviewed also mentioned how they had been involved in praying for healing before they even heard about John Wimber. In the following two accounts there was a similar sense of divine guidance involved:

. . . there was a woman with her bone structure in her feet and legs wearing away. She had arthritis flare-ups and a hip replacement but then she had an enormous abscess. The specialist said he didn't know what to do now. He couldn't put another replacement in, but it was not healing, an open wound.

She asked me to pray and anoint her with oil. I went home and prayed about it. It was so new to me – I took down the Baptist prayer book and it had a section on prayers for the healing of the sick. I felt I should meditate on Psalm 23, 'Thou anointest my head with oil . . .' The Lord said, 'I'm going to do it'; I really felt very confident and full of faith then.

A very godly man (non-charismatic) came with me, who'd been soaked in the Scriptures. He'd written out Psalm 23 and read it through. I then shared what I felt. We anointed her and she began to violently shake. In my prayers I was saying, 'Can we cool this down, Lord – I don't know what to do !' She then went very quiet and radiated. We wheeled her back to bed. When I next visited her she was really elated: they'd been plugging the wound with cotton wool but the nurse couldn't get it back in. Within two days she was healed. The doctor, who was not a Christian doctor, recorded in his notes, 'Healing after prayer by the church.'[22]

Another man I interviewed told me how in 1982, after reading a number of books on healing as well as biblical examples, he felt he should go to pray for a former colleague in a city about seventy-five miles away who had viral encephalitis. On arrival at the hospital he was told that the prognosis was very poor – in effect, that the doctors did not think it very likely that the man would survive. My informant was granted permission by the patient's wife to go in to him, but was only allowed a few minutes to pray. He then had to return home. Later he learned that about half an hour after his visit the patient had suddenly regained normal consciousness.[23]

'Signs and mercies'

When reading the Bible we often take the expression 'signs and wonders' as approximately synonymous with 'miracles'. However, in John's gospel the word 'sign' is used very specifically to point to miracles which speak to others about God – that is, they have an evangelistic import. As a result of the first sign 'his disciples put their faith in him' (John 2:11), through the second sign the royal official and all his household believed (John 4:53), and there are indications that others came to faith through most or all of the other signs.[24] However, although the signs are conducive to faith, they do not automatically produce faith. On the contrary, the same gospel describes increasing opposition which in some cases follows as a result of the signs (John 5:16; 6:66; 9:13–34; 11:47–53; 12:10–11). In the book of Acts many of the healings reported are 'signs' leading to conversions (*e.g.* Acts 3:1–4:4; 9:32–35, 36–42) but the healings provoked violent opposition too (Acts 4:5–21; 5:12–18; 16:16–24). The presence of the sign provokes a decision one way or the other (*cf.* John 3:19–21).

Another noticeable feature about these signs is that they do not necessarily conform to the pattern noted in chapter 1 whereby younger people seem to report greater degrees of healing than older ones.[25] The crippled men healed were both aged in their late thirties or early forties (John 5:5; Acts 4:22) and the man born blind was 'of age' (John 9:21). Their long-term disabilities further added to the impact of these signs, just as Lazarus was dead considerably longer than either Jairus' daughter or the widow of Nain's son.

The accounts of 'power evangelism' given in this chapter,

though anecdotal, do seem to indicate that God does tend to honour the faith of those who are willing to pray for non-Christians. Such prayer involves a greater risk of making a fool of oneself (as compared with prayer for other Christians), but it often seems to be effective. Even the one case of initially discouraging results eventually led to more positive ones later because it was seen that the Christians cared enough to pray.[26]

To offer to pray for someone who is not a Christian is in itself a form of public witness. This testimony is further backed up by the public demonstration of God's power to heal which is evident in so many of the accounts quoted earlier. Jesus said, 'In your own Law it is written that the testimony of two men is valid. I am one who testifies for myself; my other witness is the Father, who sent me . . . Even though you do not believe me, believe the miracles, that you may know and understand that the Father is in me, and I in the Father' (John 8:17–18; 10:38). Jesus probably had in mind Deuteronomy 19:15 ('A matter must be established by the testimony of two or three witnesses') when shortly after quoting that text he said, 'where two or three come together in my name, there am I with them' (Matthew 18:20).[27] When we speak for Christ, God himself adds his testimony too through 'signs, wonders and various miracles', and by the gifts of the Holy Spirit (Hebrews 2:4).

This gives one clue why prayer for healing normally involves personal interaction between two or more people. Partly it may arise from the need to discern areas of inner healing or deliverance that might be required, but the passages quoted above seem to indicate that the public testimonial aspect is equally important. If a person is healed in the presence of those who have prayed, both the prayer itself and the results are public knowledge; the results are then more likely to be attributed to God and the non-Christian may be brought to a place of decision about his or her relationship with Christ. In the few cases in which the gospels report healing at a distance, there is evidence of faith already in a member of the household (Matthew 15:28; Luke

7:9; John 4:50).[28] The 'signs' point beyond themselves in order to elicit public testimonials of faith.

To some extent this applies also within the church context, but there the faith to be elicited is of a different kind. Instead of an initial putting of one's faith in Christ, a deeper quality of faith is called for which expects God to perform miracles even using such imperfect channels as you or me. It may also be necessary to bring forth a faith which trusts in spite of continued adversities, as in the example of Job. The widow in Luke 18:1–8 also illustrates the need for persistence in prayer. Believers may also be called upon, like Christ, to 'learn obedience' through suffering (Hebrews 5:8).

For believers, divine healing seems to be motivated by divine mercy. It is given as God wills, and in particular he has a special compassion for children and younger people. Healings in a church or conference situation are what I would call 'mercy healings', gifts of divine grace. For unbelievers, divine healing is also motivated by compassion (Mark 1:41), but it is further intended as a sign to help elicit faith. When these 'sign healings' are linked with God's compassion for children, especially among the poor, some spectacular healings can result.[29]

6

HEALING IN THE LOCAL CHURCH

Issues to be considered:

To what extent might existing church structures facilitate or hinder the development of healing ministries in local churches?
How have different churches reacted to Wimber's teachings?
In what ways have clergy been affected by Wimber's approach?
What practical steps might be taken to train lay people and to develop healing ministries in churches?

John Wimber's conferences are intended to stimulate the development of healing ministries and the use of spiritual gifts both in evangelism and within the local church. However, the actual transfer of these principles from the conference to individual church situations is one of the most problematic aspects of this whole ministry.

One scenario is that of a few enthusiasts returning from one of these conferences to a church where most people lack enthusiasm for such 'signs and wonders' and are relatively sceptical of certain aspects of such a ministry. The group of enthusiasts may find difficulty in communicating their new vision. Either their enthusiasm wanes in the face of opposition or apathy, or else they eventually decide to join another fellowship and are viewed as schismatics. Consequently John Wimber's teachings are also seen as divisive.

Another scenario is the 'softly, softly' method of gradually trying to introduce change over a longer time period. This might be more successful in some congregations but in others may run out of momentum before achieving anything.

The actual chain of events does vary considerably from one church to another, but a few general patterns can be discerned. In this chapter I shall attempt to generalise on the basis of what was reported to me by those interviewed, but it should be stressed that local circumstances might influence these patterns considerably. My comments are based on second-hand reports by informants of their own church situations, but their perceptions may vary considerably according to whether they belong to the clergy or laity. It was not practical even to attempt to assess the church situations for myself, especially as I would be unable to judge the representativeness of the occasions on which I might make my visits. For example, I had been told that a particular fellowship did not normally have ministry times of the type found at John Wimber's conferences, but on the occasion I visited they did do something similar; I was assured that this was very unusual. The minister also denied any knowledge of who I was or why I had come, his decision to have such a ministry time being apparently uninfluenced by my research.

The roles of the leadership

In general, it seems that the attitude of the leadership is crucial in facilitating or hindering the development of a healing ministry in a local church. It tends to determine the extent to which opportunities are afforded for lay involvement and may also influence the overall effectiveness of the ministry.

A typology of leadership structures in churches might isolate two broad tendencies. One trend is for a pyramidal structure to be focused on one principal leader, as contrasted with looser structures in which authority is vested in a group. The hierarchical type of structure is illustrated by Roman

Catholic and Anglican clergy and is also found in some highly charismatic 'house churches'. It therefore has relatively little association with the degree to which churches are open to the charismatic movement. There is a similar diversity among churches in which major decisions are taken at a church meeting, examples of such denominations including Baptist and Congregational churches as well as the Society of Friends.

In these congregations, where authority for major decisions is vested in a group, there is more likely to be division over issues such as worship styles, the use of charismatic gifts or the development of healing ministries. Depending on the relative size and influence of the different factions, the result may be either a discontented but possibly vocal minority who seek to assert their viewpoints, or a departure of dissatisfied individuals from the church, either *en masse* or as a gradual trickle, or even a 'hung Parliament' situation in which little progress is actually made in any direction.

By contrast, where the leadership in an 'authoritarian' type of church is committed to a 'signs and wonders' kind of ministry, then it is quite likely to be implemented in practice. It may take time for the leader's ideas to be accepted, but the process is helped by a recognition of the legitimacy of that person's authority. Often it may require a programme of education through videos, audio tapes, teaching seminars or practical demonstrations.[1] Sometimes it may be feasible to encourage those in positions of responsibility within the church to attend one of John Wimber's conferences themselves, but in other cases it may be better to invite teams from other churches to give both theoretical teaching and practical demonstration.[2] Such visits are likely to be more acceptable if the visitors belong to the same denomination as those visited.[3]

However, there may also be certain socio-cultural attitudes which inhibit the general acceptance of these ideas even when the leadership is committed to them. For example, an Anglican minister working in what had been a slum community reported how when he offered to pray for someone's healing he received the reply, 'I'm not *that* bad': prayer was perceived as being for those who were about to die. Another clergyman, working in a rural district of mid-Wales, mentioned that the local suicide rate is relatively high, alcoholism is not uncommon and incest is known to occur on some isolated farms. He encounters difficulties in discussing such social problems with his parishioners because they are acutely aware of their family reputations in a community where some families have lived and intermarried for generations. Many villagers have an intimate knowledge of other villagers' family histories, going back at least two generations. The vicar is from another part of Wales, but even to him there is a reluctance to acknowledge the existence of personal problems which might damage a family's standing in the local community. If a conversation begins to touch sensitive issues the parishioner might say, 'Leave it there,' and refuse to speak any further about it.

A cross-cultural approach

The Welsh situation outlined above vividly highlights the *cultural* element in questions of church growth and development. Despite the explosion of urban population centres during the twentieth century, still the majority of people in the developing world live in villages. Where there are closely-knit ties based on kinship, residence or association, there can be strong community pressures against what may be regarded as 'deviant' behaviour. In many cultures, becoming a Christian or being filled with the Holy Spirit may count as 'deviance' from social norms. Those who do so often face the same kind of rejection as Jesus himself experienced in his home community.

We can recognise the differing values and norms of behaviour involved in such situations far more easily when they apply to a foreign culture than when they occur on our own doorsteps. In our own churches, we feel that we all ought to be 'one body', as the Bible says we are, and we therefore feel hurt when other Christians oppose us on issues we hold dear.

What we are less able to recognise is that these differences are in many cases analogous to *cultural* variations. In our rapidly changing society, generational differences may become so great as to be tantamount to differences of culture. Those brought up in more conservative, less charismatic, traditions feel a kind of 'culture shock' when confronted by the forms of behaviour and worship which often characterise those involved in the charismatic renewal. They may in addition feel insulted by what they regard as arrogance or contempt among those who think they have entered into a fuller knowledge of God.

Perhaps we may learn some lessons from the 'Judaising controversy' found in several places in the New Testament. In the early church there were cultural divergences between the Jewish and the Gentile believers, and the issue was to what extent the one group should adopt the same customs as the other. Surely, as all were Christians, they ought to be 'one' in this matter? No: at the Council of Jerusalem described in Acts 15, we read how 'The whole assembly became silent as they listened to Barnabas and Paul telling about the miraculous signs and wonders God had done among the Gentiles through them' (v.12). This conformed to the pattern experienced earlier by Peter at the house of Cornelius, where God had given his Holy Spirit to the Gentiles without their even being baptised (Acts 10:44–48). As a result of recognising the evident work of God among the Gentiles in what is now Turkey and Cyprus, the Council at Jerusalem decided that they 'should not make it difficult for the Gentiles who are turning to God' (Acts 15:19) and that they should stipulate only a few basic requirements for the Gentile believers to follow.[4] Today it may be necessary to apply the same kind of magnanimity towards other Christians whose values and backgrounds are different to ours, if we view these as equivalent to cultural diversity. As Christians we do not lose our cultural distinctions any more than we lose our sexual differences, but diversity of this kind is actually included within being 'all one in Christ Jesus' (Galatians 3:28).

Splits

Even the most tolerant of us do at times feel frustrated if we are continually in a situation where we feel our spiritual lives are being stifled. While respecting the differing 'cultural' backgrounds of those who prefer other styles of worship, we nevertheless wish for change. Essentially the two main options open to us are either to stay in the fellowship, trying to work for internal change, or to leave and go elsewhere.

None of us likes to leave a fellowship where we are well established and have close friendships. One of those I interviewed described a major split in a fellowship to which she once belonged, saying:

> I went through bereavement symptoms for a year after, because they had been my life, vision and family . . . It was devastating, not only for me. Christianity shouldn't only be a game you play where you take the good bits and leave the nasty bits. If you love people, you take the good and the bad – like in a family.

Such trauma might quite appropriately be compared with a divorce. God hates divorce (Malachi 2:16) and Jesus spoke very strongly against it (Mark 10:2–12), but in Matthew 5:32 he did include the phrase 'except for marital unfaithfulness' as an exception to his general prohibition. Is there a parallel 'exception clause' in the family of God, the church?

There are teachings in the New Testament on church discipline regarding individuals who sin (e.g. Matthew 18:15–17; Acts 5:1–11; 1 Corinthians 5:1–5, 12–13; 1 Timothy 1:20), and it is clear that there were at times disputes between groups (e.g. Acts 6:1; Galatians 2:11–14), but little instruction is provided on the circumstances, if any, in which it might be justifiable for Christians to change from one fellowship to another on account of frustrations with forms of worship or opportunities for ministry. Probably this was because there was only one Christian congregation in each city. The question is complicated today by the existence of multiple congregations within most cities, especially in countries with strongly Protestant traditions.

However, the early Christians initially worshipped along with Jews who did not follow 'the Way' of Jesus; it was only when confrontation reached acute levels that separate congregations were formed (Acts 2:46; 5:12; 13:14–50; 14:1–5; 18:5–11, *etc.*). The separation was partly on account of differing doctrinal positions, but it was also provoked by the continuing divine confirmation of the message through signs and wonders (Acts 4:5–22; 14:3). The very miracles themselves tended to produce divisions by forcing people to make decisions about them; the result was crisis and confrontation in virtually every city.

Today we find a variety of reasons why people may leave one church and join another. Two of those interviewed spoke of being unable to participate any longer in congregations where the minister had been involved in adultery; one of them also spoke of having to leave another church in which the woman minister seemed to have been a lesbian. Another person mentioned the difficulty he felt preaching in a church with the divorced ex-minister and his girlfriend up in the gallery. One couple interviewed described a vision received by the wife in which their church at the time was full of skeletons. It was a year or two later before they left that church, but in retrospect they consider the vision to have been fulfilled through the more charismatic elements gradually leaving. In their view, what is left is dry and dead.

In 1 Samuel 3–4 we read of God's warning of judgement through what is described as a vision, followed by its fulfilment. The result was 'the glory has departed from Israel'. Similarly, Ezekiel 10 describes the glory of God departing from the temple. Where there is continued disobedience to the revelation which God has given, he may indeed withdraw his glory from among those who are supposed to be his people.

The impact on churches

The churches attended by those interviewed range from traditional Roman Catholic churches across the spectrum to charismatic house churches. Whereas the Roman Catholics interviewed have no opportunity within their own churches for the development of charismatic gifts and have to seek fellowship elsewhere (at charismatic Catholic meetings), those in the house churches may have opportunities for ministry virtually every week. Those attending churches of other denominations report a variety of circumstances, ranging from Anglican churches where there are regular opportunities for ministry to Baptist churches where such opportunities are rare. One informant reported that at his Baptist church there had been a 'massive controversy', as a result of which about forty of the 250 members had left the church, others seemed about to leave and some of the deacons had resigned their posts. All those running organisations in that church have to agree with the minister on an issue before they can teach it, and there is a 'list of taboo subjects for teaching in groups'. The minister and one of the deacons had attended a conference which was highly critical of 'signs and wonders', and the minister has 'preached against John Wimber'. Those remaining in the church 'are Christians, but not filled with the Spirit', because the more charismatic ones had left.

Even in a lively, charismatic 'house church', however, there may not necessarily be an acceptance of some of the phenomena associated with John Wimber's ministry, as shown by the following account:

> After Sheffield, the leaders of [our] church felt we wanted to go on; there were no structures to stop us. On the Sunday when coming back from the Wimber conference I was preaching. God gave me the word 'compassion' to preach on. Only six of us had been to Sheffield; we came back on the Saturday and hadn't spoken to anyone about it. [On the Sunday] I relaxed and let the Holy Spirit go, and exactly the

same thing happened there as in Sheffield. People began crying, going down, shaking, eyelids fluttering – and I was absolutely gobstruck. Twenty to thirty people were moved and went down. I thought this was terrific: 'Father, we're off!'

But the reaction was also terrific. A lot of people thought it was too much and went to the elders. That killed it. They say they are with Wimber, but we've never had any manifestations since. The tin hat was put on it and they were uneasy . . . The last two occasions when I did it in church one of the elders took over and killed it dead – he talked for fifteen minutes . . . We've never had the same response again.

Some ministers who attended one of Wimber's conferences were cautious about introducing such ministries into their own churches, as exemplified by the next quotation:

Harrogate was my first Wimber conference . . . I wanted to discover more about the ministry of healing . . . Wimber's books and teachings brought a helpful background for thinking about healing, particularly his teaching on failure in this area. The ministry times were quite interesting – I'm happy to accept the validity of words of knowledge but I do so with a slight scepticism, like the instance of everyone with bone problems: such a general thing leaves it more open to question than specific things like Larry with the burned-out throat . . .

My first night I was in the overflow hall and a lot of shaking and shouting was going on. I found it a bit disturbing, if not frightening, because I was not used to it. I got to grips with it and it was helpful to hear Wimber's emphasis that it was not always demonic . . .

In the Baptist church where this man ministers, charismatic gifts are used 'virtually not at all' in public meetings, and ministry of the kind given at Harrogate takes place 'quite infrequently – a couple of times at fellowship evenings, about five times in the last eighteen months'. However, most of the eighty to ninety members of the church 'don't know a lot about it' and would be unhappy with this style of ministry 'if they saw it'. As a result, the pastor says, 'I don't think a wholesale adoption and slavishly following would be helpful – we have to discern what the Lord wants for us in this situation.'

The minister of a rural Anglican church told me that most people in his parishes know little about John Wimber because many of them are churchgoers but not 'born again' Christians. Nevertheless he has prayed for healing with certain individuals and has seen some results:

> I anointed R. when he came out of Freemasonry. He was ill with a chest infection, a pneumonic thing, quite serious, viral. I anointed him with oil and he got better the next day. It was then the Lord showed him he had to renounce [Free]masonry.
>
> Another couple got converted two years after their marriage. They couldn't have children and were thinking of adoption. I prayed with [the husband] and asked God to do something supernatural. A month later [the wife] crept up to me in church and said she was pregnant.

In other cases the pastor and other leaders in a church are committed to the new methods and are willing to risk opposition in order to bring the church on in the direction they feel God wants it to go. The success of such ventures may depend considerably on the authority structures within the church and the proportion of the congregation who are committed to change. It certainly helps if many of the key positions of leadership within the church are occupied by people sympathetic to the pastor's aims. Change initiated 'from above' generally seems to occur more rapidly than that initiated by reform movements 'from below' which seek to influence a sometimes unwilling leadership.

On occasions it seems that God may reveal himself in a special way to those who are initially opposed to the new movement of the Holy Spirit – perhaps comparable in a small way with Christ's revelation to Saul/Paul on the road to

Damascus. A curate's wife told me about a 'real basic miner' in their church who had been resistant to the charismatic movement but who during a meeting had a vision in which the room around him faded away:

At a distance he saw [this church] jampacked full and everyone praising. It was coming nearer and nearer and he felt it would go through him and out behind him. He eventually looked at it properly and it's as if a voice was saying that's what was going to happen here. God said, 'Can you see, A.?, Can you see?' – an audible voice, as if someone was speaking down a tunnel to him. He said, 'Of course I can't bloody see, I've got my hands over my eyes!' He was shaken rigid. He'd sat on the back row next to the door so he could get out when he wanted, and had had his hands on the chair in front. Afterwards he looked down for them and found they were above his head – and he was against lifting hands in prayer!

A woman who goes to a Methodist church reported that about 75% of the 150 members are unhappy with the style of ministry associated with John Wimber:

If you mention tongues it's like a dirty word. But . . . recently we were praying for inner healing and an elderly local preacher suddenly came out with such a message in tongues: he was the last person we'd have ever expected to do so, as he believed that tongues was at Pentecost only. He got a vision and the interpretation all at the same time. He'd never been to a charismatic meeting or anything, and before then he'd been quite opposed to anything charismatic . . . [His message] was something to do with one of the women and her father, and it led to some kind of a breakthrough in the inner healing.

Several pastors interviewed who had successfully managed to introduce into their churches an acceptance of healing and the use of charismatic gifts (along the lines taught by John Wimber) also reported significant church growth. Examples are as follows.

1   At an Anglican church in West Yorkshire

In the last nine months the congregation has more than doubled. The church holds 250 people and there's at least that number on a Sunday morning. There are quite a number from other churches, but 50% of the growth is from new converts. Over a hundred people have come in the last few months.

2   The curate at an Anglican church in South Yorkshire said,

The church has grown to 300 from about 150 three years ago. [The vicar's] vision is that by 1991 it should be six hundred and by 1996 up to twelve hundred.

3   At a Baptist church in North Yorkshire

The membership is about a hundred . . . Now 40% of the church are new in the last three years . . . Of these, ten to twelve people have not come from other churches and eight of these new converts have come from nowhere in the last three years; the others are more or less new to Christianity . . . In the past year there have been eight baptisms, of which five were very definitely new conversion growth, not including young people who'd grown up in the church.

[This is in a church where those who had been there a long time were 'struggling with the changes'; on the diaconate three were supportive (all elected since this minister had come), three were 'antagonistic' and three were 'not support-ive but not antagonistic'. In the church about fifty people are 'interested in renewal', thirty have a 'definite involvement in renewal' and six to ten people might manifest spiritual gifts during a worship meeting.]

4   At a 'house church' in Lancashire

From 1980 to 1982 there was zero growth . . . At the beginning we had twenty-seven adults and nine children. The latest figures are that there are 231 . . . of which 154 are adults . . . Of the new people in the church, 27% are new converts, 23% transfers from other [local] churches and 17% transfers from other parts of the country. Of the 27% new Christians, 19% are 'cold contacts', either from the streets or Billy Graham, but 81% are existing friends of people in the fellowship brought in over a period of months.[5] In the last eighteen months we've added 120 people, adults and children, growing from just over a hundred people to 230.

This coincides with: (1) Wimber, (2) the Firebird group. I'd attended a series of seminars called 'Signs and Wonders on the Streets' – taking praise and worship on to the streets and seeing quite a powerful ministry. The rate of growth of the church significantly accelerated since we went out in evangelism and have seen signs and wonders following . . . Regularly each month we've been out on to the streets.

The fact that this fellowship of 231 people should include fifty-three new converts, of whom ten are described as 'cold contacts', compares extremely favourably with the much slower conversion growth rate of many other churches. However, the growth rate of the churches cited above may not be due merely to an emphasis on healing alone. Rather, healing is one part of a 'package' which may include the use of charismatic gifts, freedom of expression in worship and the availability of small groups in which new converts can be taught, encouraged in the development of spiritual gifts and integrated into the fellowship.

The impact on ministers

Some clergy mentioned specific ways in which their personal attitudes to ministry were changed as a result of what they saw at John Wimber's conferences. A Pentecostal minister's reactions are worth quoting at some length:

It was not so much the teaching as the visual impact of the teaching in the ministry sessions . . . We had seen that sort of phenomena on a regular basis but not on that scale. Like the falling phenomenon happens about every service in our church, but screaming as hurt or occasionally demonic I've seen in my previous church on two occasions only, whereas in this meeting it was so prolific. It made a mark on my mind that there's that much pain and stress in a person's life. Usually it takes months of counselling and ministry to unravel all that stuff.

Secondly, their approach to allowing God's Spirit to move is completely different from anything I'd ever done or seen. In our church we could almost create an atmosphere – that's hard on us but at the bottom line it's probably true. Singing and the worship group effectively create an atmosphere. But John Wimber asks the Holy Spirit to come and then there's silence, so it's not a manufactured thing. That was new to us and certainly made a mark – his total confidence in the prompting of the Holy Spirit: they stood on it if God gave a word of knowledge. That impressed me . . . Harrogate encouraged me to trust the giftings of the Holy Spirit more than in the past. Before I went there I thought I did trust them until I saw these guys. Even as a Pentecostal . . . my own faith and level of expectation rose considerably . . .

Especially as I'm praying for people, when people fell my assumption had been that God had done something, but they took that as a cue that God had started, not finished. They would then minister into the situation, either by praying for a word of knowledge or by praying until God had finished. Before, people who fell got up the same but now we see a change and check up on it.

An Anglican minister also spoke of experiencing a new form of ministry for the first time:

. . . One guy was just weeping and weeping. I began to pray for him a bit . . . This guy – for one and a half hours during the lunch break the Lord exposed all he is and had been. He was very successful in pharmaceuticals . . . and all his success was because of a profound rejection complex. His problem was that he didn't want to let go of it, because all his career was built on it. In his head he knew Jesus was a better deal than his rejection complex. It went on and on, kept pouring out – like a lid off a dustbin full of worms. As a child his father and others had told him he was no good. He could visualise himself back in the situation with Jesus saying actually he's OK and alright. He did need a lot of subsequent help to reinforce this.

It was a most amazing experience because it was such a deep thing. The Lord kept giving things – he opened the guy up like undoing a zip fastener . . . It was amazing to find myself able to be used to that degree of depth because I wouldn't have rated myself as a counsellor. If he'd come to me in a different context I'd not be able to do much, but the Spirit can do much more than natural counselling. That person went through a turnabout experience in one and a half hours, and it was what the Spirit can do, not me.

A professional evangelist reported that an incorporation of a 'signs and wonders' ministry alongside his proclamation of the gospel has increased the effectiveness of his ministry in working-class areas, though he now has a problem with follow-up because most materials assume a basic level of literacy or a familiarity with using literature; there is a lack of suitable Christian videos. Several others said they had gained in confidence through John Wimber's example of dealing with apparent failure, especially regarding his reaction to the lack of immediate response to some specific words of knowledge. Some also expressed a release from a fear of failure in praying for healing because of Wimber's emphasis that the results are up to God.

A trainee missionary described how she discovered God revealing information to her about how to pray for someone else:

I was standing next to a man and knew supernaturally that he was a pastor. I knew about the problems in his church – the church had had a period of rapid growth and had then stopped growing. Then groups were backbiting because some wanted to go on and others not. A small faction was involved in evangelism but others were not so keen.

This was an inward knowledge, a feeling of what the situation was. As I spoke it out it began to become clearer, like a feeling in the mind: the words you *put around it* to *capture the feeling* and describe the impression.

He was really encouraged. I also said that God wanted to encourage him to be a support to the church and sort out the evangelism team . . . He said that was spot on – it was more like a prophecy than a word of knowledge – and he then asked me to pray for him.

Others mentioned similar experiences in which they were encouraged by the detailed descriptions of their situations given by those ministering to them.

A number of ministers received ministry themselves, especially in the area of inner healing. Often pastors feel unable, because of their position in the church, to receive ministry of this nature from other members of their congregation. A 'neutral' or anonymous place may be better suited for them. One of those I interviewed described how she had received a vision of a place which she later learned was Ellel Grange, a healing centre in Lancashire. In another vision she saw a funeral service for a minister she knew, but it was followed by a vision of him preaching, by which she knew it did not mean that he was dying. On a subsequent visit to Ellel Grange she was told that many clergymen had there received inner healing of a kind which was like their dying to self and starting anew.

Training the laity

In Matthew 10:8, Christ's command, 'Freely you have received, freely give,' is uttered in the context of commissioning his disciples to 'heal the sick, raise the dead, cleanse those who have leprosy, drive out demons'. It is important for those who have received training in healing also to train others.

The model to follow in such training is that of Jesus himself. First he chose a manageable group of a dozen people to receive both theoretical and, more importantly, practical training in this area, after which he instructed them to 'make disciples of all nations . . . teaching them to obey everything I have commanded' (Matthew 28:19–20). We are to do the same as Jesus and to teach others to do likewise.

In a church context it is practicable first to form a healing team of some kind which has been trained and is in the process of ongoing training. However, to avoid this group becoming an elitist one, it is necessary to extend such training in ever-widening circles throughout the church. Even if some of the congregation may not be called upon to minister regularly within the fellowship, each Christian should be adequately prepared to minister to non-Christian workmates, friends, relatives or acquaintances as God may lead.

Some of those interviewed who already belong to healing teams in a local church had noticed a tendency for specialisations to occur. One person may seem to be gifted in the area of physical healing, another in deliverance. Even within the broad domain of physical healing, certain people seem to be effective at praying for one kind of ailment while others may be more effective in praying for other ailments. They point out that in 1 Corinthians 12:9 the plural form is used to refer to gifts of healing.

Specialisations of this nature may arise through experience and to some extent might be reinforced by positive results in particular areas which lead to a strengthening of one's faith for repeated healings in those same areas. On the other hand, a broader spectrum of experience is also desirable in order to meet unexpected new situations outside of one's own 'speciality'. A balance needs to be obtained between a specialist on the one hand and a 'Jack of all trades and master of none' on the other.

Those involved in a healing team also need ongoing encouragement and further training as appropriate. There are some who are frightened of becoming involved in a deliverance ministry and may need gentle encouragements to assist someone who is more experienced in this area, at the same time trusting God to protect both themselves and their families. Further training might also be needed in practical aspects of counselling, especially for those involved in prayer for inner healing. The use of videos, tapes or talks by outside speakers might be helpful complements to practical experience.

Some churches have developed their ministries to the point where they send teams to other churches. A man who is often involved in such teams reported that in such situations he seems to receive more specific words of knowledge than he does in his own church. Obviously the impact of specific words of knowledge is greater from a stranger, to which may be added the consideration that within one's own fellowship there might be suspicions about ulterior motives in giving particular messages supposed to be from God. These considerations further emphasise the desirability of ministry between churches rather than confining it mainly to one's own fellowship.

Those whose model of words of knowledge is derived from Wimber's conferences often have the impression that the messages come instantly at the moment they are required. This is not necessarily the case, however. For instance, a woman at Sheffield was given a specific word of knowledge at 4.00 a.m. but was told by God to hold it until the time was right. Later that day she was told that it was time to give it out. The person it concerned had been to a different workshop that afternoon, after which she went to find a friend in the physical healing workshop. Two minutes after her arrival there, the specific word of knowledge was given about 'a lady with a worry about pancreatitis and wearing a grey raincoat'.[6]

Sometimes the person which a word of knowledge is pinpointing feels an inner conviction that the message is for him or her, which seems to confirm the external word of knowledge. At other times two different people may be given the same message, the one confirming the other. If it has already been spoken out the second person receiving it may keep quiet, but it might actually be helpful to let it be known that a confirmatory word of knowledge has also been received.

The physical facilities available in a church building often determine the extent to which ministry takes place in public view during or at the end of a service. Some of those ministering feel it is helpful for others to see what goes on so that they become used to the phenomena which might occur. Others feel that at least for some kinds of ministry it is better for those receiving prayer to be taken into a separate room.

One minister mentioned receiving criticism from some in his church that the same people go forward for ministry every week. His attitude is 'So what? They're the ones in need . . . I wish more would seek ministry too.' On the other hand, for individuals with recurring problems, especially those requiring inner healing and counselling, it might be appropriate for ministry by a small group of two or three people to take place in someone's home over a predetermined period of six sessions or so, subject to review.

The organisation of a healing team in each local church depends considerably upon the specific circumstances of each congregation. I shall conclude this chapter by reproducing some suggestions which I originally drafted for the development of such a ministry in my own church but which, with appropriate modifications, might be usefully adapted for other church situations too.

Some recommendations for the development of a healing ministry

Preparation

1   Know in advance whether or not there will be a ministry time and gear the whole service towards it: do not leave it to the last minute to decide about the ministry time at the end of the service itself.

2   Inform specific individuals that they might be called upon to pray with people should the need arise.

3   Either pair them off in advance as teams for praying with people or else allow them to choose someone else with whom they feel comfortable working together.

4   If it is known in advance what areas may be touched upon in the sermon or what words of knowledge have been received already, then it may be useful to let the team know about these.

5   If at all possible, give opportunity for the team to pray together as a group or for the pairs to pray with each other before ministering together.

6   It might be appropriate to designate 'squads' who are 'on call', perhaps on a month-on, month-off basis, the others present at a service being available in reserve if necessary.

7   It should be clear who is organising the team and who is assigning particular pairs to pray with which individuals.

8   As the ministry develops, there should be ongoing training programmes for the team and an openness to allowing others being newly trained to join the team.

9   It is *very important* that others who are not part of the official team be given the opportunity to learn alongside team members and to receive practical training, as well as having access to more theoretical teaching sessions.[7] Otherwise there is a danger of the 'team' becoming an elite group, while others who feel excluded (whether justifiably or not) might become discouraged or critical.

Words of knowledge

1   In many cases it is quite possible that God will have given words of knowledge in advance before a meeting. If so, the service should be geared towards the ministry time: the expected content of the ministry time should be allowed to influence both the worship and the preaching in terms of choice of songs or topic of the sermon.

2   It is often appropriate to ask people to write down words of knowledge and pass them to the front so that they can be given out publicly at an appropriate point in the service. In some fellowships this can act as a vetting mechanism, which

the leadership may feel is desirable, but it can also act as an unwelcome form of censorship. Prophecy is particularly problematic in this area and it is not always feasible to write it down for vetting during a service – and, indeed, some of the prophecy might come only during the process of speaking out.

3 It is very important for feedback to be given on each person prayed for. At the team feedback sessions team members should report back to the leadership regarding people prayed with – which does not mean breaking confidentiality if it relates to a very private matter. This is important for many reasons (see section below entitled 'Follow-up'), one of which is that the accuracy of words of knowledge can be assessed. Where a word of knowledge of a relatively general nature has not been responded to, it might be appropriate to ask the person who received that word of knowledge to pray further about it and ask God if there are further clarifying details he may wish to give.

4 If a word of knowledge was given out by a member of the congregation who is not at the follow-up meeting, it is usually helpful to inform that person if the word of knowledge was responded to.

5 A word of knowledge may be given out which is identical to one which someone else in the congregation has received. In such cases it should become a recognised practice for the confirmatory 'word' to be made known too. This is particularly important in cases where the person referred to in the word of knowledge may have been reluctant to come forward. Such reluctance may be overcome by a second person publicly confirming a word of knowledge already given out.

6 It often seems to be the case that a minister may be led to preach on a specific topic and to invite people to come forward for ministry who need help in that area. This may be equivalent to a generalised 'word of knowledge'. It is important to provide an opportunity for ministry afterwards rather than allowing people to 'go away and think about it' (when in most cases they will soon forget about it).

The ministry time

1   Do not assume that a person who is gifted at leading worship or preaching will automatically be the best person to lead the ministry time. Different gifts may be required, including words of knowledge, discernment and an authority in the Lord to act in the way God is leading. It may be best for the ministry time to be led by a group of two or three people together.

2   Allow God to guide regarding the most appropriate form of ministry for the occasion. Sometimes it may be that he wants to minister to people spontaneously where they are, in which case the team may move around among the congregation. At other times people might be called out of their seats through words of knowledge or general invitations for people to come forward. Often the areas of need requiring ministry will be related to the topic of the sermon.

3   Avoid stereotyped ministry times, assuming 'it has to be done this way': allow the Holy Spirit scope to use unexpected people if he wishes and it is clear that he is guiding. The Holy Spirit may anoint someone who is not a team member and tell that person to pray for someone else: if this happens, allow the non-team member to minister alongside one of the team. Be open to God's guidance about any new people he wants to bring into the team.

4   On the other hand, it is generally unwise to say to the congregation, 'Let those around you pray for you where you are' if the congregation as a whole is insufficiently trained in this area. It is indeed the practice in a number of 'house churches' to assume that the membership is sufficiently trained for anyone to minister to his or her neighbour. However, in one such fellowship I visited it was clear to me that those around a particular person seemed to have very little idea what to do. For the most part, in churches with a wide variation in the degree of training in this kind of ministry it is better for recognised team members to pray alongside less experienced people so that the latter can grow in confidence and experience.

5   Do not be afraid to refer people on to others if necessary during the ministry time itself. While on the one hand it is good to develop an all-round ministry experience in each person, it is practical also to recognise that certain individuals may be more effective in some areas than others. Among the gifts of healing, one person may be apparently more effective at praying for sensitive teeth or short legs while another may be more effective in dealing with the past hurts caused by sexual sins.

6   If the Holy Spirit is invited to come among a congregation unused to his workings, it is important for someone in authority to remain on the platform and explain or reassure people if anything occurs which might disturb them. If no authority figure is seen to be present it can be even more disturbing and lead to misunderstandings.

7   It is not always necessary for the minister to be present during the ministry time if, for example, he feels that his rightful job is to be at the door as people leave. However, he needs to be available to be called upon in an emergency. If the minister himself is not present in person, he should know that there is somebody responsible overseeing the ministry time in his absence. He must also be informed of what happens and be present at the follow-up meeting.

8   Fit the wording and style of invitations to the particular circumstances of the congregation: for example, if they have prejudices against a term like 'words of knowledge', you can instead say, 'Does anyone here have anything they would like to share about ways in which God has spoken to you recently?' This allows scope for the sharing of scripture verses as well as words of knowledge or prophecies.

9   Be explicit in your instructions about what people needing ministry are to do. It may be that some will be too shy to come forward straight away, perhaps because of the nature of their problem. It is confusing to say, 'Will all those wanting prayer please come up to the front, or, if you prefer, have a word with the pastor or a team member afterwards.' (One exception to this may be where there has been a word of knowledge regarding something very embarrassing, in which case the

leader should say that that particular person should see him or her afterwards.)

10   Respect the wishes of the person being prayed for: for example, he or she might request that a team member of the opposite sex should not be present when particular sins might need to be confessed. The leader of a meeting should be sensitive to such possibilities, especially when assigning team members to pray with particular people.

Follow-up (This is vital!)

1   Have a regular time each week, or as often as the church has occasions for ministry, when team members can report back to the leadership. This should be as soon as possible after the ministry time itself, a Monday evening probably being the most convenient. It need not last long – even as short as half an hour, or up to an hour if it is combined with prayer and preparation for the next time of ministry. Such sessions are particularly important in the initial development of healing services, after which it might be more practical to have a follow-up list of the kind mentioned by David Pytches.[8]

2   Evaluate what further steps may need to be taken in pursuing ministry with certain individuals. For example: Should they receive prayer from a small ministry team of two or three people on a regular basis for several weeks? Should this person be referred on to someone experienced in counselling? Is it appropriate to cease or curtail existing prayer teams for certain individuals? Does the house-group leader need to be informed of developments? Are there practical steps which the church may need to take in meeting some of this person's physical or social needs?

3   Allow the team to raise questions on aspects of the ministry where they encountered problems. Give advice or teaching on ways to deal with such problems or arrange for such teaching to be given in the near future.

4   Check up on areas of need expressed by those who requested prayer and see to what extent they correspond with words of knowledge that may have been given out. If there

are words of knowledge which have not been responded to, various questions may need to be asked. For example: Was there a confirmatory word of knowledge about this received by someone else? Did a word of knowledge bring someone forward for prayer, but was the ministry actually received mainly for something different? Is the nature of the word of knowledge such that a person might be embarrassed to respond to it? Should the person who had the word of knowledge be encouraged to ask God for further specific details? Are there people in the church who are known to have this problem but who did not go forward for ministry?

5 If it is clear that certain words of knowledge were accurate, encourage those who gave out the words of knowledge by letting them know that there was a response. (It is not necessary to give them further details if this would mean breaking the confidentiality of those who received ministry.)

6 Allow God to minister to the team members themselves, including the pastor. Do not let the ministry team become so involved in 'giving out' that they do not have opportunities to receive ministry themselves. Often this time of waiting upon God may simply be a time for renewal, encouragement, praise or receiving a fresh touch of the power and love of the Holy Spirit.

7 Be open to suggestions about people who may be encouraged to join the ministry team or receive further training alongside the team.

8 Plan regular teaching seminars for the team (which might need to be only once every few months or so) in order to train them further in areas where they feel weak or to remind them of aspects of the ministry which they might have forgotten.

9 Allow scope for new initiatives as God leads.

10 Do not disqualify anyone from assisting the team in ministry on grounds which may amount to prejudice. As one professional evangelist told me, 'I was prayed with by an ordinary American housewife whom I wouldn't have chosen for a team as she couldn't play an instrument, hadn't got Bible college or other training, and didn't seem very special otherwise, but she definitely knew God and knew how to pray.'

7

HEALING IN THE KINGDOM OF GOD

Issues to be considered:

*To what extent can reports of healings be characterised as
'fiction, fantasy or fact'?*
*Is it possible to dissociate healings, words of knowledge and
physical or spiritual phenomena from each other?*
*For what reasons might God heal some groups of people or
types of need more often than others?*

At the pool of Bethesda Jesus singled out one man from
among the many who were blind, lame or paralysed and
healed him alone (John 5:1–9). In Capernaum, by contrast,
Jesus 'healed all the sick' (Matthew 8:16), but the nature of
their 'various diseases' (Mark 1:34) is not specified. It is clear
from John's account of Christ's ministry that the miracles
reported have been deliberately selected for inclusion while
omitting many other cases (John 20:30–31). A similar process
of selection probably influenced the other gospel writers too.
The net result of this is a picture which tends to emphasise the
highlights and more 'dramatic' miracles in the ministry of
Jesus. Although other healings are still mentioned, they are
not given as much space as the more 'dramatic' ones.[1]
  The gospel accounts are therefore in some ways analogous
to the 'sensationalist' reports of healings today, which similarly pick out and emphasise the more remarkable cases. In
this book I have adopted a very different approach, however,

by selecting a random sample which aims to be representative of 'ordinary' healings. Admittedly these healings are not 'ordinary' in the sense that they are attributed to divine intervention, but they are at least representative of the kinds of ailments for which people have received prayer at a conference of this kind.

Among them are some which do stand out as being rather more 'dramatic' or 'extraordinary'. Examples in my random sample include the lengthening of a leg by one and a half inches, and the healing of hypersensitive teeth (pp. 37–40). Other examples from outside the random sample include the healings of an 'old whiplash injury' and of Hoffa's disease (pp. 28–30), the healing of the child with infantile fibro-sarcoma (pp. 221–228), the straightening of Jill's fingers (p. 214), the realignment of a woman's jaw (p. 221) and the restoration of a child who had been hit by a car and was not breathing (p. 230).

All these cases are difficult to account for by reference to conventional medical rationalisations such as the natural history of the disease or psychosomatic explanations. Certainly some cases are open to doubt because of the absence of available medical documentation, but even in the better documented cases, such as the healing from infantile fibro-sarcoma, it is possible to hold on to an alternative and 'non-supernatural' explanation. One *could* maintain that the cancer disappeared through 'spontaneous remission' and then argue that it is 'natural' rather than 'supernatural', but the plausibility of this view diminishes as the case in question is compared with the histories of other such tumours (see pp. 227–228). Even if the 'spontaneous remission' theory should become increasingly implausible, it is nevertheless possible to *choose* to believe it. The choice between alternative explanations is not always governed solely by rationality, but is often a matter of the *will*. It is certainly more comfortable to choose a view of the world where there is no room for the 'supernatural'.

Unfortunately for the ostrich, too many unanswered questions remain. One of the problems in attempting a study of this kind is the practical need to compartmentalise the data into chapters dealing with healing, words of knowledge or physical and spiritual phenomena. In practice, however, these are found inextricably mixed in with one another. They come as a 'package deal': one cannot take one part without the others.

What this means is that often the whole is greater than the sum of its parts. It is possible to analyse the component elements and note their similarities and differences with phenomena elsewhere, but in the end one has to come to a decision about the whole package as manifested in any particular case. Again it comes down to a question not only of plausibility but also of the will: does one *choose* to discern in these accounts the hand of God – or to dismiss them as a mishmash of hypnosis, hysteria and hallucinations?

Fiction, fantasy or fact?

In the Introduction I outlined three principal attitudes which people might take towards 'miracles'. Some dismiss them altogether as fictitious, some consider them to be fantasised embellishments of a kernel of truth and others accept them wholly as facts.

Through following up informants' accounts, some cases fall clearly into one or other of these categories. Even if some people might actually feel better, their alleged 'healings' from diabetes (pp. 36–37) or from a disc bone growing inwards and threatening to sever the spinal cord (pp. 209–210) have to be classified as 'fantasy', in the sense in which I am using that term in this book (p. 19). There are reasons for their believing themselves to have received some kind of healing, but their *interpretations* of their experiences have to be regarded as 'fantasy'. On the other hand, there are no clear cases at all of completely fictitious accounts.

There are also a number of cases which have to be regarded as *facts*, even though, again, these facts are still open to different interpretations. Among the medically documented cases, the healings from Hoffa's disease, hypersensitive teeth or infantile fibrosarcoma have to be regarded as *facts* on the basis of the medical evidence available. This does not mean that one has to accept the interpretation of those facts which sees these healings as the work of God: one can still choose to view these as, for example, 'spontaneous remission' of a cancer. However, the choice of one interpretation over another is governed not only by the plausibility of alternative explanations but also by the context of believing Christian prayer in which these alleged 'miracles' occurred. Because it is impossible to measure scientifically the relative effects of prayer versus other treatments, the therapeutic effects of prayer tend to be ignored by most doctors. However, might it turn out that the therapy the doctors rejected will become the key to understanding outcomes in particular cases?

The context of prayer is probably the only common denominator among all the variety of healings reported in this book. Those at the Harrogate conference occurred in a social environment expecting such phenomena to occur, but most of the accounts recorded in chapter 5 describe events in very different contexts. Prayer for healing might be offered in the workplace, on the street, in the home or at church; it might involve only two people or several. Sometimes the healing is instantaneous, at other times it occurs after prolonged and persistent prayer. Healings may occur with or without a 'word of knowledge', with or without 'physical phenomena', with or without the 'laying on of hands'. They occur among Anglicans, Baptists, Catholics, 'house churches' and many other denominational groups. The Spirit blows wherever he wills.

Nevertheless, there are often characteristic indications of what is perceived as the activity of the Holy Spirit. These are the equivalent of leaves stirring in the wind. Often they do take the form of 'words of knowledge' or some of the physical phenomena described in chapter 4. Sometimes they occur as 'spiritual' phenomena such as visions of Christ or of angels. At other times there is little evidence of divine activity except in the healing itself, in the context of prayer.

For most healings, the informants' own evidence cannot be dismissed. Unless there is sufficient evidence to the contrary, it is reasonable to assume that any claimed healing is founded on a perceived change in the person's condition. If medical tests happen to be available both before and after the change, they can be used to falsify or substantiate the claims. It is unlikely that many people will be reporting known fiction, but there may be some cases in which there is an unwitting elaboration of the basic facts. In extreme cases these can be counted as 'fantasy', but in most cases the actual degree of elaboration is unlikely to distort significantly the basic facts. Here we are not dealing with a game of 'Chinese whispers' in which a story is conveyed through several people, but instead we are dealing as far as possible with the informants' own accounts of events which have been important in their personal lives. Evidence from a person known to exaggerate must be treated with caution (but not necessarily dismissed altogether), and independent corroboration of the basic facts needs to be obtained whenever possible. This I have attempted to do. Even where independent confirmation is unavailable, it is nevertheless possible to obtain a subjective impression of the extent to which a person might be liable to exaggeration. Impressions of this sort during a relatively informal interview lasting at least an hour, sometimes two, can be misleading, but they do tend to be confirmed by subsequent discussions with the person's pastor. For the vast majority of cases I doubt whether there has been any significant elaboration into the realm of 'fantasy', and for this reason I am inclined to view most of them as 'facts'.

In the same way, 'words of knowledge' are difficult to dismiss as fiction. The use of statistics indicates that at least some of them have to be regarded as 'facts' in the sense of being unlikely to derive from human guesswork. There is perhaps a greater scope for subjective elaborations of words of knowledge – 'fantasy' in the sense I am using that term in this book (p. 9) – but few messages actually display any definite indications of such elaboration. The majority of 'words of knowledge' might fall in a grey area somewhere between 'fantasy' and 'fact'. However, the absence of definite evidence indicating the development of 'fantasy' leads me to believe that the majority of words of knowledge are reported sincerely as descriptions of whatever has been experienced as the source of the information. Whether the information comes in the form of a vision, a pain in a part of the body or in some other manner, it tends to be communicated with close attention to pertinent details and with little or no elaboration. The source of the information is still open to diverse interpretations, but the fact that it is received in a definite form cannot be doubted. Moreover, it also forms part of a 'package' which often leads to healing.[2]

It is important to note in addition that public words of knowledge for healing are focused, not randomised, and that there is a definite selectivity in favour of younger people. This overall 'package' contains a variety of mutually interdependent aspects.

A not dissimilar analysis could be applied to the physical and spiritual phenomena which often accompany healing. Again there is a 'grey area' which might or might not be attributable to suggestion, but there is also a range of experiences which are almost impossible to explain away by such a theory. Psychological tests indicate that most of those experiencing these phenomena are relatively stable individuals who are extrovert but not neurotic and who are unlikely to be prone to hysterical reactions. Their sensations are merely indications that *something* has been happening to them, but the nature of that 'something' is not explained by recourse to theories of suggestion or mass hysteria. Simplistic explanations are inadequate, and it is necessary to recognise that the physical manifestations are merely the epiphenomena associated with healings as aspects of the overall 'package'.

The influence of John Wimber's ministry

Prayer for healing, words of knowledge and even some of the physical phenomena such as falling or shaking have all been present in some charismatic circles for several decades at least. However, for the most part they occurred among working-class and black Christians, especially those belonging to Pentecostal churches. One of the significant effects of John Wimber's ministry has been to introduce these practices into the more traditional, 'mainline' or 'respectable' denominations.

A second area in which there has been a noticeable impact from Wimber's ministry lies in his providing a theological framework for understanding the place of 'signs and wonders' in the church. His perspective is derived from George Ladd's theology of the kingdom of God, but Wimber also provides public demonstrations of how this is applied in practice in the areas of healing and other gifts of the Holy Spirit.

Wimber's public demonstrations are in order to *teach* rather than being ends in themselves. They are followed by opportunities for the audience to put the teachings into practice during the conference itself. It is this third element in Wimber's ministry which has probably the most important and lasting impact on the participants themselves. They are far from being passive spectators, neither are they merely confined to the roles of 'patients' in the process of receiving prayer for healing: instead they themselves play active roles in praying for the healing of others.

As a result of this practical training, many are encouraged to pray for healing in their own home situations. A common result of some people from a church going to one of Wimber's conferences is that they then introduce to their congregations the idea of having a healing team or special healing services. Many churches from a wide range of denominations have been affected in this manner. Some individuals, and, more rarely, some fellowships, have also introduced healing or words of knowledge as components of their evangelism.

A further important area in which Wimber's example has had a major impact concerns his attitude to those who are not healed. His personal testimony of preaching on healing for several months, during which he became discouraged by the absence of visible results when praying for healing, seems to have been a source of encouragement to many who have followed his example. Furthermore, Wimber's clear teaching on the fact that some are not healed and his citing of biblical examples indicating the absence of healing for some of St Paul's friends (*e.g.* 1 Timothy 5:23; 2 Timothy 4:20) provide incentives for not giving up in the face of failure. Some of those I interviewed spoke positively about the encouragements imparted to their own healing ministries by Wimber's attitude that the results of the prayer are up to God: we have the responsibility to pray, but the responsibility for the healing or absence of it belongs to God. It is an attitude which is very similar to a common evangelical view of evangelism which stresses the church's responsibility for preaching the gospel but views the responsibility for the actual process of 'conversion' as a work of God the Holy Spirit.

Some of the sources of Wimber's theology derive from evangelical and Pentecostal roots which some might regard as highly conservative and even 'narrow' in terms of their denominational outlooks and theological perspectives. Certainly Wimber's theology retains an evangelical view of the importance of basing one's teaching on that of the Bible. However, his teachings have also had an impact among a much wider circle of Christians, including Roman Catholics, and have been instrumental in the development of healing ministries among those of many different theological persuasions. Although most of those influenced by him do tend to belong to evangelical kinds of churches, his influence is by no means limited to these, and is having an impact among an increasingly wide spectrum of Christians.

The focus of healing

Why some people appear to receive divine healing, and others not, is a question which many Christians have attempted to answer throughout the centuries. Ultimately, however, we have to admit that we do not know, that the mind of God and his purposes are beyond our human under-standing.

Nevertheless, I have indicated a few *tendencies* which I have noticed in the course of my research. These are by no means hard and fast rules, because there are always exceptions, but they do reveal three relatively consistent patterns.

1   Physical healing seems to be more likely to occur among younger people than older ones. It might be that this finding can be explained medically, in terms of younger people having bodies which have suffered relatively less from the effects of ageing, but, whatever the explanation, it is con-sistent with the biblical evidence from cases of raising the dead which do seem to point to a divine bias in favour of the young (see pp. 63–65).

Moreover, this is consistent with the fact that highly specific public words of knowledge almost invariably relate to *physical* healing and, instead of being randomised, are *focused* on the younger age groups. They are also associated with higher degrees of reported healings. This focusing of 'words of knowledge' in a non-arbitrary manner might be interpreted as further evidence of a divine bias to the young.

2   There are indications that God may be more likely to heal those belonging to lower social classes than the educated elite. This is consistent with the theological positions of Ronald Sider and Bishop David Sheppard, both of whom argue that God has a 'bias to the poor'.[3] Their views are commonly associated with Christian involvement in social concerns such as inner-city mission or aid to developing countries, but the same divine 'bias to the poor' appears to operate in the area of healing too. In fact the data available to me indicate that it is not so much a bias *to* the poor but more a bias *away* from the better-educated social elite, because it is they who report conspicuously lower degrees of physical healing than do all other social classes.

3   There is also a certain amount of anecdotal evidence that those who are willing to pray for non-Christians often report

relatively noticeable results. In a number of cases they felt some kind of divine leading to do so, but this is not always the case. Certainly there may be a greater risk of losing face if there are no immediately visible effects from such prayers, which is probably why many Christians shy away from praying for non-Christians. However, those who take the risk do often discover that God seems to honour their faith. Moreover, the 'sign' to the non-Christian who experiences healing tends to precipitate a decision for or against Christ; it is difficult to remain neutral once one has witnessed a work of God's power.[4]

This third generalisation is based on a smaller number of accounts and is not as amenable to statistical analysis as are the reports from the Harrogate conference, which always relate to Christians. Prayer for non-Christians seems to produce notable exceptions to the generalisations based on statistical trends among the Christian sample. Among Christians, there appears to be a selectivity towards younger and less affluent individuals, at least for physical healing, but any such selectivity is far less obvious among non-Christians.

This pattern is also consistent with the biblical evidence. When the Bible refers to the age of an older person who receives healing, there is also some indication that the person concerned was converted at the same time (*e.g.* John 5:1–15; Acts 3:1–4:22). Their healings were *signs* which led to the development of faith. Cases of healings among higher-status adults appear to have had very similar effects and to have been particularly associated with conversions among non-Jewish ethnic groups (2 Kings 5:1–19; Acts 28:7–8).

Priorities in healing?

On the whole, the degree of healing reported for deliverance is greater than that for inner healing, which in turn is greater than that for physical healing.

This generalisation applies to my findings among Christians at Harrogate, but it is unlikely to apply to non-Christians. In fact, the order might even be reversed among non-Christians. Physical healing among non-Christians is more likely to be a 'sign' to them than are other forms of healing, with the possible exception of dramatic cases of deliverance. Some, however, may find deliverance so frightening that they reject the kingdom of God (Luke 8:37), whereas physical healing is more likely to lead people to recognise and respond to the work of God (Luke 5:26).

Inner healing, especially that relating to the forgiveness of others, is probably most applicable to those who have already received forgiveness from God and as a result can extend it to others (Matthew 6:14–15; 18:21–35). It is more difficult to apply 'inner healing' to those who have not yet entered into a relationship with God. Deliverance, however, might be accomplished among non-Christians (e.g. Acts 16:16–18), but Jesus warned of the danger of more unclean spirits returning and of the person's final state being worse than the initial one (Luke 11:24–26). For this reason some Christians tend to advise against praying for the expulsion of evil spirits from a non-Christian unless the person is converted at the same time; instead, they recommend that the person first receive Christ and be filled with the Holy Spirit (Luke 11:13), so that the One who is stronger than the evil spirits can take up occupancy and drive out the previous residents (Luke 11:14–23). As long as the new owner is in residence, illegal squatters are discouraged from taking over.

A number of suggestions might be advanced to rationalise why, among Christians, prayer for deliverance appears to be more effective than prayer for inner healing, which in turn seems to be more effective than prayer for physical healing. Some possible explanations can be summarised as follows.

1   The differences are partly produced by variations in the speed of healing. Deliverance can be accomplished within a relatively short space of time, so its results are more quickly perceived. Inner healing might require longer time periods over a number of sessions, but there is often felt to be some psychological benefit after each session. Physical healing,

however, might involve a divine acceleration of 'natural' (but divinely created) healing processes, and in such cases the observable effects might be noticed only a day or two later. Therefore at the end of the Harrogate conference subjective impressions of healing showed a variation according to the types of ministries received.

This idea is at first sight very plausible, and it takes into account the fact that most of those reporting a 'fair amount' of physical healing at the end of the conference actually noticed a significant degree of healing in the longer term. (The 58% who reported an intermediate or high rate of physical healing at the end of the Harrogate conference closely correspond to the 57% of my random sample who had received prayer for physical healing at Harrogate and who reported a sustained noticeable improvement when followed up six to ten months later.) For inner healing, however, about 78% reported either high or medium rates of healing at the conference, but the proportion reporting noticeable improvements when followed up in 1987 in fact rose to 85%. Therefore the longer-term effects show an even greater increase in the effectiveness of inner healing than physical healing, and the disparity between the types of healing remains.[5]

2   These disparities are merely products of people's subjective evaluations of their degrees of healing. To some extent the very classifications themselves might contribute to this, because (1) people feel that deliverance should be associated with instantaneous healing and (2) they are also aware of the need to give physical healing the test of time. As a result they are more cautious in their self-assessments of physical healing but possibly over-optimistic about their experiences of deliverance.

This theory is also very plausible, and it is probably correct in emphasising the element of caution in self-assessments of physical healing. However, it does not account for the differences in degrees of physical healing reported by those of different generations. To do this, therefore, a further assumption needs to be made, to the effect that older people are even more cautious in their self-assessments of physical healing than are younger people. The problem with this is that it is then difficult to explain why older people should be more cautious than younger people in their personal evaluations of *both* physical healing *and* deliverance but not of inner healing.

3   God is much more concerned with spiritual health than physical health. This kind of view is perhaps associated more with those Christians who sometimes appear to lay so much stress on the salvation of souls that they seem to neglect the biblical teachings on feeding the hungry, caring for the oppressed or healing the physically sick. There is certainly some justification for this kind of theology, because all physical healing is in some sense 'temporary' in so far as all die and need to be prepared for what happens after death. Jesus commanded his followers not to be afraid of those who kill the body but cannot kill the soul, but instead to fear 'the One who can destroy both soul and body in hell' (Matthew 10:28). However, we have to recognise that Jesus did heal physical bodies out of compassion for those suffering physically (Mark 1:41). In the context of a ministry of *both* healing *and* preaching, he had compassion on the crowds and told his disciples to pray for more workers for the harvest fields (Matthew 9:35–38). Even if Jesus did put the stress more on preaching so that the healing ministry should not occupy all his time (Mark 1:32–39), he still practised both forms of ministry. There is no indication that any difference in priorities produced any variation in the degree of healing, because we assume that those receiving physical healing were 100% cured.

4   It is much easier for God to heal spirits than bodies. A view such as this would amount to heresy if expressed in a form as bald as this, but it seems to be an underlying feeling in the hearts of many Christians. They feel that physical healing is so incredible, even if they believe God can easily cast out demons. In effect they deny Christ's claim to have all authority in heaven *and* on earth (Matthew 28:18) by balancing this against the scripture that 'the whole world is under the control of the evil one' (1 John 5:19). Their attitude is similar

to the Gnostic view that matter is evil whereas spirit is good. For the Jews, by contrast, it was much more difficult to believe that Jesus could have authority in the *spiritual* realm, through his authority to forgive sins, but this was actually demonstrated to them through a physical healing (Luke 5:22–26). Our human ideas about God's abilities to drive out demons, forgive sins or heal cancers perhaps need to be reassessed according to a different perspective.

5   Perhaps the most appropriate perspective is that of death and eternity. If for the Christian death is merely the doorway to further service for Christ and worship of him in the heavenly realm, then God has the right to decide on the time for that higher calling to occur. In preparation for eternity, he also desires purer characters for all his people right now. For this reason he shows no differentiation according to age in bestowing inner healing on his people, freeing them from the burdens of sins committed by them and to them. He also desires them to be set free from demonic influence, but among older people this influence might be so closely bound up with the habits of a lifetime that they find difficulty in forsaking such behaviour patterns.

Meanwhile we know that here in this world there is plenty still to be done. Often it involves the need for physical health. It might necessitate many years of active involvement in the tasks to which God calls each one of us. According to such a perspective it is more comprehensible why God might choose to bestow physical healing more often on younger people than on older ones. The *potential* for active service might distinguish the young from the old, just as the conversion of a younger person is often viewed as not merely 'saving a soul' but as releasing the potential of a life to be lived in the service of Jesus. However, the maturing of faith and the preparation for eternity might be better accomplished, even in a younger person, by God allowing suffering in various forms, whether physical or psychological: '. . . we also rejoice in our sufferings, because we know that suffering produces perseverance; perseverance, character; and character, hope . . .' (Romans 5:3–4). Just as 'through faith' some 'escaped the edge of the sword' but others 'were put to death by the sword', and some 'were tortured and refused to be released' whereas others 'shut the mouths of lions' or 'received back their dead, raised to life' (Hebrews 11:33–37), so today some receive physical healing and others do not. For each person there are divine purposes which can be truly assessed only in the perspective of eternity.

The power and the glory

Works of God's power are often accompanied by revelations of his glory. Miracles reveal God's power in tangible forms and often provoke a recognition of his awesomeness and majesty. Christ's 'word of knowledge' about where to catch a huge shoal of fish, after the fishermen had caught nothing all night, produced a response in Simon Peter whereby he fell at Jesus' knees and said, 'Go away from me, Lord; I am a sinful man!' (Luke 5:8). Similarly, the gift of prophecy can lead to the disclosure of the secrets of an unbeliever's heart, with the result that he or she falls down in worship, recognising the presence of God among his people (1 Corinthians 14:24–25).

In the same way, 'physical phenomena' such as falling on one's face are often accompanied in the Bible by visions of Christ or his angels, as in Daniel 10:2–9, Matthew 28:2–4 or Revelation 1:12–17. The same 'falling phenomenon' accompanied the manifestation of the Shekinah as a cloud and a visible sign of God's presence and glory, filling the temple so that the priests 'could not stand to minister' (2 Chronicles 5:14, RSV).

The physical manifestation of God's *power*, apparently causing people to fall down before him, cannot be dissociated from the simultaneous revelation of God's *glory*. Similarly, the activity of the Holy Spirit in Acts 2:2–4 is described in terms of a 'sound like the blowing of a violent wind . . . from heaven' and 'what seemed to be tongues of fire' – auditory and visual phenomena pointing to the greatness of God – as well as the revelation of God's power through the gift of 'speaking in tongues'. It is noteworthy in this context that, in comparison with Paul's other correspondence, his letters to the Corinthians contain not only his most explicit teachings on charismatic gifts but also his most frequent references to angels and to personal experiences of a visionary or supernatural nature.[6] In general, there seems to be a relatively close association between spiritual revelations of God's glory and physical manifestations of his power. That they tend to occur together in a 'package' means that we need to be aware of their interrelationships.

It is certainly possible to analyse the component aspects under academic headings such as 'physical phenomena' or 'visions of angels', but it is very likely that the whole is greater than the sum of its parts. In the same way there is an intermixture between 'human' and 'divine' elements in prophecy. For example, Hosea was a Northerner who spoke with the Hebrew equivalent of a 'Yorkshire accent', so some of his words are now obscure in their meanings. They are nevertheless still believed to be divinely inspired. A very similar interaction between 'human' and 'divine' elements can be seen in the various aspects of healing, words of knowledge, 'physical phenomena' and so on. All are different aspects of the activity of the Holy Spirit expressed in his interaction with different human beings.

Beyond all of these aspects of the visible work of God lies the invisible realm of God's kingdom which can be revealed visibly through manifestations of his visible power and his majestic glory. These visible manifestations provide merely brief glimpses of the invisible power and glory which we believe lie beyond the perceptions of our presently limited senses. Healings, visions and gifts of the Holy Spirit reveal now a small part of that which is beyond us and is yet to be revealed (2 Corinthians 5:1–5; Ephesians 1:3–23). Ultimately, however, the kingdom, the power and the glory all belong to God.

Appendix A

DEGREES OF PHYSICAL HEALING REPORTED AT THE END OF THE HARROGATE CONFERENCE

In the following table, informants' self-assessments of their degrees of healing are given in numerical values as follows:

> None at all 1
> A little 3
> A fair amount 5
> A great deal 7
> Total healing 9

Where individuals bracketed together adjacent boxes, their responses are counted as being the even numbers between those given above: for example, '8' signifies that 'a great deal' and 'total healing' were bracketed together. The table shows the maximum, minimum and mean (average) degrees of healing for each condition, omitting cases in which informants left blank the degree of healing.

Informants' own categories are used in the absence of detailed medical terminology, and similar kinds of conditions may be grouped together (*e.g.* 'slipped disc' is not differentiated from 'back problems'). The responses reflect experiences of healing up to the time when the questionnaires were collected, just before the final session; any healings during the last session are excluded. (I have been told at third hand that someone was healed of blindness that evening, but I have been unable to verify this.)

	Number of cases	Max. value	Min. value	Mean
A) Skeletal disorders in:				
Unspecified	8	9	1	4.75
Back and shoulder	150	9	1	5.05
Arm	18	9	1	5.9
Hand/fingers/wrist	17	9	1	5.5
Leg or knee	43	9	1	4.65
Hip	12	9	3	5.3
Foot/ankle	28	9	1	4.6
Neck	53	9	1	5.15
Head	11	9	1	5.1
'Joints'	5	5	1	3.4
B) Arthritis or rheumatism mentioned in:				
Unspecified	16	7	1	4.6
Back	15	7	1	5.1
Arm	1	7	7	7.0
Hand	10	9	3	4.2
Leg	10	9	1	4.6
Hip	6	7	3	5.7
Foot	4	8	1	3.75
Neck	20	9	1	5.1
Pelvis/hip (Ankylosing spondylitis)	1	5	5	5.0
C) Stomach or digestive problems:				
Unspecified	20	9	1	4.85
Spastic colon	3	7	1	3.0
Diverticulitis	2	5	3	4.0
Diabetes	5	7	1	3.8
Remnant of gastric 'flu	1	7	7	7.0
'Intestinal problems'	2	7	5	6.0
Hernia	4	9	5	6.0
Bowel disorder	1	7	7	7.0
Indigestion	4	9	3	5.5
Stomach tension	1	5	5	5.0

	Number of cases	Max. value	Min. value	Mean
Colitis	3	5	1	2.3
Cirrhosis	1	5	5	5.0
D) *Eyes/sight*				
Unspecified	11	7	1	3.7
Blindness	3	7	1	4.3
Short sight	7	7	1	2.8
Glaucoma	2	7	1	4.0
Pain behind eyes	1	9	9	9.0
Conjunctivitis	2	7	1	4.0
Poor sight or blindness in one eye	8	5	1	1.75
Imperfect focus/blurring/ peripheral blindness	4	7	1	3.75
Eye squint	1	9	9	9.0
'Minor eye problem'	1	7	7	7.0
Damage to both eyes resulting from severe burns	1	3	3	3.0
E) *Ears/hearing*				
'Deafness/unspecified'	17	7	1	2.5
Loss of hearing 70%–100%	4	5	1	2.5
Loss of hearing 40%–60%	1	1	1	1.0
Loss of hearing 10%–30%	5	5	1	2.6
Distortion in hearing	1	9	9	9.0
Tinnitus/ringing or whistling in ears	3	5	1	2.3
Inability to hear in higher register	2	9	1	5.0
Oversensitivity to loud noise	1	7	7	7.0
'Partial hearing loss' not detailed further	5	7	1	3.6
Underdeveloped ear from birth	1	1	1	1.0
F) *Skin problems*				
Rash	5	5	1	3.8

	Number of cases	Max. value	Min. value	Mean
Eczema	4	7	3	5.2
Lacerations	1	7	7	7.0
Psoriasis	3	7	1	3.0
Spot on skin	1	1	1	1.0
Mouth ulcers	3	3	3	3.0
Allergic reactions (including hay fever)	8	9	1	3.8
'Overactive sweat glands'	1	5	5	5.0
Unspecified 'skin diseases'	1	5	5	5.0
G) *Miscellaneous*				
Heart	6	9	1	5.0
Irregular heart beat	4	8	4	5.5
Blood pressure	3	9	1	5.0
Bladder/kidney/urinary problems	5	9	3	5.0
Lymph glands	1	9	9	9.0
'Glandular problems'	1	3	3	3.0
High cholesterol levels	2	7	1	4.0
Lump in breast	1	7	7	7.0
Cyst-like lump	1	1	1	1.0
Circulatory conditions/ phlebitis	4	7	5	6.5
Fibrositis	1	1	1	1.0
Bronchitis/cough	5	7	3	5.0
Cold/cough and cold	6	5	1	3.5
Lung problems	2	7	5	6.0
Chest infections	3	9	5	7.0
Larynx nodules	2	7	5	6.0
Sore throats	10	9	3	5.4
Prolapse of womb	2	9	7	8.0
Haemorrhoids	1	7	7	7.0
Endometriosis	3	9	8	8.7
Menopausal or menstrual conditions	3	9	5	6.3
Pain in breast	1	7	7	7.0

	Number of cases	Max. value	Min. value	Mean
Symptoms of premenstrual tension	1	7	7	7.0
Hormonal disturbances/ morning sickness	4	7	1	4.5
Pain in 'a very private part of my body' (male)	1	5	5	5.0
Asthma	10	8	1	4.9
Breathing difficulties/ tightness in chest	10	9	1	5.2
Facial muscles	3	3	1	2.3
Muscles or swelling in feet or ankles	5	5	1	3.0
Pain or weakness in legs	3	9	1	5.0
Cyst on head	1	1	1	1.0
Headaches	12	7	1	4.0
Migraines	7	9	3	6.4
Absence of post-operative soreness	4	7	5	6.5
Symptoms of child's paralysis (vicarious prayer)	1	7	7	7.0
Multiple sclerosis	1	1	1	1.0
Loss of sense of smell	1	1	1	1.0
Bad posture	1	7	7	7.0
Varicose veins	3	5	5	5.0
Muscular tension	1	1	1	1.0
Fallen arches/flat feet	2	5	2	3.5
Sciatica	4	7	3	4.5
Muscular spasms in lower back	1	9	9	9.0
Pain in lumbar region	1	1	1	1.0
Piles	2	5	5	5.0
Loss of voice	1	3	3	3.0
'Stiff neck'	1	3	3	3.0

	Number of cases	Max. value	Min. value	Mean
Pain in right lower side of body – not yet diagnosed by doctor but received word of knowledge through picture of torn ligament in hip bone	1	7	7	7.0
Spastic condition of left side of body	1	7	7	7.0
Toothache	2	7	3	5.0
Earache	1	7	7	7.0
Numb foot	1	7	7	7.0
Severe pains in pelvis and lower back	1	7	7	7.0
Hyperventilation	1	3	3	3.0
'Neurological symptoms caused by cervical spine condition'	1	5	5	5.0
Fever	2	9	7	8.0
Anaemia	2	7	5	6.0
'Feeling cold'	1	7	7	7.0
Weak or damaged sphincter muscle	2	7	5	6.0
Cystitis	1	9	9	9.0
Lump in throat	1	3	3	3.0
Sinus problems	9	5	1	3.4
Sleeping sickness	2	9	3	6.0
Pain in rib (sternum)	1	5	5	5.0
Crohn's disease – a narrowing of the small bowel	1	5	5	5.0
Stomach ulcer	1	7	7	7.0
Bowel condition	2	7	3	5.0
Old whiplash injury	1	7	7	7.0
Damage to eyes from removal of congenital cataracts, at age of six years	1	1	1	1.0

	Number of cases	Max. value	Min. value	Mean
Constriction or blockage of nasal passages	2	5	3	4.0
Thrombosis of leg	1	1	1	1.0
Epilepsy	2	7	6	6.7
Nervous, upset stomach/ diarrhoea	2	7	7	7.0
Bulimia	1	1	1	1.0
Chronic constipation	2	1	1	1.0
Damaged vocal cords and voice box	1	1	1	1.0
Pelvic infection	1	5	5	5.0
Septic sore on amputated stump of leg	1	7	7	7.0
Neuritis (in face)	1	5	5	5.0
Thyroid condition	1	3	3	3.0
Catarrh	3	7	3	5.0
Hypoglycaemia	1	1	1	1.0
'A virus like glandular fever'	1	9	9	9.0
Nausea and vomiting	1	9	9	9.0
Strain or possible pulled tendon in groin	2	5	5	5.0
Receding gums/cold sensitive teeth	3	9	2	4.7
Damaged roots of front teeth	1	7	7	7.0
Polio-caliper on leg	1	1	1	1.0
'Obstruction in stomach, causing sickness and severe indigestion for weeks'	1	9	9	9.0
'Sickness' not further specified	1	7	7	7.0
Bleeding of vagina for twenty-five days – suspected polyp	1	9	9	9.0

	Number of cases	Max. value	Min. value	Mean
Allergic rhinitis	1	7	7	7.0
Physical exhaustion	1	7	7	7.0
Emphysema	1	7	7	7.0
'Brain' not further specified/brain aneurysm	2	8	1	4.5
Blood clots on retina of eye	1	1	1	1.0
Damage to nerves in arm	1	3	3	3.0
H) *Deliverance from spirits connected with:*				
Headaches	1	7	7	7.0
Throat problem	1	9	9	9.0
Chest problem	1	9	9	9.0
Nervous, upset stomach and haemorrhoids	1	7	7	7.0
Arthritis	1	9	9	9.0
Neck pain	1	9	9	9.0
Pain in back	1	9	9	9.0
I) *Unspecified 'physical healing'* (details left blank)	21	9	1	5.1

Appendix B

SUMMARY OF QUESTIONNAIRE RESULTS

Total number of usable questionnaires: 1890

Area of origin:

Scotland	97
North-west England	198
North-east England	165
North Yorkshire	168
West Yorkshire	301
East Yorks/Humberside	37
South Yorkshire	170
Midlands	259
East Anglia	88
Wales	31
South-west England	92
South-east England	149
Northern Ireland	9
Eire	9
Other (*i.e.* abroad)	103
Blank	14

Age of participants:

Up to 19	27	50–59	260
20–29	443	60–69	108
30–39	585	70–79	7
40–49	435	80–89	2
		Blank	23

Sex of participants:

Male	946

Female 942
Blank 2

Marital status:
Single 498
Married 1284
Widowed 35
Divorced 57
Separated 4
Engaged 7
Unspecified 5

Social class/occupation:
Social Class I (*e.g.* lawyers, doctors) 545
Social Class II (*e.g.* business managers,
  teachers) 550
Social Class III (*e.g.* plumbers, sales
  representatives) 265
Social Class IV (*e.g.* farm workers) 20
Social Class V (*e.g.* sewage plant
  attendants) 2
Unemployed 62
Housewives 278
Students 41
Retired 83
Blank 44

Present church denomination:
Anglican 668
Baptist 216
Roman Catholic 48
Methodist 80
Pentecostal 182
United Reformed Church 17
'House church'/Restoration movement 187
plus 45 other denominations represented

End of formal education:
School – left at sixteen or before 332
School – left at seventeen or eighteen 142

Technical college or equivalent 254
University (including postgraduate study) 632
Other training (*e.g.* nursing,
    apprenticeship, *etc.*) 520
Blank 10

Charismatic gifts:

	Used in the past	Used for the first time during the conference
Speaking in tongues	1638	68
Interpretation of tongues	559	8
Words of knowledge	1048	158
Prophecy	873	31
Receiving pictures during prayer	1156	102
Recognising the presence of spirits	798	96
Other	312	49

Physical phenomena:

	Experienced in the past	Experienced during the conference
Tingling in hands	959	988
Hand or arm shaking	775	846
Stiffening of body	193	206
Weeping	1197	977
Laughing	661	516
Fluttering of eyelids	455	339
Falling over	725	355
Screaming or shouting	112	81
Hot areas on body	680	723
Changes in breathing	832	752
Behaviour resembling 'drunkenness'	343	205
Other	197	295

Number who felt that a word of knowledge during the conference applied to them: 504

Number receiving prayer as a result of the word of knowledge: 422

Number conveying words of knowledge concerning another person during the conference: 582

Method of receiving the word of knowledge:

Strong intuition 440
Mental picture 175
Pain in part of body 57
Seeing words written 38
Spontaneous utterance 97
Other 63

Cases of prayer received for:

Inner healing 1275
Physical healing 867
Deliverance 171
Other areas 613

On a nine-point scale from 1 = None at all
to 9 = Total healing
Mean (average) assessments of results of prayer for:

Inner healing 6.1
Physical healing 4.8
Dcliverance 7.1
Empowering/gifts of the Holy Spirit 5.8
Any other area 5.3

Appendix C

OTHER TESTIMONIES OF HEALING

In this book I have examined 'ordinary' healings of a relatively non-dramatic nature because these are far more representative than the rarer 'spectacular' ones. In note 11 of my Introduction, note 39 of chapter 1 and note 29 of chapter 5 I have made reference to other, more 'dramatic' cases. Further examples can be found in Rex Gardner's article 'Miracles of healing in Anglo-Celtic Northumbria . . .' in the *British Medical Journal* (1983) or in his book *Healing Miracles* (1986). During my research I heard about a young lady who had been born blind but was healed at a Christian meeting unconnected with John Wimber's ministry. For this reason I excluded it from my research. Details have nevertheless been published on page 16 of the November/December 1988 issue of *Prophecy Today*. The article describes twenty-three year old Christine Newton from Durham who was born blind but after receiving prayer for healing 'felt her eyeballs grow and when she opened her eyes she could see – for the first time in her life! . . . At first her sight was dim but it has become gradually clearer each day. Now she is learning to read and write.'

A close friend of Christine's has confirmed this account and provided some supplementary details. Shortly before her healing Christine had reported to the doctors that her condition was unchanged but that she believed the Lord Jesus Christ was going to heal her. Therefore the doctors had decided to refer her to a psychiatrist. However, when she later reported that her sight had been restored they put off examining her for several months in order to have a 'specialist opinion'. At the time of writing I have not heard the final outcome.

Some of those who filled in questionnaires for me at Harrogate also provided testimonies of healing from earlier conferences, especially the Sheffield one. Again, because they were outside the scope of my research on the Harrogate conference, I did not follow them up through medical channels. However, because they were written at least a year after the events described they do provide some further evidence of the persistence of physical healings. In the two accounts reproduced below it seems difficult to attribute the healings to known medical processes.

Disappearance of a 'painful bony prominence'

At . . . Sheffield, during one of the sessions sufferers of rheumatism were asked to stand up, to be prayed for. I had a painful bony prominence on the inner side of my right wrist; after John Wimber had prayed for healing a member of the team came to pray with me and asked me which joints were affected. I lifted my wrist to show her and found that the prominence had completely disappeared. There has been no reoccurrence of this.

Healing of insomnia and of deafness

At the 1985 Sheffield conference I was prayed for by two young Americans for acute insomnia, which I had experienced from the age of approximately twenty-one years. (Was now forty-seven years old.) Both those praying for me tended to put me off their ministry, with a very casual attitude (and gum-chewing). I had only reluctantly stepped into the aisle as a result of a sharp push from my wife. As there was no apparent known reason for the insomnia, the two team members prayed. I felt nothing, so they prayed again. Still I felt nothing – but they reassured me that the Lord had ministered to me . . . [That night] I had a very good night's sleep, which I put down to real tiredness.

The next day my wife was prayed for, for deafness. She was instantly healed! That night, having gone to bed, she awoke me at approximately 1.30 a.m. I was rather irritated, as from past experience the chances of returning to sleep for me were rather slim. 'What's wrong with you?', I asked. She said that she couldn't sleep because she could hear the alarm clock ticking!! She then reminded me I was healed. I resumed sleep, and have had only *one* night in the past year when I have not slept well.

P.S. My wife still has problems with hearing too much at night!

Appendix D

FURTHER ANTHROPOLOGICAL ISSUES

In this book I have sought to address issues of interest to a wider audience than the more specialist one which normally reads the works of anthropologists or sociologists. Almost inevitably there will be specialists in some fields who will regard my treatment as too superficial, while some laymen might find certain sections too technical. The adage that one cannot please everybody all of the time is particularly true for topics like this which closely impinge on personal feelings and vested interests.

My material also has some wider implications for specialist aspects of anthropology and sociology, two of which I shall briefly address in this appendix.

The 'sick role'

Medical anthropologists and sociologists have often discussed the concept of a 'sick role' as a socially determined phenomenon. Cultures and societies vary not only in the range of ailments which they classify as 'illness' but also in their social expectations about the behaviour of a sick person. An 'illness' needs to be socially recognised as such in order for a person to assume a 'sick role' legitimately. This role has its concomitant privileges and responsibilities: for example, in the West a person carrying an infectious disease may be given the 'privilege' of time off work but assumes the 'responsibility' of avoiding the transmission of the disease to others. Problems can arise if a person seeking a sick role is not recognised as having one (*i.e.*, is suspected of malingering) or if there is no social recognition of 'illnesses' such as abnormal blood pressure which are not 'visible' on the surface and are detectable only through medical instruments. In many societies there are clear procedures for determining whether or not one is 'sick' in the view of that society. Often the crucial step in the assumption of a sick role comes through an official pronouncement by a specialist concerning the presence or absence of an 'illness'.

In this context 'words of knowledge' play an interesting part in suddenly precipitating a person into assuming a 'sick role' even if such a role had previously been unsought. Through choosing whether or not to respond to a 'word of knowledge' a person can decide to adopt or avoid a 'sick role'. If the role is assumed, it lasts only for the relatively short time during which the person receives ministry. In some conference situations, the person might receive 'therapy' from those around, who for that time period take on the 'healer' role. Shortly afterwards, however, it might be that roles are reversed, whereby those who previously assumed 'sick roles' instead take on 'healer' roles, and vice versa. In this process the public responses to 'words of knowledge' continue to determine which people assume the 'sick roles'.

Sometimes the 'illness' might be further redefined through further words of knowledge which supplement or elaborate upon the original one and might reveal the 'real' problem to be emotional or demonic rather than physical. I would add that the anthropological concept of a 'culture-bound illness', referring to illnesses recognised in a particular culture but not by outsiders, encounters anomalies when applied to demonisation. Because orthodox 'Western' or 'cosmopolitan' medicine does not recognise demonic causes for illnesses, it is in this respect at variance with possibly every other culture in the world. The general outlook which sees some illnesses as being caused by evil spirits is not 'culture bound', but the particular view which denies this concept and which is held by most anthropologists is in itself markedly culture-bound.

'Ecstatic religion'

In a book of this title well known to anthropologists and sociologists of religion, I. M. Lewis (1971) argues that in stratified state societies like our own (in contrast to some tribal societies with less conspicuous class structures), 'ecstatic religion' occurs among the oppressed and dispossessed classes of society. His choice of historical examples appears to document his case well, and it is possible that his model does apply to the roots of Pentecostalism, which were particularly strong in working-class and immigrant districts.

The so-called 'revivalist phenomena' such as shaking or falling over, which commonly occur at John Wimber's conferences, would certainly put them into this same category of 'ecstatic religion'. However, the participants at these conferences are almost entirely from the respectable middle classes. They are predominantly professional people from Social Classes I and II such as academics, accountants, clergy, doctors and even psychiatrists. Certainly this was the case at Harrogate, and it appeared to be the same at the Sheffield conference. My study therefore provides a very important exception to the sociological generalisations made by Ioan Lewis, an exception which casts considerable doubt on attempts to explain away these phenomena in terms of relative deprivation theory.

Appendix E

FURTHER THEOLOGICAL ISSUES

In this book my perspective has been that of a Christian social anthropologist who at times has delved into certain biblical issues relating to my findings. Healing ministries also raise a number of other theological questions to which others may be able to provide fuller answers than I can. In this appendix I mention some of these and also give my own personal opinions, perhaps humbly following St Paul's precedent in 1 Corinthians 7:25 ('. . . I have no command from the Lord, but I give a judgment as one who by the Lord's mercy is trustworthy'). My treatment is, however, preliminary and incomplete, because much more might be said on each of these topics.

Where can we find the prayer, 'Come, Holy Spirit' in the Bible?

This question was posed by a Baptist minister in a discussion with me about John Wimber's theology. Wimber himself also asked this question after this prayer produced some of the 'physical phenomena' which I have described in chapter 4. These actual words are not found in scripture, but for that matter neither are most of the words used by virtually every Christian in their personal prayers. The words 'Come, Holy Spirit' are also found at the beginning of the Roman Catholic prayer to the Holy Spirit: I do not know the history of this prayer, but it is possibly of great antiquity.

Certainly one of the very earliest Christian prayers was 'Maranatha': 'Come, Lord Jesus' (Revelation 22:20; cf. 1 Corinthians 16:22). If we can ask Jesus himself to come, then we can do the same in inviting the third person of the Trinity to come to us. Jesus promised that the Holy Spirit would come (John 14:15–31; 15:26–16:15), and he instructed his disciples to wait in Jerusalem until they were 'clothed with power from on high' (Luke 24:49; Acts 1:4–5). Are we to presume that the disciples were content to wait another ten days without praying for the fulfilment of these promises, for the Holy Spirit to come? Certainly later in the book of Acts we read that the Holy Spirit came on people after specific prayer to that effect (Acts 8:15–18; 9:17; 19:6).

In the later history of the church, the Holy Spirit has often been addressed in hymns and songs, some of them written before the widespread 'charismatic renewal' of the twentieth century. Words expressing the same thought as 'Come, Holy Spirit' can be found in many older hymns such as 'Breathe on me, Breath of God' or,

> Come down, O Love divine . . .
> O Comforter, draw near,
> Within my heart appear . . .
> For none can guess its grace,
> Till he become the place
> Wherein the Holy Spirit makes his dwelling.

This second example, which is from a nineteenth-century translation, actually dates from an original written by Bianco da Siena, who died in 1434. Charles Wesley (1707–1788) wrote the hymn 'Love Divine, all loves excelling', which contains the words,

> Breathe, O breathe thy loving Spirit
> Into every troubled breast.

An anonymous writer of the ninth or tenth century wrote a Latin hymn which begins, in its seventeenth-century English version,

> Come, Holy Ghost, our souls inspire,
> And lighten with celestial fire;
> Thou the anointing Spirit art,
> Who dost thy sevenfold gifts impart.

It is therefore clear, even from this limited selection, that there is a very old tradition of such prayers throughout the history of the church.

What evidence is there that the charismatic gifts have continued through the centuries?

This is too big a question for me to deal with in depth here, and I would therefore refer the reader to Appendix A of John Wimber's *Power Evangelism* (1985) or to the historical chapters of Rex Gardner's *Healing Miracles* (1986) for further details. Donald Bridge's *Signs and Wonders Today* (1985) also provides a useful introduction to this topic. On p. 165 of *Power Evangelism* John Wesley is quoted as being of the opinion that there is no scriptural evidence that God has precluded himself from working any miracles in any period of time 'even till the restitution of all things'. Commenting on 1 Corinthians 13, he writes that St Paul 'does not say, either that these or any other miracles shall cease till faith and hope shall cease also, till they all be swallowed up in the vision of God, and love be all in all'. Gardner (1986:145–147) and Bridge (1985:134–137) show clearly that 1 Corinthians 13:8–10 does not refer to any withdrawal of the gifts of tongues or prophecy at any point in history up to and including the present. They both document the continuity of gifts of healing, and Gardner refers also to gifts of knowledge and of tongues in post-Reformation Scotland. In Appendix A of *Power Evangelism* there are references to the gift of prophecy at the times both of Justin Martyr (c.100–165 AD) and of Martin Luther (1483–1546). Bold predictive prophecies are recorded of the Huguenots, and the gift of tongues was attributed to Vincent Ferrer (1350–1419). These examples happen to have been documented at the time, sometimes recorded by the persecutors of groups such as the Huguenots. We are also fortunate in having a good record of the Northumbrian saints left to us through the scholarship of the Venerable Bede, a historian of the calibre of St Luke. It is an open question how many individuals in the past had charismatic gifts (of healing, prophecy, tongues or whatever) which have simply not been documented. Among some groups the charismata might even have been common enough not to warrant special mention after a while. However, what documentation has survived generally refers to the 'famous names' whose ministries were more conspicuous and whose doctrinal positions were at the time regarded as orthodox enough for them to be canonised rather than persecuted.

The evidence is there, but it is fragmentary. I suspect that the reason for this is not theological, but sociological. It is not that God had ceased to pour out his gifts, but rather that the institutionalised church persecuted those who manifested such gifts. This certainly seems to have been the case for the Waldensian community and the Huguenots. John Wesley was of the opinion that even in the second and third centuries AD 'dry, formal, orthodox men began even then to ridicule whatever gifts they had not themselves, and to decry them all as either madness or imposture' (quoted on p. 165 of *Power Evangelism*). We can be *socialised* into expecting or not expecting the miraculous – a process which continues today in churches of *both* 'liberal' *and* 'conservative' or evangelical theological persuasions.

What might motivate opposition to the use of charismatic gifts?

In general, the persecution of Christianity by political powers has not differentiated between charismatic and non-charismatic groups unless they also happen to be differentiated in their attitudes to certain political issues. Instead, opposition to charismatic Christians as a defined group tends to come from those who represent the religious establishment.

Such a pattern can be perceived also in the New Testament. Opposition to the ministry of Jesus was apparently stronger from the Pharisees and 'teachers of the law' than from the

Sadducees. Certainly the latter did eventually combine with the former to have Jesus killed, but the Pharisees and teachers of the law seemed to have opposed the ministry of Jesus almost from the beginning (*e.g.* Mark 2:16, 24). The Sadducees were found in Galilee as well as in Jerusalem (Matthew 16:1), but they rarely questioned or opposed Jesus before his final confrontation with the Sanhedrin. By contrast, the Pharisees and teachers of the law persistently criticised and opposed Jesus, and some of Christ's strongest condemnations were directed at these groups rather than at the Sadducees (*e.g.* Luke 11:37–54; Matthew 22:41–23:39).

On the surface this might be surprising, because the Pharisees were doctrinally much closer to the teachings of Jesus than were the Sadducees. 'Liberal' ideas were held by the Sadducees, who did not believe in any resurrection, angels or spirits (Acts 23:8; Luke 20:27), whereas the Pharisees were much more conservative in their theological persuasions. The Sadducees were described as being in error because they did 'not know the Scriptures or the power of God' (Mark 12:24), a description which would not apply to the Pharisees, who staunchly upheld all scriptural references to the supernatural. They were also so zealous for their faith that Pharisee 'missionaries' would be willing to travel over land and sea in order to win a single convert (Matthew 23:15). Yet it was they rather than the doctrinally 'liberal' Sadducees who bore the brunt of Christ's strongest condemnations.

This antagonism between Jesus and many of the Pharisees might be likened to the situation in countries having several political parties, where the parties further away from the centre often reserve their harshest criticisms for those parties closest to themselves on the political spectrum. Because they are competing for a similar pool of voters, the differences between the parties tend to become emphasised through severe castigations of perceived failings in otherwise similar competitors. In the same way, voters with political views towards one end of the spectrum are more likely to move between parties relatively close to each other in many respects than to vote for a party near the other end of the spectrum.

This is analogous to the indications that Sadducees during the first century might be 'disturbed' by teachings about the resurrection of the dead (Acts 4:1–2), yet no mention is made of converts to Christianity among them. However, the Pharisees, who were doctrinally much closer to Jesus and his disciples, had members who ranged from the sympathetic (John 3:1; 19:39) to the violently antagonistic (Acts 8:1–3; Philippians 3:4–6). Their doctrinal positions were similar enough to those of the early Christians for the Pharisees even to side with Paul against the Sadducees over the issue of the resurrection of the dead (Acts 23:6–9).

Relating this now to the various reactions to John Wimber's ministry, it is clear that those most sympathetic to his teachings are to be found more among the evangelical sections of the church than among the 'liberal' sections. However, it is also from among the ranks of the conservative evangelicals that some of the most vehement critics of Wimber's ministry have arisen. These, rather than the 'liberals', feel most threatened by the kinds of practices associated with the name of John Wimber.

At least three interlinked factors might contribute to the opposition to Wimber among these factions of the evangelicals. First, their churches are among the ones more likely to lose some of their members to more charismatic churches, a process which might be accelerated if those members become influenced by the teachings of a well-known figure like Wimber. A second factor is the threat to these Christians' feelings of *security*, both theological and social. A well-defined theology which allows little or no room for the supernatural today can actually become a 'Linus blanket' for those who hold such a position. Rather than being willing to allow their existing theology to be turned on its head, such people may develop an antipathy to any kind of 'signs and wonders' teaching. An openness to the supernatural can also be threatening to them socially, because they could lose control of church situations where their influence and authority had previously been relatively secure. Reputations could be at stake! Third, the problem can be exacerbated if these people themselves suffer from major illnesses, especially those such as epilepsy or asthma which not uncommonly have demonic dimensions. Rather than facing up to the possible causes of such afflictions, it is 'safer' to rationalise away the possibility of healings today or of Christians being demonised.

Can a Christian be demonised?

Many Christians do not like to admit the possibility of a Christian being demonised, and may try to find some scriptural indication that this cannot be so by searching for texts such as Romans 8:9, 2 Corinthians 5:17 or John 8:36. However, there are also clear scriptural precedents for showing that a backslidden or wilfully sinning believer can become demonised, as indicated by, for example, Luke 22:3, John 6:70, John 13:27 or Acts 5:3. (Some might try to deny that Judas was a 'Christian', but he was certainly one of the Twelve, was entrusted with responsibility for their finances (John 13:29), was apparently regarded by the others as a fellow follower of Jesus, and seems to have participated with the others in the mission of preaching and healing described in Luke 9:1–6.) The controversial verses in 1 Corinthians 5:5 and 1 Timothy 1:20 are often interpreted as referring merely to a form of excommunication, but they might also imply some recognition that the sinning believers who were unwilling to renounce their sin were already in some sense being influenced by demons.

It should be remembered that the Greek term *daimonizomai* refers to a wide range of demonic activity or influence, and for this reason is better translated as 'demonised' than by traditional and somewhat misleading terms such as 'possessed'. Whereas 'possession' nowadays tends to bring to mind extreme forms of demonisation such as that of Legion in Mark 5:1–20, the Greek term *daimonizomai* also refers to the demonic influence over an otherwise apparently 'normal' and 'respectable' synagogue-attender (Mark 1:23), and to the cause of a *physical* rather than a mental illness in the woman who had been 'crippled by a spirit' affecting her back for eighteen years (Luke 13:11).

Demonic influence may begin with temptation, to which even Jesus was subjected (Luke 4:1–13). In this sense all Christians are exposed to demonic pressures. However, the temptations do not in themselves lead to sin unless through a deliberate choice one succumbs to these temptations (James 1:14–15). James writes of a process over time during which the desire might lead to sin, which in turn 'gives birth to death'. All Christians are subject to temptation, are liable to sin and are likely to die, but not all Christians can be said to be 'demonised' in terms of a deeper demonic influence over them.

Contemporary experience nevertheless shows that some Christians – even evangelical and charismatic ones! – do seem to need deliverance from demonic bondages or influences of some kind or other. (Some examples have been given in chapter 2 of this book, and other published examples are available elsewhere (*e.g.* Wimber 1986:111–112, 127–130; Subritzky 1986:39–51).) The demonic activity might be a result of their own sin or even be derived from serious sin committed by an ancestor and passed down the family line to the third or fourth generation. Whatever the route through which the unclean spirit has gained access to the person's life, it is nevertheless possible to expel the demon once certain conditions are met. Particularly important in this process are (1) repentance from sin on the part of the demonised person and (2) the authority vested in the person ministering through belonging to the body of Christ.

This authority given to the believer is imparted because of the victory which Jesus has won over the forces of darkness through his death and resurrection (Colossians 2:15). It is an authority which is imparted to those who belong to the church, the earthly body of Christ (Matthew 10:1; Mark 16:17), and it is an authority which the demons recognise even when it is invoked by those who do not know Christ for themselves (Matthew 7:22; Acts 19:13–16). For this reason it is only in the New Testament that the Bible gives any descriptions of the expulsion of demons from people.

Old Testament precedents for a doctrine that believers can be demonised are therefore problematic, but Wimber (1986:129) does cite the example of Saul, who had been anointed by the Holy Spirit and prophesied but after serious sin exhibited symptoms of demonisation such as 'fits of anger, murder, fear, witchcraft and suicide'. The behaviour of the old prophet at Bethel who lied to a 'man of God' but then prophesied against him (1 Kings 13:11–22) makes me wonder whether or not he too might have been demonically influenced. A similar problem occurs in 1 Kings 22:1–28, which describes the confrontation between Micaiah son of Imlah and a group of official 'court' prophets apparently led by Zedekiah son of Kenaanah. These 'court' prophets are not specified as being prophets of Baal, as were those described in 1 Kings 18 who were killed; but certainly Zedekiah son of Kenaanah was prophesying falsely in the name of Yahweh, according to 1 Kings 22:11, 24. Might these have been Old Testament counterparts to demonised charismatic Christians?

Further theological complications arise out of this passage because the lying spirit in 1 Kings 22:19–25 is depicted as coming from God. It might be compared with Exodus 20:3–6, which in the context of idolatry refers to God punishing the children for the sins of the fathers 'to the third and fourth generation of those who hate me'. Doctrines based on this passage in Exodus can easily lead to distortions or misunderstandings of the kind which were to at least some extent rectified by Jeremiah, Ezekiel and Jesus (Jeremiah 31:27–30; Ezekiel 18; John 9:1–3). Some charismatic Christians of our own day have used Exodus 20:3–6 (and similar teachings in Exodus 34:7) to provide a biblical justification for their practical experiences in deliverance ministries, because they have discovered cases of unclean spirits being passed on in families as a result of serious sin in a former gencration (Wimber 1986:130; Subritzky 1986:118–119, 123–124).

According to such a theology, the judgement referred to in Exodus 20:5 and 34:7 might be interpreted as indicating that God allows unclean spirits to enter families through the withdrawal of his protection on account of their engaging in sin such as idolatry. New Testament passages such as Romans 1:18–32 or 2 Thessalonians 2:9–12 might be used to support such a view. The method of God's judgement mentioned in Exodus 20:5 might then be illustrated by 1 Kings 22:19–23, in which God allows a lying spirit to enter into those who are supposedly his prophets.

Similar interpretations become more strained, however, when applied to 1 Samuel 18:10, which mentions an 'evil spirit from God' as afflicting Saul. An exposition which claims that this 'really' means the *withdrawal* of God's Holy Spirit, and that this was viewed as equivalent to God sending an evil spirit, tries to evade the obvious sense of the passage by attempting to avoid attributing evil to God. However, elsewhere in the Old Testament similar ideas about God can be found. For example, the words ascribed to God in Isaiah 45:7 are translated by the NIV as 'I bring prosperity and create disaster'. What is here rendered as 'disaster', and is translated as 'woe' in the Revised Standard Version, is regarded by Sanford (1982:223, n. 11) as

an indefensible translation of the Hebrew 'ra', especially since elsewhere the R.S.V. almost invariably translates 'ra' as 'evil'. We must assume that this error comes from the subjective prejudice of the translators that God cannot be thought to be the author of evil, a prejudice not shared by the Old Testament.

This problem is further intensified by the opening chapters of the book of Job, which depict Satan as actually in the presence of the Lord and given divine permission to afflict physically a righteous man. This is a problem for those who assume that the fall (or deposition) of Satan both preceded the fall of man and also at the same time resulted in Satan's expulsion from heaven. Isaiah 14:12–15 and Ezekiel 28:12–19, both of which are in the past tense, are often interpreted as descriptions of the fall of Satan because the language employed seems to refer to a spiritual ruler more than to a human monarch claiming either divine kingship or divine descent. On the surface the passages refer to the kings of Babylon and of Tyre respectively, but behind the human rulers may also be discerned spiritual rulers of the kind described in Daniel 10:13 as 'the prince of the Persian kingdom'. These spiritual rulers are not necessarily to be identified with Satan himself, who in Luke 4:5–6 claims authority over 'all the kingdoms of the world' (cf. 1 John 5:19). (Presumably political defeats of Babylon and Tyre on earth were accompanied by angelic victories over their spiritual rulers in the heavenly places.)

The timing of the fall of Satan himself is described only in the New Testament. When the kingdom of God came as an offensive thrust involving the casting out of demons through the ministries of Jesus and his followers (Matthew 11:12), the result was given in a vision in which Jesus saw Satan fall like lightning from heaven (Luke 10:18). This vision was finally fulfilled through the death and resurrection of Christ himself, shortly prior to which Jesus announced, 'Now . . . the prince of this world will be driven out' (John 12:31). Colossians 2:15 shows that other 'powers and authorities' were 'disarmed' at the same time. Revelation 12 describes the same confrontation. The 'son, a male child, who will rule all the nations with an iron sceptre' referred to in Revelation 12:5 is usually interpreted as a reference to Christ, in the light of Psalm 2 (esp. v:9), which is normally viewed as a messianic prophecy (cf. Acts 4:24–28). In Revelation 12:5 this 'male child' was 'snatched up to God and to his throne', an event which is immediately followed by a description of 'war in heaven' (v.7). The result of the contest between two opposing sets of angels (led by Michael on the one side and 'the dragon' on the other) was that 'The great dragon was hurled down – that ancient serpent called the devil, or Satan, who leads the whole earth astray. He was hurled to the earth, and his angels with him' (v.9). Satan's downfall from heaven is seen as being a result of Christ's ministry on earth 'to destroy the devil's work' (1 John 3:8) and to usher in the forceful advance of the kingdom of God.

This forceful advance is accompanied by the first mention in the Bible of the expulsion of unclean spirits who had formerly been exercising control over people. A deliverance ministry of this nature was inaugurated by Jesus, who conferred on his disciples the authority to do likewise (Matthew 10:1). It is shortly after they began to exercise this authority that mention is made of the forceful advance of the kingdom of heaven (Matthew 11:12). Nowhere in the Old Testament was this kind of authority exercised. Only with the coming of Christ, heralded by John the Baptist, is there an intensification of the confrontation between God and Satan which results in the expulsion of demonic activity from out of human bodies. Previously there were allusions to conflicts in the heavenly realms (Daniel 10:13), but now the battleground is manifested more clearly on earth too.

Perhaps some light might be shed on this process by the parable of the wheat and the weeds in Matthew 13:24–30, 36–43. At first it is very difficult to distinguish between the two types of plant, and in the same way Old Testament allusions to the influences of spiritual powers do not always clearly distinguish between those belonging to God and those belonging to Satan. (Cf. 2 Samuel 24:1 and 1 Chronicles 21:1, passages apparently referring to the same event but in the one case attributing the initiative to God and in the other case to Satan.) I would suggest that a gradual and prolonged process of differentiation was taking place, along similar lines to that described in the parable of the wheat and the weeds.

This time lapse might have been 'in order that sin might be recognised as sin', through allowing its results to come to clear fruition (cf. Romans 7:13). A similar concept can be found in God's words to Abraham in Genesis 15:16, 'In the fourth generation your descendants will come back here, for the sin of the Amorites has not yet reached its full measure.' When, four generations later, it did reach its full measure, it was to be destroyed (Deuteronomy 20:16–18), just as Christ came to destroy all the works of the evil one (1 John 3:8) and to bring about the ultimate demise of Satan himself (Revelation 20).

The parable of the wheat and the weeds similarly speaks of a sudden separation at harvest time. What previously had grown together was suddenly separated into two groups, the one destined for destruction and the other for preservation. A very similar picture is presented in Matthew 24:36–41, 25:1–13 and 25:31–46. If the first coming of Christ resulted in some kind of differentiation in the heavenly realms, his second coming will produce a similar effect on earth.

What is God's view of the church?

Outspoken critics of Wimber such as Roy Livesey or Dr Peter Masters have criticised Wimber for sharing conferences together with Father Francis MacNutt, a Roman Catholic priest, or for distributing MacNutt's book on healing at conferences such as the one in Sheffield. John Wimber has even been reported as 'putting his weight behind the Catholics'(!).

These attitudes are symptoms of a more fundamental question: what makes a person a Christian? In the New Testament there are two criteria used in defining a Christian: one is doctrinal, the other experiential. The doctrinal criterion is illustrated by Romans 10:9, 'if you confess with your mouth, "Jesus is Lord," and believe in your heart that God raised him from the dead, you will be saved'. However, the same writer also states, 'no-one can say, "Jesus is Lord," except by the Holy Spirit' (1 Corinthians 12:3), thus combining both the experiential and the doctrinal dimensions.

The experiential definition of a Christian in the New Testament lays stress on the Holy Spirit's activity in a person's life. In Romans 8:9, St Paul writes, 'if anyone does not have the Spirit of Christ, he does not belong to Christ'. A similar stress on the work of the Holy Spirit is found in John 3:3–8: it is on these experiential grounds that many 'born again' evangelicals separate themselves from 'nominal' believers.

In 1 John 4:1–3 and 1 Corinthians 12:3 the *doctrinal* test of the presence of the Holy Spirit focuses on the nature and Lordship of Jesus. Although the 'Spirit of truth' guides believers 'into all truth', he takes from what belongs to Jesus and makes it known to us (John 16:12–15); Jesus himself is 'the truth' (John 14:6). Personally, I find it difficult to believe that these words are meant to guarantee that every Spirit-filled believer will be doctrinally correct, when at the time of writing there are debates in the pages of *Renewal* magazine reflecting divergences among charismatic Christians on matters such as the role of women in the church or Christians' attitudes towards the state of Israel. When I reflect on the diversity of denominations represented at the Harrogate conference, I notice that these reflect many different viewpoints towards forms of baptism, church organisational structures, the nature of the Eucharist and many other doctrinal issues. Added to this is the variety of approaches to worship, from the contemplative/mystical to the exuberant/charismatic, a spectrum which does not always correspond to distinctions between 'liturgical' and 'free' styles of service. The outworking of one's faith in terms of verbal evangelism, social concern, healing or political activities, whether at home or abroad, brings a further range of diversity to the church.

In Acts 10 and 11 there is a detailed and repetitious account of the conversion of Gentiles at the house of Cornelius. The importance of this event is further reflected in the allusion to it in Acts 15:7–9. Its significance for us today is that the experiential criterion of who is a Christian took precedence over doctrinal prejudices. God 'purified [the] hearts' of the Gentiles 'by faith' (Acts 15:9). In order to do this he first sent an angel to Cornelius (a Gentile and 'non-Christian'), whose response to the divine instructions seems to have been more immediate and unquestioning than that of Simon Peter. Later God poured out his Holy Spirit on these Gentiles even before they were baptised, apparently overturning the neat procedural order which Peter expected from his doctrine (*cf.* Acts 2:38).

It seems to me that God's view of his church is rather wider than that to which we try to confine it by our doctrines. He pours out his Holy Spirit on women who wear hats in church and on those who do not, on those baptised as infants and on those not yet baptised at all (as in the case of Cornelius). When he freely bestows his Holy Spirit, he also seems to ignore our human distinctions between Catholic and Protestant. As yet there is little, if any, 'charismatic movement' in the Orthodox churches, but I doubt that God would not grant his Holy Spirit also to Orthodox believers who ask him (Luke 11:13).

Are we reading too much into the biblical texts referring to religious experience?

The angel who appeared to Cornelius was described later as 'a man in shining clothes' (Acts 10:30), but elsewhere we have little or no description provided of the angels who appeared to Zechariah (Luke 1:11–20), Mary (Luke 1:26–38), the shepherds (Luke 2:8–15) or Philip (Acts 8:26). Even when there is some description provided, the focus is on the content of the message delivered rather than the visual impressions (Matthew 28:2–7; Luke 24:4–8, 23).

Similarly, we have some descriptions of the content of dreams in the Bible (e.g. Genesis 28:10–16; 40:8–19; 41:1–8; Judges 7:13–15; Daniel 4:5–18; 7:1–28, etc.), but elsewhere the focus is on their import, with no description of their content (e.g. Matthew 2:12, 22; 27:19). To some extent this might be regarded as a stylistic characteristic of a particular author, but it is clear from the numerous references to dreams and angels in the New Testament that no detailed description was felt to be necessary. Nowhere in the epistles do we find instructions on dream interpretation, presumably because this was not perceived as a need. Similarly, St Paul could write to the Corinthians regarding a woman's authority 'because of the angels' (1 Corinthians 11:10), knowing that his meaning would be understood. That phrase has vexed later commentators because they do not know the kinds of teachings which the Corinthian church took for granted. We have to piece together the jigsaw from scattered fragments, by comparing it with similar references such as 1 Corinthians 6:3 (see also note 1 of chapter 3).

The fact is that our theology is based to a large extent on letters which deal with *problem areas* in the early church. We know far more about the problematic doctrines than we do about matters the early Christians took for granted. Even the detailed elaboration of doctrine in Paul's letter to the Romans is to a large extent motivated by a desire to explain misunderstandings about his controversial teachings, as indicated by Romans 3:8. However, there seemed to be no need for him to explain further his allusions to 'the power of signs and miracles' and 'the power of the Spirit' in Romans 15:19. Why was there no need for him to elaborate on these matters? Presumably these were areas about which the Roman Christians had no doctrinal problems.

Similarly, we know from Acts 14:3–10, 19:11–12, 20:7–12 and 28:7–10 that Paul exercised a healing ministry in which he often saw dramatic results, but nowhere in his letters does he provide instructions on how to pray for the sick. While personally preaching and teaching in Corinth he presumably trained those with gifts of healing (1 Corinthians 12:9), but this was not a gift he needed to give further teaching about in his later letters. His few scattered references to such phenomena take for granted that healings and miracles were taking place in Corinth, Galatia and probably elsewhere (1 Corinthians 12:9–10; Galatians 3:5 – note the present tense).

These miracles were performed 'through the power of the Spirit' (Romans 15:19). We may infer from 1 Corinthians 2:4 and 2 Corinthians 12:12–13 not only that they took place in Corinth but also that Corinth was not exceptional. Philippi was one of the cities in the area 'from Jerusalem all the way around to Illyricum' (modern-day Albania) referred to in Romans 15:19, and Paul instructed the church there to put into practice whatever they had learned, received or heard from him or seen in him (Philippians 4:9). We normally think of that verse as referring to Christian character rather than to gifts of the Spirit, but might it actually refer to both?

Paul also prayed for the Ephesians to know God's 'incomparably great power' in their own experience (Ephesians 1:19), the power which was seen in Christ's resurrection (Philippians 3:10) and which, by comparison with Acts 1:8, might be interpreted as including gifts of the Holy Spirit which are particularly important in evangelism. A similar expression is used in Colossians 1:29, but there refers to Paul's own experience of Christ's power, as also in Romans 15:19. It is noticeable that Paul himself had visited neither Colosse nor Rome at the time of writing his letters to those churches, and there is no clear indication that he was aware of 'signs and wonders' ministries in those places. Rather, he expected them as a matter of course in the churches where he himself had set an example for the believers to follow (1 Corinthians 11:1; cf. also 14:5, 18).

From the scattered references to them in Acts 16:9–10, 23:11, 27:23, 2 Corinthians 12:3–6 and Galatians 1:12 we know that Paul received a number of visions, at least three of which occurred at night and might almost be classified as dreams. However nowhere in his letters or in any other New Testament writings do we find any doctrinal exposition about visions or dreams. It is quite possible that such teaching was given to the believers while Paul or other church leaders were present in person, but that there was no need for further clarification or elaboration in letters written later. Hence a view of normative Christian life which emphasises the contents of the epistles might actually present a distorted picture of the early Christian worldview.

In the same way, what to us is an obscure reference to 'words of knowledge' would have been readily understood by Paul's readers in Corinth, who would also have been familiar with the other spiritual gifts mentioned. The fact that Paul had no need to discuss 'words of knowledge' in the depth devoted to the gifts of prophecy, tongues and the interpretation of tongues further indicates that the 'message of knowledge' was not a problem area for the believers there.

The problems arise for contemporary Christians who are unfamiliar with divine revelation through dreams, angels or 'words of knowledge' and who seek to reconstruct the common experience of the early church. Such a reconstruction can, however, be aided by a consideration of contemporary experience. This is not an 'academic' exercise like that of the archaeologist who takes clues about the meaning of past artifacts from comparisons with contemporary tribal customs (which may or may not be the same as in the past), but rather it is a dynamic exploration into the nature of God himself, who in some ways may act today as he did in the first century but in other ways may have fresh surprises for the present generation.

What did Jesus mean when he promised that those who believe in him 'will do even greater things' than he was doing (John 14:12)?

I have heard a missionary rationalise John 14:12 by saying, 'What could be a greater miracle than for somebody to come to know Christ?' But, quite frankly, this is a cop-out. The context of Christ's words shows clearly that he was not speaking of verbal evangelism (as this missionary would prefer to believe); rather, Jesus was speaking about the 'works of the Father' through miracles. Verse 11 says, 'Believe me when I say that I am in the Father and the Father is in me; or *at least believe on the evidence of the miracles themselves.*' This is immediately followed by the statement, 'I tell you the truth, anyone who has faith in me will do what I have been doing. He will do even greater things than these, because I am going to the Father. And I will do whatever you ask in my name . . .' (vv. 12–13).

The word used for greater 'things' is that normally translated as 'work' or 'works'. Commonly this Greek word *ergon* ('work'), or its plural form *erga*, is used to refer to human work or activity; it is in this sense that St Paul contrasts it with the divine work of salvation. However, its meaning in John

14:12 is best understood in the context of its particular usage by that same author. Although the word can refer to the deeds of men (*e.g.* John 3:19–21; 6:28–29; 7:7; 8:39,41), in eighteen out of twenty-seven usages it refers to the works of Jesus or of God. It clearly refers to miracles in John 7:21, whereas in John 17:4 the singular form (*ergon*) refers to the whole of Christ's earthly work. This 'work' or these 'works' are actually the works of the Father (John 4:34; 5:36; 9:3; 10:32; 17:4). Like signs, they can point men to God and provide a basis for belief (John 5:36; 10:25, 37–38; 14:10–11). It is significant that this is the word which Jesus himself normally uses to refer to miracles in John's gospel. This significance may be indicated partly by the basic meaning of the word, which can be applied to the ordinary deeds of men. 'What to men are miracles, to God and to Christ are no more than "works". This is their normal way of working' (Morris 1971:690).

Moreover, these 'works' of the Father – miracles – are also to be the 'normal way of working' for disciples of Christ (John 14:12). Jesus spoke of his disciples being sent out into the world in the same way as he himself was sent into the world (John 17:18; 20:21). That this commissioning includes 'signs and wonders' through the power of the Holy Spirit is clearer in the accounts by Mark (16:14–20) and Luke (24:46–49; *cf.* Acts 1:4–8), but many missionaries prefer to quote the great commission in Matthew 28:18–20. Even this, however, as John Wimber points out, also includes instructions to perform 'signs and wonders', because the phrase 'teaching them to obey everything I have commanded you' (v.20) – especially after the reminder in verse 18 about Christ's authority – actually includes the instructions given previously in Matthew 10:1 for the disciples to 'drive out unclean spirits and to heal every disease and sickness'.

In John 5:20–21 Jesus also speaks of 'greater works' when he says, '. . . to your amazement he [the Father] will show him [the Son] even greater things than these. For just as the Father raises the dead and gives them life, even so the Son gives life to whom he is pleased to give it.' These words were spoken in the context of the healing of the invalid at the pool of Bethesda, the 'one work' accomplished in the Jerusalem area which he later referred to in John 7:21. Whereas Jairus' daughter and the widow of Nain's son were both raised to life in Galilee, Jesus' words in John 5:20–21 *might* be interpreted as indicating a foreknowledge of the raising of Lazarus (*cf.* also John 11:4–6, 11–15) – although his subsequent words in John 5:22–30 refer to the final judgement. There are some who rationalise John 14:12 by reasoning along the following lines: 'What could be a greater miracle than raising the dead? Jesus therefore must be speaking of greater in quantity rather than greater in quality.' Such a viewpoint is a reflection of our own limited imaginations, and perhaps our paucity of 'mountain-moving faith'. Nevertheless I would concede that it is difficult to imagine a 'greater' healing than the raising of Lazarus, unless it be the raising of someone who has been dead even longer. David Pytches (1985:235) does in fact quote the case of a woman who had been dead for four days and who was raised to life.

In John 14:11, Jesus says, 'at least believe on the evidence of the miracles themselves'. Again, what is here translated as 'miracles' is literally 'works'. Do these 'works', or miracles, refer only to healing miracles, or do they also include what are often classified as 'nature miracles'? The fact that John had already recorded the turning of water into wine – through which Jesus' disciples had 'put their faith in him' (John 2:11) – as well as the 'nature miracles' of the feeding of the five thousand and of walking on water (John 6:1–21) would allow us to include both healings and 'nature miracles' as referents of John 14:11. From Matthew 14:28–32 we learn that the 'nature miracle' of walking on water was not confined to Christ alone. Historical and contemporary experience further shows that the miraculous multiplication of food is not limited to the ministry of Jesus either, and can include not only flour, grapes or squash but also cans of milk or lime used for plastering houses (Gardner 1986:13; Laurentin 1986:106–107, 119). I could also cite a letter dated February 1988 from Bryan Thompson, a missionary with Youth With A Mission.

314 HEALING: FICTION, FANTASY OR FACT?

Describing the ministry of their ship, *The Good Samaritan*, at Charlotte Amalie, St Thomas (in the US Virgin Islands), he writes, '60 people arrive for a pastor's breakfast and we watch our precisely proportioned food for the expected 35 people feed all 60 with food left over!'

The fact that these kinds of miracles do occur today also reduces the credibility of another interpretation of John 14:12, namely that it was relatively easy for the Son of God to do these miracles but that it is a more difficult and therefore 'greater' task for us to do them. Both for Jesus and for us, the 'works' are those of the *Father*; we do not do them, it is God who performs them while using us as his channels. Jesus too acknowledged 'it is the Father, living in me, who is doing his work' (John 14:10). Although Jesus had an intimacy with God which was so close that it could be described as being one with God (John 10:30; *cf*. 14:11), he also prayed for his disciples '. . . that all of them may be one, Father, just as you are in me and I am in you . . . that they may be one as we are one: I in them and you in me' (John 17:21–23). That same intimacy with God is available also to us.

Christ's words in John 14:12 about his disciples doing 'greater works' refer to miracles, not merely to healings. The category of 'miracles' – or 'signs' in John's gospel – includes healings, even raising the dead, but is wider still and encompasses the multiplication of food, walking on water or changing water into wine. In 1 Corinthians 12:8–10 'gifts of healing' are distinguished from 'miraculous powers', even if the latter may at times include healings too. Miracles might be distinguished from healings by their apparent transcendence of what we ordinarily take (or mistake) to be the 'natural' order of the universe. As René Laurentin (1986:107–108) has expressed it:

> Speak of cures, and it is still credible, those cures generated at the frontiers of consciousness where biological and psychological processes appear indistinguishable. The nonscientific term *psychosomatic* may serve to describe them. In the multiplication of food, on the other hand,

reason is assaulted. Words fail. The intellectual is at a loss for coherent speech in the attempt to integrate attested fact with the accepted order of things.

Partly this is because the 'accepted order of things' is regarded as immutable: Rupert Sheldrake (1987) has pointed out that the popular view of the 'laws of the universe' imbues them with the attributes of divinity such as omnipresence, omnipotence or eternity, but he then raises the question whether or not these same attributes were there also before the 'Big Bang' (if one subscribes to that theory of the origin of the universe). Alternatively, are these 'laws of the universe' merely temporary – provisional generalisations of how things appear to be at the moment?

It is impossible to assess the extent to which electrical malfunctions might correct themselves by 'natural' means rather than by prayer. One of those I interviewed described to me how he prayed for a faulty electric kettle, believed it was going to work, continued to thank God for what he believed would happen, and about a quarter of an hour later heard the element warming up as the kettle again began to function properly. A woman who also attended the Harrogate conference later wrote to me the following account:

Of course I have no guarantee there is not a natural explanation for these, but to me, unable to afford repairs while out of work, they were little miracles.

1 Spin drier not working. Laid hands on it and prayed, and it was alright after that.

2 Light bulb gone on sewing machine, worked after laying hands on it and praying.

3 Electric fire not working in very cold weather. Laid hands on that and prayed and it worked after that. Also the element looked as if it was new.

Even if these are not 'greater' than the miracles of Jesus, they are certainly *different*. Some healing miracles also involve a transformation of metals or even their appearance from 'nowhere'. The case of Ginny (described on pp. 272–273

of *Power Healing*) includes the unresolved question of how
she would have been able to touch her toes while still wearing
a metal-reinforced corset. One has to presume that it became temporarily flexible in order for her healing to be
demonstrated. The well-attested cases of the miraculous
filling of tooth cavities (see MacNutt 1974:327–333; Gardner
1986:175–184) involve the sudden appearance of gold and
silver fillings perfectly fitted into the cavities and bearing the
imprint of a cross. Their appearance is even more remarkable
considering the impoverished condition of most of the people
into whose mouths they materialised. Such cases seem to be
not merely 'healings' but 'miracles'. There is no record of
similar healings in the ministry of Jesus: are these possibly
examples of the 'greater works' he spoke about?

Another possible example of a 'greater work' is given in
Acts 8:39–40, which refers to a miraculous transportation
from one place to another. No parallel to this is recorded in
the life of Jesus prior to his receiving his resurrection body.
The examples of Enoch in Genesis 5:24 and Elijah in 2 Kings
2:1–18 refer to their being taken directly to heaven, not to a
transportation to somewhere else on earth. A witness to the
credibility of these accounts comes from the *physical* transportation of the body of Ivan Moiseyev ('Vanya') in 1971
from his barracks in the USSR to another world from which
he was afforded a glimpse of the new Jerusalem (Grant
1974:58–60). Another modern parallel to Philip's miraculous
transportation comes from the account quoted in chapter 2 (in
the section on 'relationships with one's mother'), in which a
four year old child is reported to have been miraculously lifted
out of the way of a charging ram. This is not dissimilar to the
angelic interventions which released from prison the apostles
in Acts 5:17–32 and Peter in Acts 12:1–19.

Miracles involving the miraculous multiplication of matter
begin with at least a small amount of the substance to be
multiplied. Nowhere does Jesus produce matter out of 'thin
air', so to speak, unless it be the miracle of the coin in the
mouth of a fish (Matthew 17:24–27). Even this, however, is
normally assumed to be a man-made coin which the fish had

found and attempted to eat, the miracle consisting in the 'coincidence' that a fish in such an unusual state should be the first to be caught at that particular time. Might it be that a 'greater work' is the faith to expect God to produce a coin out of nowhere? Consider the following account from a friend of ours:

> I don't know how old I was – very young, six or under. Every Christmas we used to get a new penny or a few new pennies; it was just a Christmas custom in our family. In the middle of the summer holidays I just started thinking of the new pennies and just wanted one. I asked my mother for one but she said you couldn't get them at this time of year.
>
> I remembered that in Sunday school the teacher said if you want anything, ask God and he'd give it to you. I sat at the bottom of the stairs by the coats and prayed that God would put a shiny new penny in my coat pocket. I put my hand in my coat pocket but no coin was there. Then I remembered my Sunday school teacher had said you should continue to pray, so I kept on praying and feeling in my pocket. I don't know if it was five or ten minutes, but it seemed a good long time. It was then that I found the penny there.
>
> I remember putting it in the palm of my hand and looking at it and it was really sort of shining. I wasn't all that surprised, just pleased because I knew all the time he'd give me one. I went and told my Mum and said, 'Look what God's given me,' and she said, 'Oh yes,' and went on reading.

Jesus said, 'I tell you the truth, anyone who will not receive the kingdom of God like a little child will never enter it' (Luke 18:17). It is easy for adults to dismiss an account like this one because it concerns a child's experience of God, but to do so might result in causing one of the little ones who believe in Jesus to sin (Matthew 18:6) – words spoken with direct reference to children. Children do seem to report miracles which adults might find hard to believe, but if we can believe adult reports of the miraculous appearance of gold and silver dental fillings among poor peasants then it is much easier to believe that God might create a shiny new penny from 'nowhere' in response to a child's persistent prayer of faith. Such a prayer is in this case an expression of innocent trust in God's providence, but it should also be mentioned that after this informant was given the new penny she then decided to pray for a two-shilling piece – but no two-shilling piece appeared!

Matthew's account of Jesus walking on water (Matthew 14:22–33) also includes Peter doing the same until 'he saw the wind', perhaps indicating that Peter could walk successfully over the water, without fear, as long as he kept his eyes on Jesus. On pp. 157–158 of Wimber's book *Power Evangelism* a parallel from the sixth century AD is recorded which, unlike the experiences of children quoted above, involved an adult. However, I wonder whether a contemporary 'greater work' might be for an adult not to walk on water but to run on air? Such an experience has indeed been claimed for our own century, as quoted by Beardsworth (1977:65–66):

Once while out in a field on a well-travelled pathway, across a neighbouring farm of low rolling hills, I was thinking deeply on the subject of Jesus as the Son of God, and some of the miracles recorded in the Bible.

I lifted my eyes heavenward and seemed to see Jesus there in the clouds before me; I began running towards him as fast as I could run – there came into my mind this question: Is this the hour – am I to go now? As long as I kept my eyes and my mind on him I kept rising, running up very fast, but not tiring at all. When I realised that I was several feet above the ground and had passed over a wagon gate across the path or roadway, I became afraid I might fall. The clouds covered him from my view. I looked earthward and was soon back down running, on the ground. No longer was he visible in the clouds, and I was once again an earthbound creature as before.

Beardsworth comments, 'Here there is no question of leaving the body: our contributor rises, body and all, "several feet above the ground" running all the while.'

An experience like this, however, is merely a brief and faint foreshadowing of that time when the fullness of healing and wholeness will come:

For the Lord himself will come down from heaven, with a loud command, with the voice of the archangel and with the trumpet call of God, and the dead in Christ will rise first. After that, we who are still alive and are left will be caught up together with them in the clouds to meet the Lord in the air. And so we will be with the Lord for ever. (1 Thessalonians 4:16–17)

NOTES

Introduction

1 In such a case as this, one has to assume that the perceptions themselves have at least some basis in reality.

2 For those unfamiliar with some of these historical figures, brief introductions can be found in Appendix A of John Wimber's book *Power Evangelism* (1985) and also in the historical chapters of Rex Gardner's book *Healing Miracles* (1986). In his article in the *British Medical Journal* (1983) Gardner includes a discussion of the reliability of Bede's account of Anglo-Celtic Christianity, a question which is also taken up by Bridge (1985:160–165). Gardner's book documents British experiences of healing from the Scottish Reformers onwards. In comparing them to the waves which gradually move up the beach, he carries back in time our awareness of the activity of the Holy Spirit in recent centuries, a perspective which is overlooked in the writings of C. Peter Wagner, followed by Wimber (1987:7, 27–32), who refers to the current wave of healings and 'power encounters' as the 'Third Wave' of the Holy Spirit in the twentieth century. It might be the 'Third Wave' of this century, but the tide has been coming in since long before the beginning of the twentieth century.

3 Masters 1987:2–3.

4 Baldwin 1987:24.

5 D. Pytches 1987:164.

6 Stafford 1986:18.

7 Sullivan 1987:27.

8 Virgo 1988:3–4.

9 An example of this process can be seen in the cases cited by Professor Verna Wright (1987).

10 *Equipping the Saints*, January–February 1987 issue, p. 10.

11 *ibid.*, pp. 11, 13. Jennings had been diagnosed at the Queen

Elizabeth Hospital in Birmingham as having sarcoidosis, 'a rare and potentially killer disease with no known cure'. He returned to the same hospital less than forty-eight hours after John Wimber had prayed for him, where blood tests and a Kveim test showed no trace of the disease and an X-Ray showed the lymph gland to have made 'a tremendous improvement', though there was still some residual damaged tissue which would eventually heal by itself. At the Eye Hospital the following day Dr Baig was very surprised to find no trace of any nodules in Jennings' eye. In a taped interview Dr Baig told Jennings:

> When I examined your eye (at first) under the microscope I found inflammation and the iris was filled with minute nodules. When I examined you again nine days later I must admit that I was very surprised that all the nodules had completely disappeared. I wrote, 'NO NODULES!' in large letters in your notes and thought it was very unusual to have seen such a big improvement in the condition of your right eye in such a short period of time. Medically I couldn't give a reason why the nodules in your eye had disappeared so quickly.

12 Gardner 1983:1932.
13 I should point out that my report on the Sheffield conference reached John Wimber via a circuitous route through Dr John White, the Christian psychiatrist and author, to whom I had sent a copy of my original article. It therefore came as a great surprise to receive a telephone call from Kevin Springer seeking permission to publish the article as an appendix to *Power Healing*.
14 I included a fourteen-page Preface to my PhD thesis (submitted to Manchester University in 1984) which discussed this issue in some depth. My comments on how one can study Japanese religion as a committed Christian also apply to a study of forms of Christian religious experience in which one may be an anthropological participant-observer in a fuller sense of that term.
15 One anthropologist has pointed out a loosely organised morass of 'beliefs' which are probably held at least in part by many anthropologists without holding a clear conceptual framework in which to incorporate them. He writes, 'not to "believe in" phenomena such as trances, stigmata, possession, levitation,

walking on hot coals without being burned or skewering the cheeks without leaving a wound – which are all above or beyond the natural, not found in nature – is surely equivalent to being a "flat-earther"' (Burridge 1969:4, n. 2). Christians too may believe that such phenomena do occur, but might attribute them in at least some cases to demonic agencies (Subritzky 1986:131–132).

16 Southwold 1983:8.

17 At the beginning of most interviews I was asked whether or not I was a Christian, and my affirmative answer seems to have reassured people when sensitive and sometimes very personal matters were discussed. However, in one case it took about half an hour to allay (perhaps not completely) one couple's suspicions. In another case an interviewee requested the interview to take place in the presence of her vicar and his wife.

18 There is some indication that the response rate was affected by language problems, in so far as those with addresses outside of Britain and Ireland accounted for 8% of those registered for the conference but only 5% of those who filled in my questionnaire. It seems that some people filled in the forms in a hurry just before they were collected in, as indicated by a comment on one form that there was insufficient time to give more details; this probably also accounts for the hundred or more completely blank forms which were scattered throughout the questionnaires handed in to the stewards. It was nevertheless considered better to have the forms collected in at the conference itself, just before the final session, than to ask people to post them to me afterwards, because this alternative method would probably have produced a much lower response rate.

There is no indication at all that one sex was more likely than the other to fill in the form, as the sex ratio was within 1% of fifty-fifty, both for those who filled in the questionnaire and for those registered for the conference whose sex could be ascertained.

It is known that in at least some cases individuals shared the conference registration fee and identity badge by going to alternate days of the conference. This was the practice of some married couples and of some friends unable to have time off work for the whole conference. It is possible that individuals who attended for only part of the conference may have felt it inappropriate for them to fill in questionnaires.

19 Three of these seven lived outside Britain, and travel expenses
    were not available for interviewing them personally. The other
    four were not available for various reasons during the periods
    when I was trying to interview people in their parts of the
    country.
        In the original random sample there were three others living
    on the continent of Europe and two in Ireland to whom postal
    questionnaires were sent but not returned. A further three
    people with British addresses at the time of the conference
    were uncontactable the following summer; substitutes for
    these were chosen by continuing to use the random number
    table. In the same way substitutes were selected for the five
    people who refused to be interviewed (sometimes giving
    reasons such as the recent death of a husband, or moving to
    another part of the country) and for the one person who was
    not available when I visited his part of the country and who did
    not send back a postal questionnaire.
20 Initially I sent out extra copies of the questionnaire I used in my
    follow-up interviews, but only 40% (eighteen out of forty-five
    people) filled these in, sometimes returning them months later.
    A slightly higher response rate of 46% (twenty-seven out of
    fifty-nine people) was obtained by sending out a letter indicat-
    ing my principal area of interest in that person's experience and
    asking for accounts of subsequent developments. Stamped
    addressed envelopes were included for all those living in
    Britain or Northern Ireland.
21 In a number of places I indicate the probability of a statistically
    significant association being due to chance alone. If there is just
    one in a hundred chance of such an association being due to
    coincidence, this is written as $p = 0.01$. In many cases it is
    sufficient merely to state that the probability is less than 1%,
    written as $p = <0.01$. In a large sample such as the 1890 people
    who filled in my Harrogate questionnaire, associations having a
    probability of chance occurrence of 1% or less are regarded as
    statistically significant. For smaller samples such as the hun-
    dred randomly chosen people followed up six to ten months
    after the conference, or for particular sub-groupings of those
    who filled in the Harrogate questionnaire, a probability level of
    5% can be regarded as statistically significant. This is written as
    $p = 0.05$. As this is the boundary marker for statistical signi-
    ficance, it is usually sufficient to state '$p = <0.05$' if the probabil-
    ity of an association being due to chance is below the 5% level.

22   Among those who filled in my questionnaire there were
     252 ministers of religion, 129 missionaries or other full-time
     Christian workers, twenty-eight identifiable wives of clergy
     (two of whom had nursing training), thirty-nine doctors, 133
     nurses, seven dentists, six pharmacists, two psychiatrists, and
     seventy-two others in health-related occupations such as
     physiotherapists, dietitians, radiographers and so on.
23   For details about the 'Restoration movement', see Walker
     1988.
24   One woman wrote on her questionnaire that this was her 'tenth
     Wimber conference'. I presume she had attended some of
     these outside Britain.

1   Physical healing

1   Smillie 1980:161–168.
2   Personal communication from David Wilson, Dean of Post-
    graduate Medical Education at the University of Leeds.
3   Professor Verna Wright, a critic of John Wimber's ministry,
    writes, 'I know a church where a person came out thrilled
    because a leg had been seen to grow half an inch. However, it is
    impossible to measure accurately a difference of half an inch in
    the leg. I have tried for years to do it, and you cannot do it, not
    even with X-rays.' (1987:7). While that may be the case for a
    difference of half an inch, Professor Wright does not consider
    cases of one-and-a-half inches or two-and-a-half inches, re-
    ports of which have been related to me and which in the latter
    case enabled the woman in question to give up wearing a shoe
    with a built-up heel.
4   The quotation is from the NIV alternative rendering of Matthew
    6:27.
5   This is Blaine Cook, one of Wimber's assistants.
6   In anthropological jargon these are called the 'emic' and 'etic'
    views respectively and to some extent these are equivalent to
    the differences between the worldviews of the Third World and
    the 'Western worldview' as discussed by John Wimber (1985,
    ch. 5). Although Wimber focuses in particular on religious
    aspects of worldviews, there can also be great cross-cultural
    differences in perceptions regarding medicine, the exchange of
    goods, social status and so on.
7   Although her opinion is presented as subjective evidence,

whereas a repeat hearing test might be viewed as objective evidence, hearing tests rely very largely upon the patient's own response (or lack of it) to certain stimuli. Whereas previously the retired missionary's hearing had been below the threshold marked by the ticking of her watch, it is now reported to be above that same threshold. If the ticking of the watch can be regarded as having a constant sound level – an assumption allowable in the present context – then this does provide a simple and objective test for measuring the person's hearing. It is very similar to the case of a person who says, 'I once was blind but now I can see.'

8   Gardner 1986:164–165.

9   See also Appendix C for further cases.

10 In his article in the *British Medical Journal* Gardner (1983:1932) writes that 'proof' of miraculous cures is 'probably impossible' but that the adjective 'miraculous' is permissible as a convenient shorthand for 'an otherwise almost inexplicable healing which occurs after prayer to God and brings honour to the Lord Jesus Christ', but in his later work (1986:206) he concludes that 'A belief in the occurrence of cases of miraculous healing today is intellectually acceptable.'

11 For an example of the healing of a cold from psychosomatic factors, see Gardner 1986:29–30.

12 The next day the man in question told my informant, 'This is the first time I've not got any pain in my feet'; he noticed it the first time when he got out of bed that morning.

13 Because of this she remained where she was during the coffee break. During the ministry time afterwards she was not involved in praying for anybody else so remained praying in tongues by herself and 'got lost in praising God – as if there was me and God and nobody else'. Meanwhile the sensations in her back were getting stronger and stronger with a heat which 'would have felt like a furnace but not uncomfortable'. She was unaware that people around her were praying for her in obedience to John Wimber's pointing her out as someone on whom the Holy Spirit was working. Ginny said:

> I didn't realise they were praying for me – I did realise he [God] was blessing me but I just thought he was empowering me for service. After a while I realised others around me were praying. I opened my eyes and saw myself eyeball to eyeball with a man who said God was working on my back. I

wondered how he knew and then realised [God had] been doing it all night . . .

I've always had a back problem since childhood because even before I couldn't touch my toes. There was only one way to find out – do it. I went into the aisle and did it. I had a corset with 8 metal rods in it – my brain stayed with my toes! It was not as if 3,000 people were there but as if God was dealing with me since I went into the building. God did do something that night – a purely *physical* experience . . .

In addition to receiving healing for her back, Ginny also discovered that she had been healed at the same time of a bowel problem. Moreover, she no longer has any pain at all in her leg or foot, a problem which had been present even after her operation and for which the healing is not attributable to her surgery.

14 In John 5:14, Jesus tells the crippled man who had been healed, 'Stop sinning or something worse may happen to you.' This might be interpreted as implying that the healing was also conditional upon a moral reform. We may also distinguish between temporary healings and conditional healings, in so far as those who are brought back to life might be healed 'unconditionally' in terms of their moral lives but their healing is still in some sense 'temporary' because they eventually die again for one reason or another. David Pytches (1985:232–253) does however cite one modern day case of raising the dead in which the man's continuing life was said to be conditional upon repentance in his family. The family repented and the man lived for another thirty years.

15 It is noticeable that Samson's strength was a gift of the Holy Spirit, as indicated by the repeated expression 'the Spirit of the Lord came upon him in power' (Judges 14:6, 19; 15:14) and the comment in Judges 16:20 that 'the Lord had left him'. It is important to note that the outward manifestation of super-human strength can be from the Holy Spirit, in this case, but can also be from demonic sources, as in the case of Legion (Mark 5:2, 4). The outward manifestation does not in itself prove its origin and it is important to examine the context and results of the gift in order to discern its source. (I shall discuss this further in chapter 4.) Samson's weakness was his being attracted to Philistine women, although in Judges 14:4 his desire to marry such a woman is reported to be 'from the Lord, who

was seeking an occasion to confront the Philistines'. Even after sleeping with a prostitute his strength did not leave him (Judges 16:1–3) but it did so after his hair was cut in contravention of the specific instruction given through an angel in Judges 13:5. This raises the question of whether or not there are specific sins which might lead to an immediate withdrawal of God's grace and to what extent God continues to be merciful towards us while our behaviour falls short of the standards normally expected of us. (Compare also the teaching of Jesus about divorce in Matthew 19:3–9.)

16   Gardner 1986:189.

17   To contemporary eyes the passage in 2 Kings 2:23–24 appears to involve an excessive punishment for the youths' jeering at Elisha's baldness, but it should be noted that these are 'youths', not young children, who would have been socialised in a culture which accords high respect to older people. People brought up in East Asia or West Africa who have lived and worked in Britain have told me how shocked they were at the disrespect paid to older people in this country. (Sometimes missionaries to such cultures have unwittingly caused offence by appearing to have a relatively disrespectful attitude to older people.) In this cultural context the youths' jeering at Elisha violated the expected respectful behaviour which the Bible itself advocates and which many other cultures today practise more than we do in the West.

18   Gardner 1986:164.

19   I shall not here delve into the question of whether or not healing is 'in the atonement', a question which hinges in particular on the exegesis of Matthew 8:16–17. The theological questions have been discussed to some extent by Rex Gardner (1986:159–164) and more recently in some depth by Tom Marshall (1988, esp. ch. 3).

20   Some people who have reflected on the growth and vitality of many churches in countries where they have suffered oppression have suggested that perhaps the church 'needs suffering' in order to purify it. However, even if there has been a substantial growth in the numbers of Christians in China in recent decades, the same pattern of growth during persecution has not necessarily been the case for the churches in some countries with a predominantly Muslim population.

21   The parallel quotation in Luke 14:34 follows teaching in verses

25–33 on discipleship in which Jesus makes it clear that to follow him may involve suffering and hardship.

22   His article 'Why Must Christians Suffer?' has also been published by British Youth For Christ in the April 1988 issue of their publication *Frontline* (p. 6). Further teaching by Wimber on this theme is contained in his tape series 'Trials, Testing and Suffering', available from Vineyard Ministries International.

23   Billheimer 1977. One type of 'explanation' for illnesses which is not often mentioned is the idea that God can use it as a form of guidance. (This might be behind Paul's comment in Galatians 4:13.) An example of this occurred in my own experience in 1988 after moving to a different town, where we wanted to visit a number of churches before deciding which one to join. One Sunday I woke up feeling nauseous and sick, as a result of which my wife decided to revisit a church we had already attended instead of going to a new one without me. That afternoon the church was having a March of Witness and one of the organisers promised our eldest son to keep some tracts for him to distribute. I was well enough to accompany Daniel, then aged five, on the March and supervise him as he gave out the tracts. He was actually much more effective than many of the adults because those who were hesitant about receiving literature from an adult were much less inhibited about taking it from a child. In this instance my illness meant that God was able to use my son more effectively.

24   Vickery 1986.

25   Thalidomide is an example of a therapeutic measure, while an example of unintended side-effects from a preventative measure is the effects of whooping cough vaccine on certain children.

26   See Exodus 23:19b and Deuteronomy 14:21b (*cf.* also Leviticus 22:28). The traditional Jewish interpretation of this prohibition on boiling a kid in its mother's milk is that one should not eat meat and dairy products together. This has led to an elaborate series of rules on how long to allow in between eating them so that they do not mix in the stomach, in addition to the practice of keeping separate dishes for meat and milk products. If this were the meaning of the verse, why is it not spelled out far more explicitly, as other dietary and ceremonial laws are? Moreover, in Genesis 18:3–8 it is clear that Abraham served meat and milk together which were eaten without objections by his visitors, one of whom is identified as 'the Lord'. This was

before the Mosaic law was given, but why should the Lord accept such a meal at one time and later ban it? I prefer to interpret the verses in Exodus 23:19b and Deuteronomy 14:21b as meaning 'Do not use as an agent for death that which God created to be an agent for life.' In the same way a cloak taken as security for a debt was to be returned at night (Deuteronomy 24:13), charging of interest on 'money or food or anything else' was forbidden (Deuteronomy 23:19; Leviticus 25:37) and land was to return to its original ownership in the year of Jubilee (Leviticus 25:8–28). What God has provided for life, let not man exploit for personal gain to the detriment of others.

Although most iatrogenic illnesses are unintended there are nevertheless examples of medical techniques being corrupted for political ends, as in Hitler's concentration camps or in the abuse of psychiatry in the USSR as a means of detaining religious believers. Many Christians would also regard abortion and euthanasia as corruptions of the medical techniques which were originally developed in the interests of preserving life.

27 Lock (1980:136) refers to this in the context of East Asian herbal medicine, which Christian missionaries have tended to look upon with suspicion because of the theories of yin and yang, *etc.*, which have become mixed up with it. However, one can accept that a Creator God made the plants containing their own remedies against side-effects without necessarily accepting all the theories which have grown up regarding the use of such herbs.

A possible danger in genetic engineering which seeks to enhance desirable traits is that in so doing it might eliminate elements which are important for counteracting unanticipated side-effects.

28 The New International Version has footnotes which say 'or excessive interest' as an alternative reading to the main reading of the texts which forbids charging of interest altogether. Perhaps it is precisely because we would find it so hard to live without banks and building societies that we try to circumvent the obvious reading of the texts. Similarly Matthew 25:27 is used to justify the practice of lending money at interest, but it should be remembered that (1) this seems to be a 'second best' alternative to the kind of investment of the others (who today might have bought shares in businesses, which involves sharing also in the risks) and (2) we do not take the parable of the

shrewd manager in Luke 16:1–15 as normative behaviour: instead we interpret it as praise of shrewdness, not of dishonesty. (In fact, it might be that the manager had been letting the debtors off the interest which they owed and which his master had charged illegally, but this interpretation may be reading too much into the text.)

29 Vickery 1986:77.

30 Similarly, New Testament teachings advocating forgiveness, love, forbearance, humility and so on can be said to be 'preventive medicine' obviating the need for 'inner healing'.

31 This connection between age and the incidence of people seeking physical healing is statistically significant ($p = 0.0002$) but is not surprising in view of the incidence of degenerative diseases in the older population.

32 $p = <0.001$.

33 Michael Flowers and John Sloan, two medical consultants who have commented on the initial draft of this chapter, have suggested that my findings reflect either the greater *responsiveness* of the young or else the fact that among older people the 'healed' state is 'often one of residual degeneration, hence lesser changes, whereas in the young much more dramatic changes occur'. John Sloan relates this also to the comment by Walter Stockdale quoted earlier (p. 57) about God healing us into dying bodies.

34 One effect of this is that the high numbers of older people reporting lesser degrees of healing tend to swamp out the minority with higher degrees of healing when overall statistics are presented.

35 There are unanswered questions about the demographic structure of the population at that time, in terms of average life expectancies. How common was it for a person to reach the ages of forty, fifty or more? What proportion of the population died in infancy or childhood? Is it fair to assume the population had an age range similar to that of many Third World countries of today, or did Jewish ritual practices such as ceremonial washing actually reduce mortality and produce greater longevity?

There is at least some evidence that life expectancies in biblical times were not as short as those in many developing countries today. Among the patriarchs life spans of 175, 180 and 110 years are recorded for Abraham, Isaac and Joseph respectively (Genesis 25:7; 35:28; 50:22, 26). Such longevity might be attributed to a pastoral, nomadic lifestyle in some cases, but Joseph did not have this for most of his life. Going on to the New Testament, there is the example of Anna in Luke 2:36–37, which is translated either 'she had lived with her husband seven years after her marriage, and then was a widow for eighty-four years' or ' . . . and then was a widow until she was eighty-four'. Perhaps such an individual was exceptional, but from 1 Timothy 5:9 it is clear that it was not uncommon for a widow to be agēd at least sixty.

More circumstantial evidence for relatively high life expectancies comes from the consideration that medieval Jews were sometimes blamed for causing the Black Death because they suffered fewer fatalities on account of the hygienic aspects of their purification practices. The Mediterranean diet is a very healthy one, based largely on wholegrain, olives and grapes plus fish more than meat. For the majority of the population who lived in villages – and even the 'cities' were often the size of small towns of today – there were fewer problems of sanitation and overcrowding which gave rise to the short life expectancies found among inhabitants of British slum areas during the nineteenth century. Similar problems are faced today by many residents of the squatter settlements or 'shanty towns' which have sprung up around most major cities of the Third World. The shorter life expectancies of such people are not to be compared with those of people in biblical times whose conditions of life were in many respects substantially different.

36 Gardner 1986:84–85, 138–140.
37 Pytches 1985:232–239.
38 In chapter 5 I shall argue that major exceptions to these generalisations do occur when healings take place in evangelistic contexts as 'signs' to unbelievers.
39 In chapter 5 I quote the case of a boy who was hit by a car after which 'he was not breathing and was blue'. Although a doctor in the car behind said it was 'serious', it would be difficult to prove that the boy was in fact 'dead' because almost immediately his father commanded him in the name of Jesus to start breathing, and he did so.

The April–May 1988 issue of *Pray for China*, citing the January–February 1987 report from 'Asian Outreach', reports two cases of the raising of the dead. One involved a four year old girl, an only child, who had been dead for twenty hours. As a result of this incident 'many people came to know the

Lord . . .' The other case involved 'a little boy, the only child of a Christian mother and a non-Christian father'. The father had told the boy's mother to take their son away and unless the boy came back to life she was never to return. After the child had been dead ten hours God raised him to life again in answer to his mother's prayers. As a result the father became a Christian and took a month's leave from his job in order to travel with his wife and son testifying to God's power. It is reported that within that month about forty thousand people became believers.

Some years ago I also read an account of an African evangelist who commenced a series of evangelistic meetings by the announcement that if anyone in that town died that week, they were to be brought to the final meeting, where God would raise them to life. At the last meeting the evangelist preached with the corpses of a young boy and an old man lying in front of him. Then the evangelist prayed and both were raised to life: the old man was allowed to die again shortly afterwards but the young boy remained alive. Unfortunately I am unable to trace where I read this account.

40 Abraham and/or Sarah experienced healing from infertility when Abraham was about a hundred years old, but he then lived for a further seventy-five years.

41 $p = <0.01$.

42 $p = <0.001$. For example, comparing the actual number with the expected numbers it is found that among those with university education there are 110 cases of little or no healing as compared with an expected value of 96.14, whereas the 74 people reporting a great deal or total healing falls short of the 88.18 expected value. For the medium range, however, the actual value of 71 is very close to the expected value of 70.67. There is therefore a definite downward shift in the reports of healing among the higher-educated.

43 This is particularly so among those reporting a great deal of or total healing, the 51 people in this range being far more than the 35.96 mathematically calculated expected figure. It should also be noted that those who left school at fourteen or fifteen show less than expected degrees of healing, but this is probably on account of more older people being in this group.

44 Gardner 1986:114–115. Gardner discusses this in the context of refuting the view that the miracles of Jesus were performed to demonstrate his status or divinity.

45 Quoted by Gardner (1986:202–205).
46 Laurentin (1986:21) quotes a Catholic priest working among the Mexican poor, who remarked, 'Proofs of the miraculous you will find only for the rich: there never are any as regards the poor.' However, a few days later this same priest came across photographs documenting the healing of a child who had been unable to walk.

2 Inner healing and deliverance

1 Gardner 1986:30–31.
2 Bennett 1984:21–22.
3 Some possible theories are: (1) Luke or an early scribe copying Luke simply overlooked this line by mistake. (2) Luke was a medical doctor and not a psychiatrist so he was more interested in recording cases of physical healing. (But he seems to be aware of 'inner healing' in Luke 5:20 and the distinction between 'medicine' and 'psychiatry' is a modern one.) (3) Luke did not believe that inner healing was part of the commission of Jesus. (Nevertheless, he did believe that Isaiah 61:1–2 did apply to Jesus.) (4) Luke was quoting from a text in which that line had been missed out for some reason. However, the Septuagint, which Luke was probably quoting, does contain this passage. On balance, I would consider the first theory – that of an accidental omission – to be the most plausible.
4 See also the section in chapter 1 which raises the question of whether or not healings can be conditional.
5 Bennett 1984:36–45.
6 Hunt and McMahon 1985; Livesey 1987:107–120.
7 Wimber 1986:285, n. 1.
8 MacNutt 1974:327–333; Gardner 1986:175–184.
9 Gardner 1986:184.
10 McBain 1986:97.
11 Penfield 1952.
12 Sheldrake 1987.
13 Ritchie 1978:48–53.
14 The links by sex and age are both so highly significant that the probability is 0.0000, meaning that such a correlation has a probability of occurring by chance less than one in ten thousand times. Overall, 40% of the sample reported receiving some kind of prayer for inner healing, but the proportions are 33% of

the men and 47% of the women. There is a steady drop in the percentage of people who received prayer for inner healing from 56% of the teenagers down to 26% of those aged sixty or over.

15   Differences in the degrees of healing reported by women versus men are also highly significant ($p = 0.0000$). For the correlations with both social class and education $p = <0.01$. Although relatively more younger people received prayer for inner healing, the actual degree of healing reported does not differ significantly according to age.

16   *Faith in Leeds*, the report of the Leeds Churches Community Involvement Project, reports that twelve of the city's thirty-three wards are wholly or partly in the city's urban priority areas. These twelve wards contain approximately 75% of the city's houses needing repair, 60% of the city's unemployed people, 60% of the supplementary benefit claimants, 55% of the crimes reported in the city, 50% of the manual workers, 50% of the city's single parents and 40% of the elderly living alone. Similar statistics could be presented for other British cities.

17   In working class areas the Roman Catholic church has remained relatively strong but in the nineteenth century was largely catering for Irish immigrants. Similarly, some West Indian Pentecostal churches have remained active among a particular ethnic minority of the working classes. A relatively high proportion of those from lower social classes who were at Harrogate actually belong to house churches; it remains to be seen whether these fellowships (perhaps aided by emphases on 'power evangelism') will have a significant impact among the English working-class population.

18   There were forty-eight people who received prayer for inner healing, of whom eleven had prayer for two different areas and one person for three areas of need.

19   Another person interviewed was apparently present praying for this man and her account corroborates his description well:

I was praying along with a team member for someone . . . It was something in his past life about his marriage, he needed to confess to someone and hadn't. We really saw the Holy Spirit touch him – a lot of physical signs . . . and a whole change of his face as he received forgiveness. I had a feeling

like a ton of bricks was taken off him. That time I saw the
Holy Spirit manifest physically so obviously.

20 1 Chronicles 4:10.

21 Another man was told similarly that it was 'not lust but a desire
    for comfort'.

22 In the first week or two he did notice a discolouration in his
    urine which seemed to be from semen, but he has not had any
    natural emissions during sleep.

23 M. Pytches 1987; Bennett 1984.

24 I am not here entering into the theological issue of whether or
    not everybody ought to be able to speak in tongues; rather, I
    am presenting the empirical facts as they have been reported to
    me concerning actual human experience.

25 An example of a 'blockage' came from another informant, who
    described praying for a girl who had 'had an abortion a long
    time ago and had forgiven the guy but not herself'. After
    receiving ministry for this area of inner healing, she then
    received the gift of tongues a week or two later. In another case
    recounted to me, the daughter of a practising Freemason was
    unable to receive the gift of tongues until the demonic influence
    from Freemasonry in her family had been broken.

26 The one who gave out the word of knowledge did not know the
    person who responded to his name being specified.

27 He went on to describe how he had taped someone else praying
    in a tongue which sounded like an Indian language. Later he
    played the tape to someone else who identified it as Bengali, his
    translation being almost verbatim with the interpretation on
    the tape. The translator also remarked, 'But he was singing it so
    must have been drunk'!

28 Kissell 1986:109, 111.

29 Wimber (1986:131) writes that 'drug and alcohol abuse com-
    monly open the door to demonic influence'. Subritzky
    (1986:93, 111) describes ministering deliverance from spirits
    of smoking. He writes that these addictions 'sometimes arise
    from sheer habit' and at other times come from 'a sense of
    unworthiness or frustration' (p.111). Their hold over a person
    may nevertheless result in a demonic bondage of some kind.

30 M. Pytches 1987:113.

31 ibid., pp. 58–59.

32 ibid., p. 120.

33 Her husband also testified to a change in his wife since the
    conference, saying 'it has become obvious' to him that his wife

'has a lot more peace nowadays, a lot more ability to . . .
maintain an emotional stability'. Their pastor observed that
she had become 'much more freer now and much more open.
Harrogate certainly helped a lot with that – a major step
forward.'

34   In chapter 4 I cite the opinion of evangelist Don Double that
the way to discern whether or not the experience of 'resting in
the Spirit' is psychologically or humanly induced is through the
resultant effects. However, the case quoted here indicates that
the effects of ministry to deep areas of the subconscious might
not be discernible on the surface.

35   C. S. Lewis (1960:63) writes that if two people who discover
that they have common interests which are not shared by most
others also happen to be of different sexes, 'the friendship
which arises between them will very easily pass – may pass in
the first half-hour – into erotic love. Indeed, unless they are
physically repulsive to each other or unless one or both already
loves elsewhere, it is almost certain to do so sooner or later.'
The fact that the erotic element is mixed in with other types of
love makes it very difficult at times to discern the extent to
which one is motivated by each kind of love, compounded by
an unwillingness to admit to the erotic side. One woman
mentioned in a letter that her husband claims she has ruined
his ministry by her complaints about his counselling
another woman late at night in his car. 'The heart is
deceptive above all things' and we do not like to face up
to all the hidden motivations behind apparently altruistic
behaviour.

36   In 1 Peter 5:14 this is described as a 'kiss of love', which conveys
the meaning of the kiss, whereas the term 'holy kiss' describes
its form. What is 'holy' in one culture might be seen as 'unholy'
in another, as illustrated by northern Pakistan, where men may
kiss other men on the cheek or neck but would not kiss a
woman in public. To them, the practice of publicly kissing the
opposite sex, as in many Western churches, might be viewed as
immoral.

37   I do not wish to imply by this that it is impossible for a deep and
sincere love to develop between two people of opposite sexes in
the church family who are not married to each other. Jesus had
an apparently very close friendship with Mary and Martha as
well as with their brother Lazarus. A number of women
travelled with Jesus and the Twelve (Luke 8:2–3), one of them

being 'Joanna the wife of Chuza, the manager of Herod's household'. It sounds as if Chuza was alive and active in his job, which means that his wife travelled around with Jesus and the Twelve in what we have to assume was a non-adulterous but relatively close friendship.

[In view of the misrepresentations by some people of what John meant in referring to 'the disciple whom Jesus loved', it is worth pointing out that this disciple was probably Jesus' cousin. The link of kinship is a sufficient reason for there to have been a special affinity between them of a non-sexual nature. This connection is established if we follow the traditional identification of 'the disciple whom Jesus loved' as being John the son of Zebedee and also the author of the fourth gospel. Comparing Matthew 27:56 and John 19:25 it is quite likely that 'the mother of Zebedee's sons' was Jesus' mother's sister. (As two sisters would not both have been called Mary, she is probably the Salome mentioned in Mark 15:40.) This would also explain why John, as Christ's mother's sister's son, was entrusted with the care of Jesus' mother, John's aunt (John 19:26). John would also have been related in some way to Zechariah and Elizabeth (Luke 1:36–45), which would explain how John was known to the high priest (John 18:15). It is even possible that John's own name was chosen by Zebedee and his wife after Zechariah and Elizabeth had set a precedent in naming their son John, so the connotations of the name itself would have reminded Jesus of his other relative who had been beheaded because of his prophetic ministry.]

38 A similar comment was expressed about masturbation.
39 See Hay 1982, 1987:173–174.
40 Greeley and McCready 1974:18. (For a more accessible summary of their results see Greeley 1975:61.) Their 'twice-born factor' refers to a particular kind of mystical or religious experience described in terms of bestowing 'new life', feelings of 'being bathed in light', passivity – in which the 'Other' is perceived as the 'active' agent in the relationship – and 'ineffability', a sense that words are inadequate to describe the experience.
41 On a nine-point scale the mean (average) scores of psychological well-being were 5.9 for those whose 'principal' experience was the presence of God as compared with 4.6 for those who had at some time in their lives been involved with spiritualism. The average for all others was 5.7. Using a statistical

technique known as the analysis of variance, the difference between these groups was found to be statistically significant (p = <0.05). On a ten-point scale measuring satisfaction with life, the average scores were 7.5 for the 'presence of God' group, 6.5 for those having had spiritualist involvements and 7.1 for all others. Although this is consistent with the pattern found for psychological well-being, the difference between the groups was not great enough to be statistically significant. (The same overall pattern was also discovered using two different scales of altruism.)

42   The mean (average) score in the Harrogate sample was 6.3 on the scale of psychological well-being and 7.3 for satisfaction with life.

43   One of these also ranked below 5 on the 'satisfaction with life' scale, the only other person to do so being a recently divorced woman.

44   Such stress factors among those interviewed who rank relatively low on the scale of psychological well-being include long-term illness in a spouse, lack of healing for oneself and a difficult relationship with a parent.

45   Jesus often used debt relationships as a metaphor for sin (e.g. Matthew 6:12; 18:21–35; Luke 7:40–49), but in spiritualising this metaphor we too easily lose sight of its practical application. 'Forgive us our debts, as we also have forgiven our debtors' is even more forcibly expressed in Luke 6:35, 'Love your enemies, do good to them, and lend to them without expecting to get anything back.' When expressed in practical monetary terms, this teaching goes against the grain of our debt-ridden society. Forgiveness, or 'wiping off the debt', is often difficult in some family situations of perceived injustice, as illustrated by a woman I interviewed who felt she had made a bad choice in choosing some inherited jewellery and silver. She recognised that her feelings that her sister had got the better share 'may crop up again', even though at the time of the interview she thought the issue was not disturbing her.

46   Anthropologists have a number of theories about the origin of the 'incest taboo', one of the few social institutions which appears to be found in all cultures, their theories tending to focus on either parent–child or sibling incest rather than trying to account for both types together. The sexual abuse of children by parents involves a breach of trust and authority producing a public outcry similar to that which can follow the

discovery of a pastor's sexual relationship with a parishioner. However, incestuous child abuse is far more damaging in its effect on the child, who is not only unwillingly coerced into the sexual involvement (in most cases) but is also damaged emotionally, psychologically, socially and sometimes also physically (La Fontaine 1988:13). This makes incestuous relationships with a child very different to adulterous relationships between consenting adults. I would suggest that the 'incest taboo' could actually arise from a recognition of the damaging effects which such activity can engender in cases of parent–child incest. The evidence for psychological damage is not so clear for sibling incest (*ibid.*, p. 6) but I would not rule out the possibility that it could lead to a tendency to promiscuity in later life. Wimber (1986:137) mentions incest and 'various forms of child abuse' in the context of disturbed family relationships as possible symptoms of demonisation. Whereas most anthropologists would be sceptical of a theory of the origin of the 'incest taboo' as a means of averting demonisation, I suggest it here as a personal hunch. Even if it does not lead to demonisation, it certainly leads to deep inner hurts and emotional or psychological damage when the victim is a child.

47 Some examples given of how this gift operates in the experience of one informant are worth quoting:

> Different spirits appear in different forms. Perversion is like a crocodile – I know it well because I've dealt with it on two occasions. On a homosexual prostitute it had a greenish, long snout; usually I can see the eyes.
>
> Sometimes I can see a look in people's eyes – something not quite right, a peculiar look in the eyes. I've often seen a blackness about a person and prayed, 'Lord, what's going on?' and a word comes to mind such as 'permissive'. Whether it's a sin that hangs on to someone, or a demon, there *is* something there . . .
>
> Spirits of affliction usually look like a black lump on a person, like a small animal clinging on to the person. Myself and A. and another girl all agree together independently – that's been reassuring. Sometimes it's just a matter of approaching someone and saying, 'I think you have a problem with—.' I did that once and he dealt with it; I don't know what he did but it went without any heavy deliverance.

48   For example, after my wife and I had been in Japan only a few
     weeks we visited a mountain on the summit of which there is a
     large Buddhist temple and around the sides of which are
     located many Shinto shrines. We had not prayed for spiritual
     protection as we wandered around the forests on this hillside
     but we discovered that soon we were bickering in a manner
     which was unusual for us. When we finally suspected that it
     might have something to do with the spiritual atmosphere of
     the place and prayed against any such attack we immediately
     felt a sense of release from whatever had been affecting us.
        On another occasion I went, in the course of my research, to
     observe a dance held one night at a Shinto shrine. Although I
     had prayed for protection for myself, and my wife Ruth had not
     been with me, shortly after I returned home she began to have a
     series of nightmares throughout that night. From such experi-
     ences we learned 'the hard way' of the need to pray for
     protection if one goes to places where there might be intense
     spiritual activity of a non-Christian nature.
        For another example of demonic forces associated with a
     place rather than a person, see Subritzky 1986:1–2.

49   Hereditary spirits are mentioned by Wimber (1986:132) and by
     Subritzky (1986:67, 118). Subritzky gives examples of demonic
     activity as a result of ancestors being involved in Freemasonry
     or Hinduism (*ibid.*, pp. 41, 47–48, 123–124). A rather different
     approach to hereditary spirits is that advocated by McAll
     (1982), whose theology is not one familiar to most evangelicals
     (*cf.* pp. 88–97) but whose methods do seem to be effective. He
     uses the Eucharist in a way which seems to produce deliverance
     from at least certain kinds of hereditary spirits; I do not know
     whether or not baptism for the dead had the same result in the
     early church (1 Corinthians 15:29). In Appendix E I raise some
     of the theological questions surrounding the use of Exodus 20:5
     by Wimber and Subritzky as a biblical text to justify their
     theology of hereditary spirits. Whatever theological position
     one might hold regarding this area, one has to take account of
     all the empirical evidence, especially that assembled by McAll
     regarding some kind of spiritual influences (which do seem to
     be hereditary) and the healing (physical as well as psychologi-
     cal and spiritual) which does often accompany ministry in this
     area.

50   The problem is compounded if the presence of a demon can
     have physical effects not only on the body but also on the genes.

Hence recent claims by doctors at the Middlesex hospital to have discovered a possible genetic cause of schizophrenia does not in itself rule out the possibility of a demonic aspect too. Demons may appear to be localised in certain parts of the body and their expulsion might be accompanied by physical emissions such as foul odours, deep exhaling, yawning or vomiting (*cf.* Wimber 1986:242–243). Their physical *effects* might be misinterpreted as physical causes if they affect physiological mechanisms – as, for instance, in the claim that at least some homosexuals have that tendency because of a hormonal imbalance. The question arises whether the physical phenomenon is a cause or a result of the sinful behaviour pattern. By analogy with the case of a man with one leg about four inches shorter than the other whose deformity began about the same time as he became homosexual, and was healed when he repented of the homosexuality (see Subritzky 1986:108), I would suggest that in many cases it is the sinful behaviour which produces the physical effects and not vice versa.

51 This 'Western worldview' has also come to influence official thinking in some non-Western nations, as illustrated by reactions to Archbishop Milingo's deliverance ministry in Zambia. Two Western scholars who have conducted research on this ministry conclude:

> . . . the national government seems itself reluctant to acknowledge the existence of spirit possession or to offer a remedy for it. Even the Church . . . has refused to recognise the phenomenon except when Archbishop Milingo occupied the see of Lusaka . . . The Church . . . is not perfectly equipped to deal with popular spiritual needs . . . [It] does have the potential to deal with these, but is unwilling to do so because of the problems it poses in both the theological and political spheres. (Ter Haar and Ellis 1988:205)

52 An example of a mental illness produced by a virus is *kuru*, a disease which was transmitted through cannibalism among the Fore people of New Guinea (Glasse and Lindenbaum 1976:48–51; Mathews 1976:100–102).

53 Czaplicka (1914:309–315) describes features of what at the time was known as 'Arctic hysteria' – a term not often used by contemporary psychiatrists – which includes the manifestation of 'supernatural strength' (pp. 314–315), glossolalia (p. 311) or

'howling like a dog' (p. 309), features strongly reminiscent of demonisation.

Compare also the account quoted earlier of a woman diagnosed as having 'puerperal psychosis', whose description of herself in a mirror resembles that of a demonised woman described on p. 111 of *Power Healing*. On p. 112 she is reported to have 'felt like a spectator' during her experience, and similar words were used by the woman with 'puerperal psychosis' in describing her state to her minister.

54   Research on the relationship between religious experience and schizotypy is currently being conducted by Mr Michael Jackson of the Alister Hardy Research Centre, Oxford. He informs me that for psychiatric criteria there are two alternatives: the American system, *Diagnostic and Statistical Manual*, version 3(b), or the English system, *International Classification of Diseases*. The American system describes 'schizotypal personality disorder' and 'borderline personality disorder', as contrasted with schizophrenia, but the British system does not provide for this distinction.

55   Hay and Heald 1987, Table 1; Hay 1982, 1987:152; Hay and Morisy 1985:217; Krarup, n.d: 11.

56   See the NIV footnotes in numerous places in the gospels and Acts which state the Greek word is literally 'unclean' where the main text uses the term 'evil' spirit. In Mark 7:1–23 the same word refers to the eating of food with ceremonially unwashed hands, but Jesus applies it to what comes from 'within, out of men's hearts', such as 'evil thoughts, sexual immorality, theft, murder . . . [etc.]'. It is noticeable that these are the kinds of attributes also used to describe the activities of dirty ('unclean') spirits.

57   Links with fortune-telling were less clear, but it should be pointed out that thirty-eight out of 108 nurses (35%) had been involved with either spiritualism or Ouija boards and a further twenty-one had consulted a fortune-teller. As occult involvements usually lead to demonisation, this is a good indication of the extent of demonic influence in our society. Moreover, this does not indicate the frequency of demonic influence via alcohol or drug abuse and, being a largely female sample, does not indicate the extent of demonic influence from Freemasonry.

58   Masters 1987:31.

59   Grant 1974:59.

60   The reader can give his or her own interpretation to the
     following account from a Roman Catholic man followed up
     after the Harrogate conference:

> When my youngest son's girlfriend ['J.'] was killed in a car
> accident, I was praying and asked the Lord if he would allow
> J. to comfort my son M. in some way. I had an immediate
> sense – I saw without seeing – that she came from the side of
> the chair and sat on the floor. She had long blonde hair,
> looked up and said, 'Tell M. not to worry because I'm with
> the Lord. The Lord is always with M. and I'm always with
> M.' I had never met J. but M. later said she never sat on
> furniture, always on the floor.
>
> M. was very much in the Lord's presence. He had an
> experience of her being sat on the back of his motorbike. He
> felt her put her feet down at the back. This released him from
> his grief. (He could tell when someone at the back was
> dragging their feet; this startled him and he turned round and
> knew it was J.)
>
> Three weeks before her death J. had almost died in another
> accident but 'after three days she regained consciousness and
> asked M. if his mum and dad had been praying for her. "That's
> why I've come back," she said, and she came to the Lord after
> that.'

61   Prayers for the dead are said in some Anglican and Orthodox
     churches, a practice which some evangelicals find strange,
     but which might be a modern equivalent to the practice of baptism
     for the dead mentioned in 1 Corinthians 15:29. (The practice
     was obviously one with which Paul's readers were well ac-
     quainted.) Some comments on the theology of praying for the
     dead are provided by McAll (1982:88ff.) He notes that Heb-
     rews 9:27–28 ('Just as man is destined to die once, and after
     that to face judgment, so Christ was sacrificed once to take
     away the sins of many people; and he will appear a second time
     . . .') does 'not specify when judgement will occur – it could be
     taken as happening parallel to the second coming of Christ'.
     (McAll also cites evidence from the catacombs showing a
     practice of praying for the dead among Christians from the first
     century onwards.) Luke 16:26 refers to a 'great chasm' between
     the rich man in Hades and the place where Lazarus was with
     Abraham, but no such chasm is mentioned in verses 27–31 as a
     reason why Lazarus should not go to warn the rich man's living

relatives; the reason given instead was that the living already have Moses and the prophets. Hebrews 12:1 might be interpreted as meaning that the people of faith in the past are aware of events on this earth now: 'we are surrounded by such a great cloud of witnesses'.

62   Hay and Morisy 1985:222. In my study of nurses, those reporting the presence of the dead were mostly enrolled nurses and auxiliaries rather than registered nurses (Lewis 1987, Figs. 1 and 2).

63   In the ministry of Elisha we read of raising the dead (2 Kings 4:8–37), the miraculous multiplication of bread (4:42–44) and oil (4:1–7), healing from leprosy (5:1–14), words of knowledge (5:26; 6:9, 32) and fulfilled predictions (3:17–19; 7:1–2). The floating axe-head (6:5–7) is the closest Old Testament parallel to walking on water, and the prevention of people from recognising Elisha or their surroundings (6:18–23) parallels those who on the road to Emmaus were 'kept from recognising' Jesus (Luke 24:16). Jesus and Elisha both on occasion used negative prayers (curses) as well as positive prayers (Mark 11:12–14, 20–21; 2 Kings 2:23–24), a modern parallel to which is recorded by David Pytches (1985:112).

64    $p = <0.01$. Receiving a deliverance ministry is reported by 4% of the men and 7% of the women.

65   Among the 1444 people for whom a social class can be assigned – which excludes housewives, students and retired people – the proportions receiving deliverance ministries were between 4.5% and 5% for all groups except those in social class 3, where the proportion was 9.4% ($p = <0.05$). When compared with the proportions of each social class receiving prayer for inner or physical healing, it is found that there is far more deliverance received among those in social class 3 ($p = <0.001$).

66   The percentages reporting high degrees of healing through deliverance are:

    Age group
    Teens and twenties   90%
             Thirties   74%
             Forties   74%
           Fifty plus   45%

This produces a very significant difference ($p = <0.001$).

67   Matthew 17:15 specifies that the boy was an epileptic, but the parallel passage in Mark 9:14–28 specifies that the cause of the

epilepsy was an evil spirit. Jesus asked how long he had been like this and was told, 'From childhood.' One of John Wimber's team who visited Leeds after the Harrogate conference told the story of a very severe case of epilepsy which was healed after God gave a supernatural insight into its cause – namely, that there had been one or more unsuccessful abortion attempts while the child was still in the mother's womb. 'Inner healing' going back to the time in the womb was necessary in order to heal the subsequent epilepsy. Such cases make me wonder how often epilepsy is associated with traumas within the womb. A possibly analogous case concerns a young man who either from birth or shortly afterwards had a partial paralysis of his left side and subsequently developed epilepsy. He was prayed for at Harrogate but the symptoms remained. However, when following him up later I learned that he had never received prayer about the time when he was in the womb next to his twin who had died before birth.

68 The same problem applies to inner healing in general because ministers whose opinions were solicited about observed changes in some of their congregations often mentioned other times of ministry for such people in addition to the Harrogate conference. As they often regard inner healing as a process which takes time, the contribution of any one factor is difficult to assess.

3   Words of knowledge

1   A similar problem arises in 1 Corinthians 11:10, where Paul refers to angels, without further explanation, in a discussion about women's headgear. The phrase 'because of the angels' seems mysterious to a modern reader but must have referred to a concept well known to Paul's readership for him to have referred to it in passing in this way. Dr Philip Payne, who recently taught at Gordon-Conwell Theological Seminary, argues (convincingly, in my view) that Paul is here referring to believers judging angels – an idea mentioned earlier in 1 Corinthians 6:3. Furthermore, the word used for 'authority' (*exousia*) in v.10 always refers to holding power of one's own, never meaning a 'symbol of authority over oneself'. Payne interprets the verse to mean that a woman has the authority or right to do with her own hair (which in v.15 Paul calls her

'glory') whatever her conscience directs – whether to wear it up, cover it with a shawl or put on a veil – just as she also has authority over angels. In the same way, Paul's reference to the 'message of knowledge' needs to be understood by comparison with whatever other New Testament passages may shed light on it. Other elucidating passages may also take for granted that the reader knows about the nature of this spiritual gift, accounting for the absence of specific teaching on it, so the expositor may become liable to the charge of reading unwarranted assumptions into the text.

2 If in John 8:1–11 Jesus was writing on the ground the sins of those who accused the woman caught in adultery, beginning with the sins of the eldest among them, this may be a further example of the 'word of knowledge' in Christ's ministry.

3 See Wimber (1985:44–46) for a modern example of a 'word of knowledge' having this result.

4 He was also aware of the sin of Gehazi (2 Kings 5:19–27) and on another occasion admits to the absence of any supernatural insight from God about the reasons for another person's distress (2 Kings 4:27).

5 Baldwin 1987:26.

6 Applicants to the conference supplied only their names and addresses on their registration forms, sending them to the Christian organisation in Hove which had invited Wimber to come to Britain and had organised the conferences in Brighton and Harrogate as well as a one-day 'Celebration of the Kingdom of God' in London. Although those attending were encouraged to have either attended a 'Part I' conference or to have listened to tapes of one, there were still some who had not done either of these. In any case, the organisers of this conference were a different group to those who had organised the Sheffield conference over a year previously, so it is highly unlikely that any fraud was involved in terms of collecting information about people through other channels.

7 On one of the questionnaires a sixty-two year old woman reported that she saw 'a light of healing' on Janet's skirt 'which I never thought possible'. In an interview with her in 1987 she also said that one of her friends had seen the same light, which could not be attributed to any 'natural' source.

8 In the above calculation I have not accounted for the obvious implication that the person involved has a physical ailment at all. Between a quarter and a third of those attending this

conference received prayer for some kind of physical condition, but it is possible that a healing conference like this one has attracted to it a disproportionate number of people who are ill in some way. However, the smaller the proportion of the population who have an ailment, the higher is the corresponding multiple by which the total probability is to be further multiplied. For example, if a quarter of the population has a physical ailment, then multiplying by this factor the three million to one probability figure obtained in the example produces a probability of twelve million to one. If a fifth of the population has a physical ailment, the corresponding probability factor rises to fifteen million to one.

9   For advice on the statistical analysis employed in this example I would like to thank the Statistical Advisory Service of the University of Leeds, Department of Mathematics.

10 Baldwin 1987:28.

11 It is possible that some people filled in the ways they have received words of knowledge in the past, but the intention of the question was to elicit information on how they were received at the conference. Most people understood the question to mean this.

12 A few of this miscellaneous group are almost unclassifiable by the descriptions written in on the questionnaire, such as 'engulfment' or 'the person had said before it was God's time for deliverance and filling at the conference'. A phrase such as 'looking at the person, seeing it on her' might refer to a strong intuition, or (more probably) a type of empathy.

13 The example described in Wimber 1986:270–271 involves one person feeling her friend's emotional pain in a way analogous to the 'word of knowledge' which comes by feeling another person's physical pain. I remarked that such phenomena are particularly appropriate in a context where the participants all belong to the body of Christ, in which, 'If one part suffers, every part suffers with it' (1 Corinthians 12:26). I wonder whether or not words of knowledge conveyed in this manner are analogous to the referred pain sometimes encountered by medical doctors, in which a problem in one area of the body is manifested by pain elsewhere. We need to be wary of reading too much into the metaphors used to describe spiritual matters, but it is clear that St Paul's repeated use of the human body as a metaphor for the church probably derives from Paul's initial conversion experience when Christ said to him, 'Saul, Saul,

why do you persecute me?' (Acts 9:4); in persecuting the church, Saul was actually persecuting Christ (*cf*. also Matthew 25:31–45). Just as Jesus suffered vicariously on behalf of the church, and believers may vicariously receive one another's pains, so too the afflictions of believers might constitute a form of continual suffering for Christ himself (Colossians 1:24; *cf*. Philippians 3:10).

14   I give this example because I once had a word of knowledge in which I saw a number followed by a symbol used in Japan to indicate a person's age. This was comprehensible to me, but would not be to many others. I was confused when later I saw another number in the middle of two squares and I did not know if it referred to the person's current age or (more likely) to the age when they felt 'blocked in'. Two other examples of words of knowledge coming to people in a position to understand them are first: 'I saw in my mind's eye a statue of Our Lady. As I have a Roman Catholic background I knew what it was, and it helped me to understand the other person's problem.' And second (From the former drama teacher):

> . . . I was . . . joining in ministry with a group of teenagers. The Lord told me to get away from the group, there were other things to do. I was attracted to an Indian couple at the top . . . Both were praising the Lord and seemed quite happy . . . then my eye caught something. The Indian woman in praising the Lord did a particular movement of her hand. I shared with her that in Indian dance (which she'd been brought up with and taught by her grandmother) . . . it's either religious or sexual, no happy medium. The very fact I'd been drama trained and recognised a little movement as part of Indian dance . . . It was a matter of counselling – it had to be handed over completely to the Lord . . . Confirmation of that came from the man – he nodded complete agreement to what I was saying. He realised that this was right.

15   I have twice written to this missionary to ask if he can remember the details of the chemical formula but I have received no reply.

16   These examples are taken from Soal and Bateman 1954:313, the 'intrinsic percentage scores' in these cases (when adjusted for discrepancies with statistical probability, *etc*.) being in these cases 8.8 and 9.9 respectively.

17 See Boerenkamp 1985.

18 Some spiritualists, espccially those calling themselves Christian spiritualists, may take a fourth position and deny that the spiritualist messages are from demonic sources, perhaps even attributing the source to God or to intermediaries (including those identified as dead relatives) said to be speaking on God's behalf. I find myself unable to go along with this idea because: (1) there are strong biblical commands against trying to communicate with the dead (*e.g.* Exodus 22:18; Leviticus 19:26b, 28, 31; 20:27; Deuteronomy 18:9–13); (2) in my study of nurses in Leeds I found statistically significant links between spiritual experience and psychological well-being whereby those whose principal experience is the presence of God had average scores of psychological well-being higher than average but those who had previous involvements with spiritualism ranked lower than average; (3) the ways in which a spirit manifests itself in a spiritualist context is very similar or identical to that described in Christian contexts as demonisation, and I know of cases in which mediums have been delivered of demons through the agency of Christians.

19 This appears to be the kind of approach taken by Masters (1987:28, 29, 35), who refers to 'words of knowledge' as examples of clairvoyance.

20 A possible example of this is Kelsey (1977), whose appendix lists 'extrasensory experiences in the New Testament' and describes them as 'clairvoyant' or 'telepathic' etc.

21 The probability values are 0.0106 for age, 0.0011 for marital status and 0.0256 for sex. If 0.01 is taken as the boundary of significance for a sample of this size, then the links with marital status can be regarded as significant, with sex as not quite significant and with age as so close to the border that it is probably significant.

22 The probability values are 0.0004 for sex, 0.5844 for marital status and 0.0181 for age. The age distribution shows a peak among increasing age groups.

23 Although there are no statistically significant links between words of knowledge and either sex or age, the link with marital status is virtually significant – but in a different direction than might be expected. The greatest divergences from the expected values (as calculated by a standard mathematical procedure) come among single people – who report having words of knowledge *less* frequently than might be expected – and

widows who report having them *more* frequently than expected. Does a social status component operate in the recognition of these gifts, so that widows are less likely to be recognised as having the gift of prophecy but the not dissimilar gift of 'words of knowledge' is open to them? (The probability values of the linkages are 0.2369 with age, 0.2865 with sex but 0.0158 with marital status.)

24 This association is highly significant: $p = <0.001$.

25 Even identical ('monòzygotic') twins – and most twins are not identical when detailed tests are performed – have very similar environments which can produce similar influences upon them, except in very rare cases of twins being brought up separately from soon after birth.

26 For further details on hemisphere differences see Springer and Deutsch 1985.

27 Moreover, none of these seven have any regular current musical or artistic pursuits, though two have learned to play an instrument to a limited extent in the past. It is also noticeable that five of these seven are men.

28 The same informant also described how he believed God had guided him to locate quickly the area in a computer operating system which was causing problems for a customer. This can be compared with a case quoted by Pytches (1985:103–104) in which a technical problem at a power station was diagnosed by a word of knowledge. Similarly, a twenty-five year old woman during the Harrogate conference had a word of knowledge described as 'picture of a man's house with a problem – central heating needed fixing and was causing him problems'.

29 Of the hundred people in my sample, 33% had received at various times both 'warnings' and words of knowledge, a further 10% had received 'warnings' but no words of knowledge and another 34% had received words of knowledge but no 'warnings'. The remainder reported neither of these kinds of experiences (including among these one man who wrote in question marks for both the 'Yes' and 'No' columns of the warning or 'premonition' question). I should point out that I asked all informants, including those interviewed in person, to fill in this question in writing, thereby minimising any 'interview effect'. In the same question were items on a variety of other spiritual experiences, including the one about having strong 'promptings' to action.

30 This process of taking hold of passing thoughts at the periphery

of one's mind has relevance for one's personal times with God. One of those I interviewed mentioned how he had been previously taught to clear his mind of all distractions during his personal devotional times but he now realises that this practice may also blot out the 'still small voice' of God. (It is important to recognise the difference between 'distractions' and divinely prompted thoughts: see McAll 1982:43 for an example of initially unrecognised divine prompting.)

31 In October 1986 for an unknown reason I awoke one Wednesday night and started thinking about the coming Sunday evening's service when the words came to me, 'Sarah, your mother wants you to write to her.' At that time I did not know of anyone of that name at church who was not still living at home, but when it was given out on the Sunday evening (to a congregation of perhaps 150 or so) it turned out to fit exactly a particular situation. This was my first 'word of knowledge' which I felt sure was from God, and I believe it was given to me because I was in a position to counsel Sarah from my own personal experience of having had a difficult relationship with my step-mother.

32 Samuel's experience seemed to have been auditory but in 1 Samuel 3:15 it is actually referred to as a 'vision'.

33 Note that these are regarded as the *causes* of trauma requiring inner healing: they are not clinical descriptions of psychiatric disorders such as 'schizophrenia'.

34 These percentages are based on the responses of 204 people who (1) thought that a public word of knowledge had applied to them, (2) received prayer in response to it and (3) indicated their subjective assessments of the degree of healing they had received. In the sample the correlation between higher degrees of specificity in words of knowledge and greater amounts of reported healing is statistically 'noticeable'. This means that it is not quite significant among this group but it may turn out to be significant if a larger sample were available.

35 An unpublished report by Douglas G. T. McBain of Manna Ministries Trust, London, and C. E. Fryer, the minister of Ilfracombe Baptist Church, Devon, showed that at John Wimber's 1984 conference in London fewer claimed healings as a result of a word of knowledge than those who claimed healings without a word of knowledge. Because they do not analyse this result according to the specificity of the words of knowledge involved, I suspect that the larger numbers who

respond to a general word of knowledge might swamp out statistically those who respond to a more specific one. It is likely also that those who ask for prayer without having had a word of knowledge about their conditions start off with a higher level of faith or expectancy than those who go forward in response to a more general word of knowledge with an attitude of 'There's no harm in trying.' Some caution may be necessary in evaluating the findings of McBain and Fryer because their analysis is based on a response rate of only 31% (*i.e.* 645 out of 2065 registered delegates), so its representativeness is considerably open to question.

36 I telephoned her to ask if she had been to her optician in the meantime but she had not.

37 This correlation is statistically significant: $p = <0.05$ (and is virtually at the 0.025 level).

38 Her physical healing was sustained for about a year after the conference, until she had a subsequent fall and again damaged her lower back. As no X-Rays were taken between the conference and her later fall, no medical verification of her healing is available. However, her own testimony points to a very substantial improvement and is worth quoting:

> . . . When during the workshop Blaine Cook was given a word of knowledge for a lady who had broken her back in the summer at the third bone from the bottom, I knew it was me. I couldn't believe it, I didn't quite know what to think. I was nervous, but excited and also full of doubt.
>
> As I received prayer I can't really remember what happened . . . At one point I wondered whether it was my imagination or whether I really had felt a 'click' at the base of my spine or not. However the pain that I had had since the accident did not disappear, though I think it got less. Then later on that day while I was dancing in the aisles I slipped down a step and banged/bruised my back again.
>
> Then the following week while I was at home writing to my missionary friends I was telling them about the conference, and suddenly I realised that I had no pain in my back. I dropped what I was doing to check it out. I did everything possible to make my back hurt – but it didn't. I knew that it had been hurting when I sat down – the doctors had said that I would always have some pain.
>
> Suddenly it came to me as clear as crystal, 'When God says

he wants to do something then he does it.' I realised on a deeper level than I have before that it was God who had given the word of knowledge to Blaine Cook and that it was God who wanted to heal my back.

From that day onwards I had no more pain in my back except on two separate occasions when the pain may just have been very bad backache – making it difficult for me to stand up or sit down. I think it may have been God warning me not to do silly things.

Since I received this form I have been away on holiday and while I was away I had another epileptic partial split-second blackout and I fell on my back awkwardly again and so now I once again have constant pain in my coccyx. It happened on a Sunday and was not as bad as last year and so I did not have an X-Ray taken. When I saw my doctor when I returned home he did not send me for an X-Ray as he said I'd obviously damaged my coccyx (and nothing could be done). I do not believe that I have broken it like last time but I do believe there is a possibility that I have cracked the bone again.

39 Although the specificity of words of knowledge does not show a statistically significant link with either social class or education, it should be borne in mind that the social class classifications are based on occupation. 'Housewives' are not classified by social class. Therefore the statistics by social class tend to be weighted on the male side. I find it remarkable that two women receiving very specific public words of knowledge should relatively soon afterwards experience financial difficulties on account of their husbands' becoming unable to work for different reasons.

4 Physical and spiritual phenomena

1 See Wimber 1986:221–222.
2 *ibid*. This might be what Douglas McBain (1986:40) refers to as 'the vibrating hands of those who minister'.
3 Wright 1987:8.
4 *ibid*.
5 Baldwin 1987:25.
6 When I suggested this at a conference in Leeds in 1987, a medical consultant countered it with the remark that 'it is the

same God'. This is of course true, just as it is the same God who is addressed in a Russian Orthodox church, a Brethren assembly and a Pentecostal meeting. However, the differing expectations of how that God might make his presence known to the believers surely has a great effect on their differing experiences of the sacred.

7   I understand that the meetings at Leeds Grammar School following the Harrogate conference in 1986 were felt to have been better organised along these lines. Study materials were provided and a small fee charged to cover these, though it is likely that this would have had the effect of discouraging those who might have attended out of casual curiosity – and who might have attended the meetings at St George's in 1985 where no fee was charged.

8   Moss and McEvedy 1966:1295. I am grateful to Dr Tony Holton for bringing this article to my attention.

9   Symptoms of other cases described as mass hysteria have on occasion included crying, laughing, 'abnormal movements', convulsions, tremor, vomiting, palpitations, coughing, headaches, flushing, running, walking around, paraesthesia, pain, false belief and several other phenomena (Sirois, 1974: Table II).

10   Eysenck and Eysenck 1969:155 report that the EPI (an improved version of the Maudsley Personality Inventory or MPI) consists of 108 questions to measure neuroticism and extroversion, besides a separate lie scale, but on p. 171 of the same book the EPI is said to contain forty-eight items measuring neuroticism, forty-eight measuring extroversion, and a lie scale of eighteen items. If I had administered the EPI as a written questionnaire I doubt if I would have had a satisfactory response rate, considering the relatively low response rate to my postal questionnaires. Written questionnaires have the advantage of equalising any 'interview effect' from the way in which the questions are asked, but I am assuming that any such effect will be constant as the same person did the interviewing in each case. These practical problems are more easily overcome when conducting research on schoolgirls who can be given a questionnaire to fill in during school time than when interviewing personally during their spare time a random sample of people living throughout Britain.

11   Eysenck and Eysenck 1969:83.

12   Following Eysenck and Eysenck (1969:80), 'Yes' replies are counted as two points, 'No' replies as zero and '?' (an inter-

mediate or uncertain category) as one point. This produces two scales, each ranging from zero to twelve, on which the half-way boundary is taken as lying between points six and seven.

13 Might it be that levels of neuroticism tend to decline the longer one has been a Christian? This question would need to be answered by further empirical research, but if at least some neurotic behaviour is a response to situations of stress then alternative ways of coping with stress may lead to decreased neuroticism. Dr Herbert Benson (1984) has argued that both prayer and meditation produce in the body a 'relaxation response' which has measurable effects in reducing blood pressure and cholesterol levels. It is the physiological opposite to the 'fight or flight' response which is often triggered off by stress situations. This 'relaxation response' among those who pray might also account for the statistically significant finding that cardiac arrests are relatively less common among church attenders (Comstock and Partridge 1972).

14 Dr Richard Turner observes:

When a diagnosis of hysteria is made one has to ask the question why an individual should develop a particular symptom at that point in time, and for what purpose. In fact, hysteria as a psychiatric diagnosis is now used very much less frequently than it used to be, as it is recognised that many symptoms are direct consequences of physiological or pathological change rather than psychologically mediated. (Personal communication; letter dated 4 July 1988)

I have included this discussion of hysteria in this chapter because a popular or 'lay' view is that some of these phenomena may be a form of mass hysteria. This term has actually been used to describe what happened at a meeting led by some of Wimber's team.

15 Testing independently the item for tingling in the hands and comparing those reporting it at the conference with those not reporting it, there is a statistically significant difference whereby those ranking higher on the extroversion scale report this experience much more than those ranking lower on this scale ($p = {<}0.025, {>}0.01$). However, taking all those who have ever experienced this (which is often interpreted as a sign of an anointing for a healing ministry) it is found that there is no significant difference according to extroversion. The difference may be due simply to the fact that 66% of the 'high

extroversion' group reporting this during the conference had already experienced the same phenomenon previously, as had also all four of the 'low extroversion' group.

16   Richards 1984:4–6. Richards also (on p. 8) distinguishes between falling forwards and falling backwards. I regard this as important because falling forwards may in some cases be interpreted in the light of the common Oriental practice of prostration before gods, kings and high officials (*cf.* Wittfogel 1957:152–154).

17   I reserve judgement about the 'authenticity' of this message because it is not impossible to attribute it to her overhearing the comment of an American man who believed he had a 'word of knowledge' about what God was doing. Her account is as follows:

> While I was down I heard in a very definite physical way (not just a feeling), 'The time hasn't come yet for your healing but I'm going to teach you to hear my voice in a more definite, deeper and surer way so that people will be brought into my glory and will know me in a deeper way.' An American man and an English man were next to me and the American told the English man that this was what God was saying. But I hadn't heard it in an American accent. So I don't think it was my subconscious.

She does believe that from that time on she has heard God more clearly and has been given a number of quite specific 'words of knowledge', further indications to her mind that this experience was from God.

18   With a sample size of 1890 people the relevant level of probability for statistical significance is more appropriately taken at $p = 0.01$ rather than 0.05. In Table 4.5, statistically significant associations mean $p = <0.01, >0.001$; highly significant associations mean $p = <0.001$. There are also some marginally significant associations ($p = <0.05, >0.01$) as follows:

	Age	Sex	Marital Status
Tingling in the hands		F	D, W, S
Hand or arm shaking		F	
Screaming or shouting	Y		S
Hot areas on the body			D, W, S
Behaviour resembling 'drunkenness'	Y	F	

19 Dr Richard Turner, personal communication.

20 Two younger women I noticed at Sheffield and one whom my wife noticed during the team visit to Leeds in 1985 had patterns of breathing, vocalisation and flushed expressions strongly reminiscent of sexual orgasm. There was no external stimulation of their sexual organs but their central nervous systems were being stimulated in a different manner to produce superficially similar symptoms. (I know of no cases at all of men ejaculating while believing themselves to be under the influence of the Holy Spirit.) These few cases reminiscent of sexual experience among women may be attributable to the fact that both changes in breathing and hot areas on the body are significantly linked with younger age groups and with women. A few who happen to combine these features during a time of ministry might appear to resemble women experiencing a sexual climax, but it should be borne in mind that similar physiological changes such as increased respiration and heartbeat or flushed expressions can also be produced by running or by many forms of strenuous work. If younger people are more likely to react in these ways it may be simply a product of physiology: apparent similarities in result do not mean that the causes are the same by any means.

21 John's vision in Revelation 1:13–16 resembles in several details the description of a vision received by Daniel (10:5–6) which his companions did not see even though they experienced the affective response of terror, fleeing and hiding themselves, as if they had seen it (v.7). I shall discuss the significance of such emotional responses to unseen presences in the final section of this chapter. Daniel describes his own physical responses to the vision as, 'I had no strength left, my face turned deathly pale and I was helpless. Then I heard him speaking, and as I listened to him, I fell into a deep sleep, my face to the ground' (vv. 8–9). This sounds very like what happened to John on Patmos, and might be equated to a trance. In both cases the one seen in the vision reaches out a hand to touch either Daniel or John, in Daniel's case explicitly telling him to stand up again. Jesus did the same to the boy who appeared dead to the bystanders (Mark 9:27), but presumably sufficient time must have elapsed while the boy was on the ground for people to reach the conclusion that he had died. Daniel's account of falling into a 'deep sleep' might also suggest that he was on the ground for an extended period. (His 'deep sleep' might have been reported to

him by those who ran away and hid themselves, who presumably also told him that his face turned 'deathly pale' – a detail reminiscent of the boy who was thought to be dead.) It should not be taken for granted – as Richards (1984:8) does – that those who fall are immediately brought back to a standing position and not left lying on the ground for a while.

22 Sanford 1982:98–101.

23 This illustration was related to me by someone who attended a meeting in Nottingham at which I was invited to speak, but I have so far been unable to track down the reference.

24 Gardner 1986:118.

25 If 'credulity' is the 'mirror image' of 'faith', but with negative connotations, I wonder what the corresponding word would be for 'suggestibility'? Are such people 'independent', 'strong minded' – or 'pig-headed'?!

26 My list of phenomena has been given earlier (above Fig. 3), but the one item I did not include which had been mentioned at Sheffield was 'Glistening'. Blaine Cook suggested this was a result of 'light perspiration and light flickering on sweat', the sweat being a result of hot areas on one's body.

27 Barely a month prior to the conference Wimber's book *Power Healing* was published and was freely available to all participants on arrival at the conference. Although on p. 218 Wimber refers to 'something like electricity' coming from his hands it is unlikely that many would have read this passage by the time they filled in my questionnaire.

28 Perry (1987:13–14) mentions cold spots as one of the phenomena sometimes associated with 'poltergeist' activity. One case reported to me in which a cold area was noticed on someone being prayed for involved a young Japanese man who belongs to Tenrikyō, a Shinto-derived 'new religion'. The initial prayer for healing of a neck problem produced no alleviation of pain, but on further counselling it was discovered that the symptoms began at around the time this young man became more actively involved in Tenrikyō. He was advised that healing would follow his turning away from Tenrikyō to Christ, a step he has not yet taken.

29 Wimber 1986:227.

30 The only scriptural analogy I can suggest is the experience of Zechariah, who became dumb because of unbelief when a miracle was promised (Luke 1:20–22). Luke 1:62 ('they made signs to his father') also seems to indicate that Zechariah

became deaf, so in this case deafness and dumbness may have resulted from a divine rather than demonic cause, as was the case elsewhere (Mark 9:25). The outward manifestations do not necessarily reveal the spiritual source of a phenomenon.

31 Compare this with the following account sent in to the Alister Hardy Research Centre in Oxford (an institution conducting research on religious experience):

> The 'golden light' . . . has for many years taken the form of a glowing golden ball in my cupped hands, pulsing with warmth and power. At the end of a Communion Service I have wondered what it meant, and, unable to answer my own question, have tipped my hands in the direction of the departing priest asking that it would be used to enable him in his work that day. I just knew that the gift was not for me. That 'golden light' at an early morning Communion was often there while my eyes were closed – when I opened them the sunlight through the east window was dull! I cannot explain these 'glimpses'. Something 'other' happens and one is suddenly aware of an experience which brings a deeper, richer quality to one's worship: a reality far beyond everyday existence, and which even a vivid imagination could never conceive . . . They have certainly done much to consolidate my own commitment to a Living Loving God . . .

32 One woman on the back of her questionnaire described two visions, as follows: (1) 'During worship at the first session I saw a very pure, white lamb superimposed on the red curtain above the stage.' (2) 'When John Wimber asked the Lord to show us the state of the church I saw a very thin, puny, tree which was in danger of being blown down and was trying to prop itself up. It was white and anaemic looking.'

33 One woman I interviewed said that at her Baptist church, 'one night when the worship was particularly anointed my husband, standing beside me, said, "Can you feel the wind of the Spirit?" I felt it go past and someone else on the other side said they had felt a wind too.'

A similar account comes from a service at another church where I was present. Two people sitting near to me felt a breeze at a particularly moving point in the service whereas I noticed nothing of the kind. It might be significant that one of these two people is blind, and so is probably more aware of non-visual sensations.

34   The reference is to Elisha taking over the mantle and ministry of Elijah (2 Kings 2:13), as well as to the call of Elisha when Elijah threw his cloak over him (1 Kings 19:19).

35   Memories of the conference afterwards often retain a general impression and recall of certain significant events without being able to remember exactly what happened on any particular day unless notes were taken.

36   Dr John White, a psychiatrist and author of several Christian books, has commented that some of these experiences are similar to those recounted by medieval mystics. I wonder to what extent there are social factors which allow the *report* of mystical experiences more at some times and places than at others. Certainly many people who have such experiences today are afraid to relate them to others for fear of being misunderstood, ridiculed or considered mad (Hay 1982, 1987:163–164; Hay and Heald 1987, Table 4). It is possible that the experiences themselves occur relatively commonly in each century but that reports of them may be affected by social factors. Perhaps the same might be true of the incidence of charismatic gifts throughout the centuries except that these are even more likely to be affected by social constraints: whereas mystical experiences may be 'individual', many of the charismatic gifts are effective only in interaction with others for the benefit of the church as a whole.

37   It is possible that her experience of watching Blaine Cook was related to her prior wish, a parallel case being that of George Ritchie (1978), who at the beginning of his near-death experience found himself out of his body and heading towards a city which just prior to his 'death' he had been longing to go to.

38   See, for example, Green 1968; Sabom 1980.

39   Hay 1982, 1987:141.

40   Compare the experience of Moses in Exodus 34:29–35.

41   I am citing Mr Livesey's name because it is possible that he might express such opinions in one of his books.

42   Beardsworth 1977:66–67, 71, 74.

43   It is worth noting there that some near-death experiences have a structure similar to that of the book of Revelation. There may be an encounter with a glorious presence who might be identified as Christ, followed by revelations about others (*cf.* Gardner 1986:138) or visions of the future of this planet (Ring 1980, ch. 8; Grey 1985:122–133). Some also think they are in heaven, but the detailed description by George Ritchie (1978)

mentions a pleasant place which he at first mistook for heaven and which actually turned out to be a building that would be constructed on this earth some years later. It was only after this that he was given a far-off glimpse of a 'city of light' resembling that described in the closing chapters of Revelation.

44 Grant 1974:58–62.
45 However, one informant who mentioned experiencing 'isolation/terror' when the Holy Spirit was invited to come interpreted this as 'probably a word of knowledge about future ministry'.
46 See also Wimber 1986:124–125.
47 Ring 1980:94–95.
48 Compare also the experience described by Colin Urquhart (1974:90), who when announcing a hymn had said, '. . . we are joining with the whole host of heaven in praising God. Let us ask the Lord to make us aware that we are part of that great worshipping company as we sing'. During the second verse he heard a trumpet. Then he writes:

> I listened more intently and realised that I could hear not one trumpet, but several, blending beautifully with the organ. (Afterwards) . . . several people confirmed that they too had heard the heavenly trumpets . . . Later . . . our organist said to me, 'Something strange happened to the organ; the trumpet stop refused to work during that hymn. It was working perfectly up until then; it worked perfectly afterwards, but it would not work at all during that hymn.'

49 Compare the account quoted earlier (pp. 192–193) of the young man who was taken from the Sheffield conference in an ambulance and who said, 'if it hadn't been so unusual I suppose humanly speaking I'd have tried to stop what he was doing . . .'
50 Beardsworth 1977:116, 131.

5 'Doin' the stuff'

1 $p = <0.001$. For example, there were sixty-eight people in Social Class II who reported high degrees of anointing, as compared with an expected number of 50.4, while the six people ¡o reported low degrees of anointing were considerably less than the expected number of 15.2.

2   $p = <0.05$, which is significant with a sample size of 108.
    (Chi-square $= 6.04$ with 2 degrees of freedom.)
3   Of the thirty-nine people in health-related professions who
    reported some degree of anointing, thirty-one reported a high
    amount and the remaining six reported medium or low
    amounts. Comparing this with the sixty-nine others in Social
    Class II reporting degrees of anointing, thirty-seven reported
    high amounts and thirty-two medium or low amounts. This
    difference is statistically significant ($p = <0.02$).

    It might be suggested that the high degree of anointing
    among nurses and other predominantly female health-related
    occupations is actually due to differences of sex rather than
    occupation. However, this is not borne out by an analysis of the
    reported degrees of anointing. Although women do show
    higher amounts of anointing than do men, as would be ex-
    pected from the numbers of nurses, physiotherapists and
    health visitors who are women, the overall difference between
    the sexes is not great enough to be statistically significant.

4   This statement is not meant to discourage ministers or doctors
    from becoming involved in healing ministries. For deliverance
    ministries, it is good to follow the advice of Bishop David
    Pytches, who writes that it 'should never be engaged in without
    authority from the leaders of the church' and cases of demon
    control requiring deliverance should be referred to the church
    leadership (1985:202, 207).

5   He does not use this expression on p. 13 of *Power Evangelism*,
    but he does describe how on reflection he felt cheated after his
    first church service because he 'had joined Christ's army in
    order to do his works'.

6   See Wimber 1985:12.

7   The consultant also provided copies of the patient's clinical
    notes. The relevant passages are as follows:

    18.3.87 . . . His back feels fine but he is aware of some
        radicular pain in the right leg consistent with L 5:
        certainly having screwed the 5/1 facet joint firmly
        together we may well have produced some entrap-
        ment of the root although SLR is normal. I think we
        have just got to see if the nerve settles but put him
        into a single hip spica involving the right leg.

    25.3.87 . . . Since mobilising in his spica incorporating the
        left leg he has developed moderately severe pain

down the back of his left thigh not below the knee. This has not been really relieved by 2 days of bed rest. X-Rays show the screws in a good position. For re-X-Ray just to check if there has been any movement and continue with bed rest.

27.3.87 . . . No change on X-Ray . . .

1.4.87 . . . He has got unpleasant sensations in the legs and one must wonder whether in firmly tightening the fusion, we have produced any compression of the cauda equina. Suggest that we do a radiculogram as we did not specifically explore the nerves.

2.4.87 *X-RAY REPORT*
Myelogram:
The examination proved somewhat difficult owing to the previous surgery and the extensive spinal deformity. There is an anterior indentation on the thecal sac at L 4/5. There was poor filling of both the right and left L 5 nerve roots present, though this was somewhat more apparent on the left side. It was a little difficult to demonstrate this clearly owing to the scoliosis at this level. No other abnormality was demonstrated on this examination . . .

8.4.87 . . . Pain does not appear to be settling, mostly in the back of the right thigh and pelvis today? For decompression next week if he has not settled.

This is interesting insofar as I suspect he had a protrusion all along which he compensated for by bending forward to the left slightly. We have now put him straight and screwed him straight and as a consequence the previously asymptomatic central protrusion has become disabling. Fortunately no bone is over the midline and decompression should not be difficult and I would like to defer this until my return from holiday.

9.4.87 DISCHARGE: To be readmitted.

6.5.87 READMITTED . . .
Admitted for decompression but attended a Christian meeting 10 days ago and has dramatically

improved since. No left sciatica, some residual right thigh pain only.

NO tension signs and can extend spine and stand upright.

Urged (and told) to wear his support . . .

1.7.87   Present situation is that he is aware of toothache-like discomfort in his lower back but does not appear to have any radicular pain. We carried out a 3 to 5 fusion which failed to fuse at 5 to 1. We demonstrated abnormal movement at 5 to 1 and corrected this using screws. We were concerned that in tightening up the 5/1 level we produced root irritation but this seems to have settled but the myelogram suggested that he had a central disc protrusion and when this was strained it created a degree of symptoms.

O.E.

Good lateral flexion in his upper lumbar spine and indeed forward flexion is surprisingly good considering the extent of the fusion, excursion being some 4″. S L R full with slight discomfort.

All reflexes are present.

X-RAYS

Show a very solid fusion now with considerable thickening up of the fusion mass on the concave side extending into the alar.

I have advised him to get back to pretty normal activity and I will see him again in 6 months.

8   In a later clarificatory letter the doctor wrote:

I think . . . that she was anxious and depressed and that her feelings manifested themselves as pain/tension in the neck. I initially treated her as a case of cervical spondylosis – trying non-steroidal antiarthritic drugs and physiotherapy. These were very unsuccessful. She then saw her own GP . . . who made the right diagnosis of depression, was put on antidepressants and she made a recovery a week or two after starting them, which is what we would expect with these sort of tablets. However, the psychological support of people praying would have been also important, although not as any direct intervention of God. I . . . feel that she was healed by the antidepressants rather than prayer.

This case is not dissimilar to one cited by Gardner (1983:1929) for a much more convincing case of what appears to be divine healing in which the subsequent history of the condition forced sceptical doctors to assert that the original diagnosis was mistaken. Owing to such problems of doctors redefining the nature and causes of conditions in the light of subsequent events, Gardner considered that 'even in well-documented cases where patients and doctors are available for questioning and medical records can be examined, proof of miraculous cure is probably impossible'.

9 See Wimber 1986:269. (The figures I cite there are to be reckoned inclusively rather than exclusively: the 71% who reported some measure of healing after ten sessions of prayer include the 30% who received such ministry on only one occasion.)

10 He also gave other accounts of children or young people in their fellowship being very effective in praying for healing.

11 Some time after this the informant's daughter said that she had overheard a conversation about God in which the boy who had been healed of asthma was saying 'I know there's someone,' based on his experience of healing. Three years previously the daughter had been pushed into some stinging nettles by the gang of which that boy was the leader and as a result she began to pray for him.

12 She could not remember the date exactly, but thought it was in September. I would consider Thursday 1 October was the probable date of her earnest and prolonged prayer.

13 Gardner 1986:40–41.

14 The consultant quoted from Allen 1977:319, which states:

The fibromatoses are a group of non-metastasing fibrous tumours that tend to invade and recur locally after attempted surgical excision; they may be multiple and familial; after an initial period of rapid growth, their growth rate decreases and they may eventually regress spontaneously; they may be complicated by contractures and are sometimes associated with diseases of other organs.

15 Allen 1977:320. He also adds that amputation of the limb is 'rarely justifiable'. In L.'s case this might have been necessary if the tumour had not disappeared, because his consultant described it as a 'large lesion infiltrating around the nerves and

arteries of the forearm' and 'the median nerve was running into the tumour', making it impossible to cut out by itself.

16   Allen 1977:308.

17   Allen 1977:308. (Allen's remarks are based on the evidence of only eleven cases of this kind of tumour.)

18   Allen 1977: 305.

19   Chung and Enzinger 1976:729.

20   L.'s consultant had ended his letter of 27 January 1988 with the sentence, 'I will be extremely interested to hear your views and to see how you present it in any forthcoming publication.' I accordingly wrote back to him, referring to Chung and Enzinger's article and pointing out how remarkable L.'s recovery was when compared with other cases. The consultant apparently felt he needed to justify his decision not to operate when he wrote back to me:

> The decision not to treat him was based on a clear understanding that tumours called infantile fibrosarcoma behave in a way completely unlike other tumours in children. I am certainly aware of several other cases that have not appeared in the literature but I have been told about anecdotally in which a biopsy or an incomplete excision was performed and where the tumour appeared to resolve spontaneously. If either I or . . . the surgeon involved had felt that this course of action could put L.'s life at risk then we would have had no hesitation recommending an amputation . . .

In retrospect, it is fortunate that the consultant and surgeon did choose not to operate or to use any other form of treatment, because that would have pre-empted even the possibility of 'spontaneous remission' or of divine healing. The Christian believer might interpret the consultant's decision as divinely ordained in order to allow scope for divine healing. In the same way the hand of God might be discerned in the way the Christian visitor by 'mistake' went to the house where this baby had cancer instead of going to the street which had been allocated for visiting that week.

21   Note that the prayer relieved the pain but apparently did not cure the mumps. My wife and I have been told by John Wimber that prayer often may speed up recovery from childhood illnesses rather than give instant healing.

22   The Consultant Orthopaedic Surgeon who dealt with this case

did not send me copies of his clinical notes, but instead wrote me a letter giving the following details:

> Mrs W. has a long and complex history of rheumatoid arthritis with multiple joint involvement and it would require a book in itself to give all the details of her condition. She came under my care in October 1975 because of her arthritic right hip and in November of that year the joint was replaced. All remained well until November 1978, when she developed infection in the hip for no obvious reason. She had an intermittently discharging sinus over the outer side of the hip for a long time and in July 1979, the prosthesis previously inserted was removed and replaced with another, using antibiotic impregnated cement. All seemed well until the beginning of November 1979, when she had more pain in the right hip associated with a temperature and then developed an abscess over the hip, which discharged. She was treated with antibiotics and in January 1980 the discharge subsided and she has not had any further suggestion of infection in that joint.

23   The hospital sent me a copy of a letter sent to the patient's GP which confirmed the severity of the case and the fact that he made a 'good recovery'. In brief, the illness started with the onset of pyrexia [fever] and perspiration cough with sputum production. Photophobia [painful reaction to light], headache and double vision ushered in the meningoencephalitis and shortly before admission to a local hospital his 'thought processes had become rather confused' and his wife noticed a tendency for him to drag his right leg when walking. This hospital found him 'pyrexial but without distinct neck stiffness on admission, but there was nystagmus and truncal ataxia. Physical signs and radiographs confirmed the presence of right lower lobe pneumonia.' Blood tests were unable to identify the type of organism affecting him.

As his consciousness level deteriorated, along with respiratory effort, he was transferred to a larger hospital. There he was found to be 'unresponsive to any verbal command.' His breathing was shallow and continued to deteriorate until soon he was put on a ventilator. There were persistent signs of a right lower lobe pneumonia. 'Although he was moving all four limbs there was a hint of flaccidity in the right arm and leg, with loss of reflexes on that side suggesting perhaps a developing left hemisphere lesion [*i.e.* the left half of the brain, controlling movement on the right side of the body, probably became affected].' A scan 'did not show an abscess but rather a diffuse breakdown of the blood brain barrier compatible with a meningeal exudate'.

Details were provided of the drugs used in order to combat the disease in the hope that at least one of them might be effective against the unknown organism. The letter made no mention of any sudden regaining of consciousness, merely stating that the patient's progress 'really was one of general recovery' and 'by the time he left the Unit he was fully recovered apart from some residual lethargy of course . . .' There was no indication at all of the recovery being attributable to any other factor apart from the medical treatment provided by the hospital.

24 In John 5:14 the man healed at the pool was told to 'stop sinning' – a call to repentance. (*Cf.* also Mark 1:15, where repentance is linked to belief.) After the feeding of the five thousand, the people began to say, 'Surely this is the Prophet . . .' (6:14); the next day Jesus gave further teaching about who he is, which some disciples found hard to accept. The man born blind described in John 9 came to a definite faith after his healing (9:38), and after the raising of Lazarus 'many . . . put their faith in him' (11:45). The resurrection account in John 20 focuses at the end on Thomas, who is told, 'Stop doubting and believe' (27, somewhat reminiscent of John 5:14); the chapter concludes by stating, 'Jesus did many other miraculous signs . . . which are not recorded in this book. But these are written that you may believe that Jesus is the Christ, the Son of God, and that by believing you may have life in his name' (vv. 30–31).

25 An exception in John's gospel is the royal official's son (John 4:46–54). We do not know the ages of Lazarus in John 11 or of Aeneas and Dorcas in Acts 9. These healings are 'signs' which led to others coming to faith, whereas the deliverance of the slave girl in Acts 16 produced direct opposition and only indirectly led to the jailer's family coming to faith. (It can be assumed he would not have believed had it not been for the events surrounding the earthquake.) It is noticeable that in Acts 16:18 Paul did not attempt any deliverance ministry for 'many days', and seemed to do so in the end in response to continued provocation.

26 See case (c), p. 217.

27 Compare verses 16 and 20 of Matthew 18.

28 In John 4:46–53 the royal official did demonstrate some kind of faith in persistently begging Jesus to come to heal his son (vv. 47 and 49). This is similar to the woman's persistence in Matthew 15:22–28. The royal official also demonstrated faith when he 'took Jesus at his word' and acted upon Christ's instruction (John 4:50). However, afterwards 'he and all his household believed' (v.53) as a result of the healing. (Some kind of initial faith might also be indicated by the behaviour of a royal official seeking help from an itinerant preacher who used to be a carpenter.)

29 Rex Gardner (1986:181) quotes the case of an eleven year old village girl in southern Chile who was miraculously given beautiful fillings with silver crosses on, plus new teeth growing into areas where she had gaps, whereas an Indian Mapuche Lay Reader was not given a new tooth and had to sell a cow in order to buy a false tooth. On another occasion (Gardner 1986:177–178), several people were given fillings having the form of a silver cross set in each tooth, but a little boy whose 'high-pitched, hysterical voice' mounted above the others was granted a tooth into which was set 'delicately but quite distinctly, a golden cross'.

The February 1987 issue of *U Magazine*, which caters for Christian students in the USA, has on p. 13 an article, by Kate Semmerling with Andrés Tapia, about a healing miracle in Haiti. Kate describes how as part of her nursing training she helped at a clinic set up for the 200,000 destitute people who live off food picked out of the city garbage dump on the outskirts of Port-au-Prince. A mother brought to the clinic a boy named Jean, aged five or six, who sat on his mother's lap. Kate writes, 'his legs distressed me the most. They were very thin and small with almost no muscle; I could easily put my fingers around his ankle and his knobbly knees protruded grotesquely. He could not stand or walk. Most likely he had been a polio victim.' The mother asked Kate if she could make Jean walk again, to which Kate tried to explain that there was nothing she could do. When the mother pleaded again, 'Can't you try anything,' Kate sighed and offered to pray for her 'a God-bless-this-woman type of prayer that would send her on her way'.

Her account of what happened then is worth noting at some length:

A part of me, however, believed in God's supernatural ability to heal, so I put my hands on the little boy's legs and prayed, 'Dear God, please come and do your work here.'

Even before I finished the prayer I felt a strange sort of energy – something like electricity and heat – going through my hands. When I looked at Jean's legs my eyes nearly popped out: his muscles and skin and bone were expanding – as if someone were blowing up a balloon! The Haitian lab technician I worked with and I stood by incredulous as the leg continued growing . . . I had never seen anything like this happen before.

After a few more mind-blowing minutes the skin had ballooned out to the right size from the top of his hip to his toe, and his legs had also gotten longer. The growth had even covered up his knobbly knees! Yet Jean's legs still did not look very solid. A few seconds later, however, they started firming up as the muscles underneath the 'balloon' grew.

After about five minutes the growing stopped. His legs looked completely normal. We were all in shock.

Jean crawled off his mother's lap, stood up and walked around. All of us stared in silence. After several seconds I got my voice back. All I could say was, 'Oh, my God, look at this!'

Jean's mother looked at me with tears running down her face. 'Look at what God has done,' she said quietly. 'My son can walk.' She seemed to be in shock. She then picked up her daughter in one arm, held Jean's hand in the other and walked out the door. And to every person standing in line she said, 'Look what God has done – my son can walk!'

The people in line were amazed because they all knew Jean was crippled. Every patient who came in after that excitedly asked, 'Can you pray for *me*?'

. . . After that experience I decided to pray more often for my patients in the course of treating them medically. During the rest of my time in Haiti I saw a deaf boy regain his hearing, a girl recover from pneumonia instantly, and several children who were on the brink of death revive completely within a few days . . .

6   Healing in the local church

1   See, for example, Urquhart 1974:16–36 or Huggett and Huggett 1984:67–68.

2   Barry Kissell (1986) describes such 'faith sharing' teams sent out from an Anglican church outside London to a variety of host churches throughout Britain.

3   It is possible that sometimes the teams which visit local churches (by invitation) after John Wimber's conferences might provoke stronger negative reactions among certain British people simply because the visitors are American. Those who bring the same message but belong to the same nationality as the recipients might be regarded with less suspicion, particularly if they belong to the same denomination.

4   It might be reading too much into the text of Acts 15:20 to speculate to what extent the items prohibited are those which are particularly susceptible to being vehicles for demonic influence on new believers. Certainly sexual immorality is widely regarded by authorities on demonisation as a channel through which Christians might become demonised (Wimber 1986: 130–131; Subritzky 1986:76). In Deuteronomy 7:25–26 we read, 'The images of their gods you are to burn in the fire . . . Do not bring a detestable thing into your house or you, like it, will be set apart for destruction. Utterly abhor and detest it, for it is set apart for destruction.' For such reasons it is important to destroy household articles which have been associated with the occult, including Freemasonry, in order to break any demonic hold which they may continue to exert over a person, even over a Christian (Subritzky 1986:117, 138, 257–262). Might it be that 'food polluted by idols', mentioned in Acts 15:20, falls into the same category? (The 'meat of strangled animals' and 'blood' would be associated also with food sacrificed to idols.) This is a contentious issue, as Paul recognised when writing to the Corinthians (1 Corinthians 8). His rule was that it was a matter of individual conscience, provided that one person's actions do not cause problems for another. Hence the eating of food which had been sacrificed to idols did not necessarily confer any demonic influence upon the eater, who in many social situations would have been unable to refuse such food without causing offence to a host. Nevertheless it was certainly a matter which was of considerable concern in the early church (*cf*. also

Romans 14:2–3, 13–23; 1 Timothy 4:3–5). In Revelation 2:20 there is condemnation of teaching (described in v.24 as 'Satan's so-called deep secrets') which misleads Christians into sexual immorality and the eating of food sacrificed to idols. Again these two items are linked (as in Acts 15:20 and 29), but the specific area of repentance called for in Revelation 2:21 concerns immorality, with no repeated mention of food sacrificed to idols.

5   The percentages quoted can be converted into real figures. If there are 195 people who have been added to the church since its foundation, then the 27% of these who are new converts amount to 53 people. Ten of these are what the pastor described as 'cold contacts'. It may also be appropriate to mention in this context that many of those at the Harrogate conference belonging to Social Classes III to V also belong to 'house churches' or similar kinds of fellowships, indicating that such churches have probably made a greater impact in 'working-class' areas than have some of the established churches.

6   An analogous case reported to me in a different context concerns a woman with a hiatus hernia who had told her husband she would know she was healed when she could eat a bag of chips at nine o'clock at night. It was around that time one evening that a word of knowledge was given out at a meeting where she was present, saying that someone with a digestive problem was healed, and that it would be appropriate, by way of celebration, to go out and buy a bag of chips!

Other examples of the variety of ways in which words of knowledge can operate are given by David Pytches (1985:101–105).

7   Ian Smale (of 'Ishmael' fame) has many stories of children being effective in praying for healing.

8   Pytches 1985:277.

7   Healing in the Kingdom of God

1   Compare Mark 1:29–34 with the more detailed descriptions in Mark 5:1–20, 21–43; 8:22–26; 9:14–29 or 10:46–52.

2   At other times words of knowledge can lead to a conviction of sin in a person's life and subsequent repentance.

3   See Sheppard 1984 and Sider 1977.

4   In this context it seems significant that in Mark 16:17–18 the
     word 'signs' is used to refer to driving out demons, speaking in
     tongues, picking up snakes, being unharmed by deadly poison
     and healing the sick. The one biblical account of being un-
     harmed by a snake bite, in Acts 28:1–6, was certainly a *sign* to
     the Maltese, but they misinterpreted it to mean that Paul
     himself was a god. Similarly, in John 2:23–25 it is recorded that
     many people saw the miraculous signs Jesus was doing and
     'believed in his name. But Jesus would not entrust himself to
     them, for he knew all men . . . he knew what was in a man.'
     Immediately afterwards we read of Nicodemus, who says to
     Jesus, 'no-one could perform the miraculous signs you are
     doing if God were not with him', but Jesus responds to this by
     telling Nicodemus he must be born again. These signs are
     conducive to faith, but they need to be supplemented by a
     personal experience of God through being 'born of the Spirit'
     (John 3:8).
        A modern case of being unharmed by poison as a *sign* to
     unbelievers concerns a Muslim man in Turkey who was con-
     verted to Christianity. Because of his faith in Jesus, his family
     tried to poison him and were amazed when the poison had no
     effect.
5   The number of cases of deliverance in my random sample is too
     small for meaningful comparisons to be made between the
     short-term and longer-term perceptions of degrees of healing.
6   See, for example, 1 Corinthians 6:3; 11:10 and 13:1 for Paul's
     references to angels. In 1 Corinthians 2:4–5; 14:14–19 and
     2 Corinthians 12:1–6 (which many commentators think is
     actually alluding to Paul himself) Paul refers to supernatural
     experiences of his own.
        Although the letter to the Hebrews also contains detailed
     references to angels, the general scholarly opinion is that it was
     written not by Paul, but by someone else (possibly Apollos).
     No Pauline authorship is ascribed to it in the Greek manu-
     scripts, and most modern translations based on these do
     not follow the Authorised Version's assumption of Pauline
     authorship when giving a title to the letter.

BIBLIOGRAPHY

Allen 1977	P. W. Allen, 'The fibromatoses: A clinicopathologic classification based on 140 cases', *American Journal of Surgical Pathology* 1 (1977), pp. 255–270, 305–321
Baldwin 1987	Robert Baldwin, 'Signs and Wonders – A Personal Medical View', *Journal of the Christian Medical Fellowship* (January 1987), pp. 24–28
Beardsworth 1977	Timothy Beardsworth, 'A Sense of Presence' (Religious Experience Research Unit, Manchester College, Oxford), 1977
Bennett 1984	Rita Bennett, *How to Pray for Inner Healing for Yourself and Others* (Eastbourne: Kingsway Publications, 1984)
Benson 1984	Herbert Benson, *Beyond the Relaxation Response* (New York: Times Books, 1984)
Billheimer 1977	Paul E. Billheimer, *Don't Waste Your Sorrows* (Fort Washington, Pennsylvania: Christian Literature Crusade, 1977)
Boerenkamp 1985	Hendrik G. Boerenkamp, 'A Study of Paranormal Impressions of Psychics', *European Journal of Parapsychology* 5 (1985), pp. 327–371
Bridge 1985	Donald Bridge, *Signs and Wonders Today* (Leicester: Inter-Varsity Press, 1985)
Burridge 1969	Kenelm Burridge, *New Heaven, New Earth* (Oxford: Basil Blackwell, 1969)
Chung and Enzinger 1976	E. B. Chung and F. M. Enzinger, 'Infantile Fibrosarcoma', *Cancer* 38 (1976), pp. 729–739
Comstock and Partridge 1972	G. W. Comstock and K. B. Partridge, 'Church Attendance and Health', *Journal of Chronic Diseases* 25 (1972), pp. 665–672
Czaplicka 1914	M. A. Czaplicka, *Aboriginal Siberia* (Oxford: Clarendon Press, 1914)

Eysenck and Eysenck 1969	Hans J. Eysenck and Sybil B. G. Eysenck, *Personality Structure and Measurement* (London: Routledge & Kegan Paul, 1969)
Gardner 1983	Rex Gardner, 'Miracles of Healing in Anglo-Celtic Northumbria as Recorded by the Venerable Bede and his Contemporaries: a reappraisal in the light of twentieth-century experience', *British Medical Journal* 287, 24–31 December 1983, pp. 1927–1933
Gardner 1986	Rex Gardner, *Healing Miracles: A Doctor Investigates* (London: Darton, Longman & Todd, 1986)
Glasse and Lindenbaum 1976	R. M. Glasse and Shirley Lindenbaum, 'Kuru at Wanitabe' in R. W. Hornabrooke (ed.), *Essays on Kuru* (Faringdon, Bucks: E. W. Classey, 1976)
Grant 1974	Myrna Grant, *Vanya* (Eastbourne: Victory Press, 1974)
Greeley and McCready 1974	Andrew M. Greeley and William C. McCready, *The Mystical, the Twice Born and the Happy: An Investigation of the Sociology of Religious Experience* (Chicago: National Opinion Research Center, The University of Chicago, 1974)
Greeley 1975	Andrew M. Greeley, *The Sociology of the Paranormal: A Reconnaissance*, Sage Research Papers in the Social Sciences, Studies in Religion and Ethnicity Series, No. 90–023 (Beverly Hills and London: Sage Publications, 1975)
Green 1968	Celia Green, *Out of the Body Experiences* (Oxford: Institute of Psychophysical Research, 1968)
Grey 1985	Margot Grey, *Return From Death* (London: Routledge & Kegan Paul, 1985)
Hay 1987	David Hay, *Exploring Inner Space* (Oxford: A. R. Mowbray, 1987)
Hay and Heald 1987	David Hay and Gordon Heald, 'Religion is Good For You', *New Society*, 17 April 1987
Hay and Morisy 1985	David Hay and Ann Morisy, 'Secular Society/Religious Meanings: A Contemporary Paradox', *Review of Religious Research* 26/3 (1985), pp. 213–227
Huggett and Huggett	John and Christine Huggett, *It Hurts to Heal* (Eastbourne: Kingsway Publications, 1984)
Hunt and McMahon 1985	Dave Hunt and T. A. McMahon, *The*

Seduction of Christianity – Spiritual Discernment in the Last Days (Eugene, Oregon: Harvest House Publishers Inc., 1985)

Kelsey 1977   Morton Kelsey, *The Christian and the Supernatural* (London: Search Press, 1977)

Kissell 1986   Barry Kissell, *Walking on Water* (London: Hodder & Stoughton, 1986)

Krarup n.d.   Helen Krarup, *Conventional Religion and Common Religion in Leeds, Interview Schedule/Basic Frequencies by Question* (University of Leeds Department of Sociology, Religious Research Papers, No. 12)

La Fontaine 1988   J. S. La Fontaine, 'Child sexual abuse and the incest taboo: practical problems and theoretical issues', *Man* (n.s.) 23/1, March 1988

Laurentin 1986   Rene Laurentin, *Viva Christo Rey!* (Milton Keynes: Word Books, 1986)

Lewis 1960   C. S. Lewis, *The Four Loves* (London: Collins Fount, 1960)

Lewis 1987   David C. Lewis, 'All in Good Faith', *Nursing Times* 18–24 March 1987, pp. 40–43

Lewis 1971   I. M. Lewis, *Ecstatic Religion* (Harmondsworth: Penguin Books, 1971)

Livesey 1987   Roy Livesey, *Understanding Deception* (Chichester: New Wine Press, 1987)

Lock 1980   Margaret Lock, *East Asian Medicine in Urban Japan* (Berkeley: University of California Press, 1980)

MacNutt 1974   Francis MacNutt, *Healing* (Notre Dame, Indiana: Ave Maria Press, 1974)

Marshall 1988   Tom Marshall, *Foundations for a Healing Ministry* (Chichester: Sovereign World Ltd, 1988)

Masters 1987   Peter Masters' articles on 'Divine Healing: The New Emphasis', *Sword and Trowel* 1 (1987) The Metropolitan Tabernacle, London

Mathews 1976   J. D. Mathews, 'Kuru as an epidemic disease' in R. W. Hornabrooke (ed.), *Essays on Kuru* (Faringdon, Bucks: E. W. Classey, 1976)

McAll 1982   Kenneth McAll, *Healing the Family Tree* (London: Sheldon Press, 1982)

McBain 1986   Douglas McBain, *Eyes that See: The Spiritual Gift of Discernment* (Basingstoke: Marshall Pickering, 1986)

Morris 1971	Leon Morris, *The Gospel According to John*, New International Commentary on the New Testament (Grand Rapids, Michigan: Wm B. Eerdmans Publishing Co., 1971)
Moss and McEvedy 1966	Peter D. Moss and Colin P. McEvedy, 'An Epidemic of Overbreathing Among Schoolgirls', *British Medical Journal*, November 1966, pp. 1295–1300
Penfield 1952	Wilder Penfield, 'Memory Mechanism', *American Medical Association Archives of Neurology and Psychiatry* 67 (1952), pp. 178–198
Perry 1987	Michael Perry (ed.), *Deliverance* (London: SPCK, 1987)
Pytches 1985	David Pytches, *Come Holy Spirit: Learning to Minister in Power* (London: Hodder & Stoughton, 1985)
D. Pytches 1987	David Pytches, 'Fully Anglican, Fully Renewed' Kevin Springer (ed.), *Riding the Third Wave* (Basingstoke: Marshall Pickering, 1987)
M. Pytches 1987	Mary Pytches, *Set My People Free: Inner Healing in the Local Church* (London: Hodder & Stoughton, 1987)
Richards 1984	John Richards, *Resting in the Spirit* (Weybridge: Renewal Servicing, 1984)
Ring 1980	Kenneth Ring, *Life at Death* (New York: Coward, McCann & Geoghegan, 1980)
Ritchie 1978	George G. Ritchie with Elizabeth Sherrill, *Return From Tomorrow* (Eastbourne: Kingsway Publications, 1978)
Sabom 1980	Michael B. Sabom, *The Near-Death Experience: A Medical Perspective* (Philadelphia: J. B. Lippincott, 1980)
Sanford 1982	John A. Sanford, *Dreams: God's Forgotten Language* (New York: Crossroad Publishing Co., 1982)
Sargant 1973	William Sargant, *The Mind Possessed* (London: W. Heinemann, 1973)
Sheldrake 1987	Rupert Sheldrake, *Religious Experience in a Living World*, The Alister Hardy Memorial Lecture (Oxford: The Alister Hardy Research Centre, 1987)
Sheppard 1984	David Sheppard, *Bias to the Poor* (London: Hodder & Stoughton, 1984)
Sider 1977	Ronald J. Sider, *Rich Christians in an Age of*

	Hunger (London: Hodder & Stoughton, 1977)
Sirois 1974	Francois Sirois, *Epidemic Hysteria*, Acta Psychiatrica Scandinavica, Supplementum 252 (Munksgaard, Copenhagen: 1974)
Smillie 1980	I. S. Smillie, *Diseases of the Knee Joint* (Edinburgh: Churchill-Livingstone, 1980)
Soal and Bateman 1954	S. G. Soal and F. Bateman, *Modern Experiments in Telepathy* (London: Faber & Faber, 1954)
Southwold 1983	Martin Southwold, *Buddhism in Life* (Manchester: Manchester University Press, 1983)
Springer and Deutsch 1985	S. P. Springer and G. Deutsch, *Left Brain, Right Brain* (Oxford: W. H. Freeman & Co., 1985)
Stafford 1986	Tim Stafford, 'Testing the Wine from John Wimber's Vineyard', *Christianity Today*, 8 August 1986, pp. 17–22
Subritzky 1986	Bill Subritzky, *Demons Defeated*, International Edition (Chichester: Sovereign World Ltd, 1986)
Sullivan 1987	Leonard Sullivan, 'John Wimber at Harrogate', *Catholic Gazette* 78/3 (March 1987), pp. 26–27
Ter Haar and Ellis 1988	Gerrie Ter Haar and Stephen Ellis, 'Spirit Possession and Healing in Modern Zambia: An Analysis of Letters to Archbishop Milingo', *African Affairs, Journal of the Royal African Society* 87/347 (April 1988), pp. 185–206
Urquhart 1974	Colin Urquhart, *When the Spirit Comes* (London: Hodder & Stoughton, 1974)
Vickery 1986	Kenneth Vickery, *Choose Health – Choose Life* (Eastbourne: Kingsway Publications, 1986)
Virgo 1988	Terry Virgo, 'More than "a healer"', *New Frontiers*, April/May 1988, pp. 3–4
Walker 1988	Andrew Walker, *Restoring the Kingdom* (London: Hodder & Stoughton, 1988)
Wimber 1985	John Wimber with Kevin Springer, *Power Evangelism* (London: Hodder & Stoughton, 1985)
Wimber 1986	John Wimber with Kevin Springer, *Power Healing* (London: Hodder & Stoughton, 1986)
Wimber 1987	John Wimber, 'Introduction' to Kevin

Springer (ed.), *Riding the Third Wave* (Basingstoke: Marshall Pickering, 1987)

Wittfogel 1957   Karl Wittfogel, *Oriental Despotism: A Comparative Study of Total Power* (New Haven, New York: Yale University Press, 1957)

Wright 1987   Verna Wright, 'A Medical View of Miraculous Healing' *Sword and Trowel* 1 (1987) The Metropolitan Tabernacle, London

INDEX

[References to conditions listed in Appendix A (pp. 277–283) are excluded.]

Sheffield 13, 14, 17–18, 34, 50, 133, 140, 149, 161, 164–166, 174, 184, 192, 206, 208, 213, 215, 219, 242–243, 252, 289, 293, 306, 321, 346, 357, 361
Shekinah 187, 274
Sheldrake, Rupert 76–77, 315
Sheppard, David 268
shoulder pain 23, 27, 31, 156, 221
Siberian tribes 121
sick role 291–292
Sider, Ronald 268
signs 19, 59–60, 159, 201, 232–234, 269, 270, 314, 331, 368, 373
skeletal problems 155–156, 243
sleeping patterns 82, 100–101, 126–127, 289–290
Sloan, John 7, 330
slum areas 237, 331
smoking 82, 109
snakes, picking up 373
social classes 66–67, 79–80, 86, 124, 204, 249, 266, 269, 285, 293, 334, 344, 353, 361–362, 372
Society of Friends 17, 237
sodomy 120
songs 164, 207, 254
spastic colon 23, 25
speaking in tongues 79, 82, 93–94, 105–108, 129, 143, 182, 205–206, 228, 245, 274–275, 286, 310, 335, 341, 373
spinal problems 23, 26, 31, 156, 158, 160–161, 209–210, 262, 352–353, 362–364
spiritualism 122, 140–142, 181, 338, 342, 349
splits in churches 240–241
stigmata 185
spontaneous remission or regression 223, 226, 261, 263, 366
Stockdale, Walter 57, 330
stomach 218
stress 54, 69, 80
stroke 220
Suenens, Cardinal 172
suffering, theology of 58
suggestion or auto-suggestion 55, 76, 164, 166–167, 182–191, 265
Sullivan, Leonard 11

Tapia, Andrés 369
tears 85, 107–108
teeth, 73–74, 316–318, 369
telepathy 141
temple 220
tendons 23, 118
tension 81, 86–87
testimony 233
theological issues 18–20, 58, 141, 157, 266–267, 294–319
'Third Wave' 320
Thompson, Bryan 313–314
throat 118, 219, 243
tongue 221, 230

training of healing teams 250–259
trance 181–182, 357
transportation 90, 195, 316, 318
transvestism 118
tumour 222–228
Turner, Richard 7, 195, 355, 357
'twice-born factor' 115, 337
twins 350

ulcers 70
United Reformed Church 285
unloved, feeling of being 81
Urquhart, Colin 10, 361

Vanya 123, 195, 316
visions 75, 91, 188, 197–199, 241, 245, 250, 263, 265, 274–275, 310, 318, 351, 359, 360
visualisation 72, 76

Wales 238–239
weight 186–187
weightlessness 198
Wesley, Charles 295
Wesley, John 296–297
West Indian churches 66, 334
whiplash injury 28, 50, 261
White, John 7, 31, 360
whooping cough 210–212
will 261–262
Wilson, David 7, 44, 324
Wimber, John 10, 11, 19, 20, 34, 48, 49, 51, 55, 58, 69, 72, 86, 89, 91, 95, 104, 113, 117, 119, 122, 129, 132, 133, 136, 141, 145, 149–151, 161, 163–166, 171, 183, 189, 191–193, 198, 207–208, 215, 228, 231, 235, 242–245, 247–249, 265–267, 288, 289, 293, 294, 296, 302, 303, 306, 312, 318, 359
wind 188–189, 197, 198, 274, 359
words of knowledge 9, 11, 12, 52–53, 63–64, 88, 118, 129–161, 205, 230, 243, 248–250, 252, 254–255, 259, 262–265, 268, 274, 286–287, 292, 310–311, 339, 345–353, 372
  associated with musical or artistic pursuits 142–146
  development of 146–150
  private versus public 131, 132, 156
  reception of 137–140, 265
  relationship with healing 154–161
  specificity of 131–137, 156–158, 160, 351–352
  statistical analysis of 132–137
  verification of 150–154
worship 91, 164, 186, 237, 240–241, 248, 254, 359
worthlessness, sense of 77, 90
Wright, Verna 163–165, 183, 324
wrist 289

Zacchaeus 130